BRVEGEL

OR THE WORKSHOP OF DREAMS

BRVEGEL

OR THE WORKSHOP OF DREAMS

CLAUDE-HENRI ROCQUET

TRANSLATED BY NORA SCOTT

THE UNIVERSITY OF CHICAGO PRESS
CHICAGO AND LONDON

CLAUDE-HENRI ROCQUET, professor of aesthetics and art history at the École Nationale Supérieure des Arts Décoratifs in Paris, has published widely in art, literature, and theater. His conversations with Mircea Eliade, *Ordeal by Labyrinth,* are also published by the University of Chicago Press.

The University of Chicago Press, Chicago 60637
The University of Chicago Press, Ltd., London

© 1991 by The University of Chicago
All rights reserved. Published 1991
Printed in Mexico

00 99 98 97 96 95 94 93 92 91   5 4 3 2 1

ISBN 0-226-72342-9 (cloth)

Originally published as *Bruegel, ou l'atelier des songes,*
© by Editions Denoël, 1987.

Library of Congress Cataloging-in-Publication Data

Rocquet, Claude-Henri.
    [Bruegel, ou L'atelier des songes. English]
    Bruegel, or, The workshop of dreams / Claude-Henri Rocquet ;
translated by Nora Scott.
        p.   cm.
    Translation of: Bruegel ou L'atelier des songes.
    Includes bibliographical references.
    1. Bruegel, Pieter, ca. 1525–1569.   2. Painters—Flanders—
Biography.   I. Title.   II. Title: Workshop of dreams.
ND673.B73R6413   1991
760'.092—dc20
[B]   91–16718
                                                                          CIP

This book is printed on acid-free paper

For Annik

CONTENTS

"The Painter and the Connoisseur," about 1565, Albertina, Bildarchiv der
Österreichischen Nationalbibliotek, Vienna

On the twenty-first of May, 1527, Charles V was preparing to celebrate the birth of his son, Philip, at Valladolid and throughout all of
Spain. But the banners were soon to be folded away: the imperial
army was sacking Rome and besieging the Castel Sant'Angelo, where
Clement VII was in residence. Lutheran lansquenets, his majesty's
faithful troops, were gathering in public squares shouting, "Vivat Luther Papa!" These hornet-striped devils were burning the town, pillaging, raping women in the streets and convents, killing for the fun
of it. They donned mitres and threw relics and hosts into the Tiber.
They took a Christ from one of the altars at Saint Peter's and dressed
him up as a lansquenet. They used crucifixes for target practice. They
cut down a priest for refusing communion to a donkey. And yet, before three years were out, the pope would crown Charles, in Bologna,
amid the pomp and celebrations that were the mark of this century.

Charles of Luxemburg was the grandson of Maximilian of Austria
and the great-grandson of Charles of Burgundy, or Charles the Bold
as he was also known, archduke of the Western Empire. He was born,
with the century, in Ghent. He inherited the throne of the Lowlands,
then that of Spain. The Fugger banking family financed his election
to the Holy Roman Empire, over the king of France. He was more
powerful than Charlemagne, Alexander, or Cæsar. He was to be the
defender of Christendom. He would crush Turk and heretic alike. He
would plant the Catholic faith firmly in the freshly conquered New
World. His device was "Plus oultre." And his motto: "The sun never
sets on my empire." These were the device and motto for a king of
Babel.

This would be Peter Bruegel's world.

Bruegel left no portrait of his wife or his children or his friends. It
is generally thought that he occasionally placed himself among his
figures, but there is no proof. Engravings of him by friends have little

in common. I would like to see him in his pen drawing of an elderly, shaggy painter, in a bowllike felt hat, his eyebrows bushy, his gaze bitter and grave: a Leonardo da Vinci retired from the world. But it is probably a picture of the Painter pestered by a foolish Client. Had Bruegel been a playwright rather than a painter, his works would have been attributed to others, so few clues did this man leave about his life. All he left was his work. Bruegel, like Shakespeare, remains unknown.

The passages in which the Flemish Vasari, Karel van Mander, speaks of Bruegel are more legend than history. When the painter died, his eldest son, Peter, was not yet five, and John had just been born. Their mother was to die nine years later, in 1578. Van Mander did not publish his *Life of the Most Illustrious Painters of the Lowlands* until 1604. It seems that he never met Bruegel. Where, then, does he get his information? No doubt from painters who knew him. Perhaps from Hans Franckert, a Nuremberg merchant, "a good and excellent man, who often stopped late at the Bruegel home and who saw him every day." From the few details that had come down, and by letting his imagination work on the paintings he had seen, he invented a plausible life.

This is what I, too, have done.

I revisited the meadows of my childhood, the gray sea a dozen leagues from Bruges. I traveled through Bruegel's paintings, a country unto themselves. I read Guicciardini's *Description of All the Lowlands*, a rare book in which an Italian contemporary, who mentions Bruegel's name, depicts the world in which the painter lived. It was in this world that I saw him. I did not follow him across the Alps, or through Italy or into Sicily: that period of his life will remain a distant glimmer.

One of Bruegel's engravings is entitled *Elck* (Everyman). It depicts every man as unknowing, but self-seeking. Each man who watches the sea, the fire, the seasons, who wonders that he is alive and that he must die, is, in fact, everyman. It is no lie to give him a name. The reader can usually tell what is invented and what is known. I have tempered fiction with respect. I have let my reveries well. At times I have hesitated before taking a certain path, and yet it shone like that nocturnal linden, in the Forêt de Soignes, under which the novices from the hermitage met their spiritual father, illuminated. Something which I hold to be supernatural, however, allows me to think that my least cautious reveries have been approved by the unseen.

1

THE TRIP TO HOLLAND

Often physical towns and fortresses do not last as long as their more fragile images, which lie hidden from the gnawing light of day, sometimes for centuries, in the libraries and museums of other towns: figures fashioned from a little ink, water, and dust, intact amid the ruins—paper butterflies bearing worlds to safety on their wings. In Besançon and Boston, three pen-and-sepia drawings show, on the far side of a body of water in the middle distance, part of the old walls of Amsterdam. Bruegel has delicately traced towers, pepper-pot and pinnacle turrets, gates and ramparts, stone or wooden bridges, a house hidden by foliage, a hut perched on stilts. It is like looking at a mysterious island. And one can imagine Peter Bruegel drawing from a boat. This is not his country: perhaps some dream country where he will never live. He fixes it with a tender, meticulous eye. He sees the water shimmering and slipping past the rounded walls, the expanse of the sea fanning out through the gates to the Baltic countries with their harsh winters, to Norway and Russia. Does he see, as he sketches, the tiny buildings he will one day paint at the foot of the tower of Babel; does he dream of the clay moats, the ramparts with their gates where Bablyonian ships tie up in rows. A hush hovers above the slate-topped turrets. Perhaps it would be pleasant to live in this town, with its bouquet of towers bathed in silvery light. Solitude, soothing, beneficent, and calm, in the boat with the industrious cries of gulls overhead.

This view of Amsterdam is not a faithful rendition of what the contemporary traveler saw. Bruegel took pleasure in letting his pen follow the bend of the shore, the arches and porches, the curves and openings of the arcades. He took pleasure in the lip and the moldings of each tower, in the prismed facades, in the delicacy of the distant balconies. The details are exact. But his imagination may have rearranged the buildings and, as an artist disposes on the table the bottles and pitcher he is about to paint, so may Bruegel have moved

Sint-Anthoniespoort somewhat closer to the Svych Utrecht tower. Perhaps he did not even visit Amsterdam. Perhaps he merely used drawings by mapmakers the likes of Anthonie van den Wijngaerde or Cornelis Anthoniszoon. They would first make scrupulous drawings from the subject, then rework them into isometric projections, bird's-eye views of the vast countryside—tiny windmills on the horizon, polders, hamlets, and the main town in the foreground, with its coat of arms inscribed in the clouds. So one of the keepers of the city archives assumes. And one is sometimes forced to turn to archives: the Svych Utrecht tower was destroyed last century, and it has been a long time since ramparts have enclosed Saint Anthony's gate, now the Weighhouse, in Nieumarkt Square. But would Bruegel have included the date 1562 in his drawing if he had not stood before the walls and dikes of Amsterdam that year?

That was the year Dirck Volckertzoon Coornhert served as one of the three syndics of Haarlem. If Bruegel did come to Amsterdam, if he traveled in Holland at all, I imagine that he stopped in Haarlem and that he may just have made this trip especially to meet Coornhert. No doubt he did not come to see the alderman, but the engraver and poet, the author of somewhat mordant comedies, the man who translated Plutarch, Boethius, and the *Odyssey*—sea-blue Ulysses speaking in the accents of mariners of the mists and chill (I love this Irish-hued Odyssey where Penelope is Isolda). Coornhert does not receive him at the town hall amid classic busts, marbles, and heroic tapestries, but at home, in an austere, studious, almost poor house with Cornelia (to marry this daughter of the people, he had to break with his patrician family, abandoning all hope of an inheritance). He invites him to their home, along with a few friends, for a hearty meal of mussels and herring (it would be surprising indeed were his closest friend, the poet Herman Spiegel, not there that day); late that evening, they are alone, among the books and the proof sheets suspended overhead. Coornhert was an excellent engraver and etcher, but the engraving and drawing were largely for his own pleasure, as when he played the harpsichord or the recorder, and to earn his living when his pen did not suffice. Above all, he was a man of books and, because it was not right to neglect the public welfare and peace, he was a man of action. So he would appear later in an engraving by his pupil Goltzius: the eyes of a philosopher, a willful mouth. Coornhert and Bruegel were about the same age; it might be said that they were much alike, even in the face. But one was apt to be talkative, the other, as we know, laconic. One made an effort not to run on; the other reminded himself to talk.

For at least seven years Coornhert entertained close ties with the *Familia Caritatis*, which had formed in Antwerp around the figure of Hendrick Niclaes: their purpose, in those stormy times of discord, those quarrelsome times of strife, was to lead a life of prayer and good works, with a simple and pure heart—a family, a house of love, as in the days of the first disciples, when the Gospel exhaled a breath of springtime over the world. He had often received Hendrick Niclaes in this very place. They had written; Niclaes's letters were there, in the Spanish leather chest, between the medical texts and the gardening manuals (perhaps it would be wiser to hide or destroy them). The excessively tense Niclaes had finally tired him. He sought nothing so much as peace of mind. He longed to know only that which prepared and preserved it. That was why the example and ideas of Sebastien Franck constantly sustained him. "Remember, Turks and pagans were all, like you, created in the image of God, and they are the work of God, just like the Germans, for God instilled his image in all men alike, and he engraved his laws, his will, his Word in their hearts." Coornhert had inscribed Franck's maxim on one of the shelves in his library; as though he had to remind himself. He read it aloud, and sighed (but his sigh was like a cry): "The heart of man is one and everywhere the same, and we accept these quarrels and wars among us, we who believe in Christ."

The house is full of books. They cover the study walls, flow over into the workshop, pile up on the harpsichord; they slip into the kitchen between the pots of salt and flour. Some stand on the stair, against the wall. A few lie open on tables. At the foot of tall, heavy, ribbed tomes, huddle pocket-sized volumes; the chestnut or ivory-colored leather bindings are broken by spots of blue or white brochures, light reflected from their pages: the works consort as, in town, palace columns and vendors' carts, the elevated discourse of the learned and the small change of idle talk, the fleeting confidence, the short-lived cry. Certainly Coornhert preferred at times to do without rather than not to have some pamphlet from Geneva or Madrid. A treasure house of learning, of poetry. The books gleam in the lamplight. They shine in the candlelight. The street, visible through the small bottle-green panes, is still. Bells ring the hours. Rare, occasional footsteps sound in the night. Later they may be those of patrolmen. Their thick hands slip between the books, splaying the boards as if to quarter them.

Bruegel brings news of Antwerp. Christopher Plantin has closed his printshop and left the city. Antwerp has not recovered from the bankruptcy of 1557, and credit is suffering. They say that Plantin has gone to Paris in search of lenders. But it was probably to escape an impending arrest. Other members of the *Familia Caritatis* have gone into hiding, have left town, taken refuge in England or France. The image comes to Coornhert's mind of the death threats posted by the emperors' men, long ago, when he was seven. Had he dared look at those twenty Anabaptist heads, shipped from The Hague in a herring barrel and impaled at the crossroads at Wolewick, their rotting to be a preachment to Amsterdam? Or perhaps this was only a memory of something he had heard. But he does remember what happened in 1535. One night in early May, while most of the dignitaries were sitting down to a formal banquet at the town hall, a ragtag band of Anabaptists, mercenaries, and visionaries stormed the building. A few guests escaped and raised the alarm. In the wealthy quarters, inhabitants barricaded the doors with wardrobes and armed themselves with pistols. Some ran for the ramparts, their diamonds in a sack under their shirt, and escaped through the fields. Coornhert can still see his father, white faced, attempting to reassure the household, scouring the garden for a place to hide. His mother, standing under the blackened crucifix on the mantle, had opened the Bible at random and, having crossed herself, was reading a Psalm. The servants chorused "Amen!" whenever she paused for breath. Suddenly the house was filled with the smell of smoke, and they all prayed as they watched, through the windowpanes, the reddening sky. Screams and hymns wafted on the wind, now near, now far, like a storm; and thudding, the sound of axes hacking at doors. And laughter—and cries. The Saints, swords aloft as they had been seen once before, rampaged through the town, breaking in wherever inspiration led them, setting fire to houses, slitting the throats of sleepy idolaters on their doorsteps. Ivy-crowned Adamites ran naked, singing in the streets. Many of the poor had begun ransacking the burning houses. The silver plate clashed as they dragged their great sacks over the paving stones. The next morning, everyone knew that the great square and the streets around the town hall were blocked with sacks of hop flour and sandbags: behind these barricades and in shelters made from beams, clustered burghers, sailors and the local militia. The town hall was not only a symbol, it was the bank, and it held enormous gold reserves in its coffers. Soldiers repelled the rebels toward the port. The Anabaptists holding the town hall fired on the advancing troops. Since the start of the attack they had been waiting for reinforcements that were to come from Yselstein, a small town nearby. They did not want to admit that all was lost. Had the others not heard the shooting and the tocsin? Had they not seen the night sky like a field of poppies, and the smoke? Something was keeping them, but they would come and would take the square. Amsterdam would be a second Munster. The rich would lay their fortunes at the feet of the righteous and would beg for the true baptism. Everything would be shared. The banners of justice would fly over Holland. The gold of Amsterdam would pay the troops. The attack surprised and disconcerted them. Van Geel, their general, climbed to the roof of the town hall and, looking out to sea, hailed John of Leiden bellowing insults at the pope and Luther and at all those watching from below; he prophesied, he blasphemed. A ball from a musket pierced his head. Jacob van Kempen, his lieutenant, whom the rebels had greeted throughout the night with cries of "Long live the new bishop!" was found a few days later hiding in a latrine barrel. Crowned with a gold paper mitre, dressed in shirtsleeves, hands and arms trussed to his side, he was exposed for nearly a week in the great square. From his platform, enthroned in his own urine and excrement, he watched the tortures and the executions, which lasted three days. He saw everything, he heard every cry. Recanters were beheaded. The stubborn were burned. The misguided of an evening were paraded about in burlesque costumes. A few girls who had harbored deserters were thrown into the Amstel and drowned. Adamites who had been recognized were hanged in front of their homes, naked as they had lived. The carnival was growing stale. They finally came to Van Kempen and some of the Munich leaders. For his lies, they cut out his tongue; for his sacreligious baptisms, they severed his right hand; the executioner tore out his heart and flung it by the aorta into his face. In the end, they picked up a hand, an arm, a few other remains, and nailed them to the gates of Amsterdam. Everywhere, in the city, in small towns, on farms, suspects were arrested, questioned, executed. The repression spread to the other provinces. Coornhert witnessed all this at close range or from afar. He saw the quaking figures of the night stand in broad daylight before the pyres and the sticky chopping blocks and watch with satisfaction the pathetic catch put to death; few felt pity. Would his life have taken the shape it did had he not seen so closely, so early, what a hell man can make for himself, that gives the lie to all his words and prayers? He was thirteen, then. Now he is forty. He thinks he will see worse.

"They say that Van Geel paid the soldiers who took the town hall and those who were to join them with the regent's silver," says Bruegel.

"So you know that? Yes, he went to Brussels, dressed as a merchant, and he led Mary to believe that he had recanted the false doctrine, that he had fled Munster only to denounce the folly of John of Leiden and would return to fight him. He asked for two regiments to subdue Westphalia and recapture Munster before Luther's friends got to it. The regent let herself be persuaded. He returned to Amsterdam, took rooms in a hotel emblazoned with the emperor's arms, made friends with the burgomaster. I sometimes remind my colleagues at the town hall of this story. Once Amsterdam was taken, Munster was delivered, and Bockelszoon, known as John of Leiden, perhaps the master of the world."

"For a time," replies Bruegel.

Bruegel is standing by the bookshelves.

"I can hear them," says Coornhert, "babbling in vast debate. And I dream of one day collecting the contradictions into one great book. It would be a sort of synod. All those would-be Christians killing each other would finally make their peace."

"It will be a fine book," says Bruegel. But I doubt it will calm the waters. Where the Gospel does not suffice, can any philosophy do better? The theologians will agree on paper, thanks to you; but what about the others?"

But he does not go on because he sees the sadness in this kind man's eyes and that he is ready to lay down his life for the love of freedom and truth, for his faith in the Spirit present in every man, even if so many forget.

"The kingdom within . . . ," Coornhert begins. Then both fall silent.

Dirck Coornhert accompanied Bruegel back to the inn. They walked along the canal. A red moon rolled across the Haarlem sky. "This man still has something of his childhood," Bruegel thought to himself. As he walked, he observed the kindly face beneath the peasant hat, with its floppy brim and braid. He mulled over their conversation. Above all, he reflected on the paintings Coornhert had shown him, just before they left. Bruegel could not say who had done them. Coornhert watched Haarlem as it slept, the dark water slapping in the canal, beneath the moon, and he wondered if he would be allowed to live out his life in this town and to die in his own house. For these two men, who could have become fast friends, this was no doubt their only meeting, and it has left no trace in history.

2

He has nothing pressing to do. He likes these trails where men's clogs and cattle's hooves have worn depressions from which puddles reflect patches of sky. Between the hedgerows, he follows the tracks of herds whose feet have left their hieroglyphics in the drying mud. Who knows if the bird-tracks in the snow, the starlike footprints, and those hoofmarks in the mud are not another bible, which we could read if only we knew how. The priests of Etruria and Rome, soothsayers who saw omens in the flight of birds and the beating of wings, or in the configuration of entrails and clouds, read nature's dreams as though they were our own. And who knows whether nature does not know more than man, who is distracted by the tinkling of a bell from what Time is crafting in its cavernous workshops? The bohemian and the gypsy palmreaders often predict our path. And the astrologer traces among the planets the cipher of our birth and the bent of our days. Is it any more futile to believe that animal tracks or the crossing of straws would tell us, if only we could read them, beneath what roofs or skies our steps will take us as we go, or come?

Tranquil paths lead through pastures, from one cottage to the next. The clouds unravel like evening wool, colored by the fire, like wool died many purples by the glow of embers. It was along these same paths that fiery-eyed prophets rose up and passed; on these paths, so peaceful that a bird, undisturbed by our approach, stalks in front of us, that prophets walked, called from their smith, their stable, their oven—the Bible in their mouth and in their belly, in the grip of the Spirit, they would say. Smitten by the Spirit, intolerant of all servitude, and of all the tiara- and mitre-crowned heresies. They had risen up, like Amos, the cowherd; they had left their stable and plow, at once, like Elisha. They stood in the rainbow and the stormy light of the Apocalypse, on the brink of the millennium of justice, prophets and martyrs! Two by two, they went, and the market towns thought Enoch and Elija had come back at last. They went bathed in this light of meadows and lucerne. And in order that the shell of the old world crack the quicker, in order that the New Jerusalem shine the sooner, rid of the dung and the dregs of the days at hand, these prophets came with steel and fire to the cities, the palaces of bishops, the homes of princes.

I can see Bruegel on these roads of Holland where John of Leiden marched on Munster, his New Jerusalem, of which he made a short-lived realm of orgies and killings, of madness. I can see him dreaming of the father he never knew. Was it he, the man he had sometimes glimpsed as a small child, at his mother's side? His mother never spoke of him. Did she tell him that his father had died as he himself opened his eyes? And yet he remembers a man who held him on his lap, who sat him on his shoulders and who carried him about, his eyes level with the leaves and rooftops. A dark beard, a deep voice, a broad, strong hand which held his own or rested on his head. A voice saying to him: "My child," or "little Peter." A man leaning toward him, sitting on a bank, weaving straws or grasses into crowns and rings. I see Bruegel dreaming of his father, of that man: did he follow one of those prophets of brotherly love and justice, the visible kingdom of Christ on earth? Did he die at Munster, massacred by John of Leiden's axes for having risen up against that frenzied king of sham?

3

He has nothing pressing to do. He goes from town to town. He enjoys the solitude of these wanderings, the silence, dreaming down roads and paths, along fields. Once again he feels the well-being of his bachelor voyage. He travels light. He walks in the shelter of his broadbrimmed hat, and it is a pleasure to sweep it off upon entering the inn and, sitting down, to hang it, glistening with rain, on his knee, and to be a man stopping a moment to enjoy the slow, familiar local life and then to leave, with a self-possessed air. He takes a seat in the far corner of the room, or near the fire, and looks out the cloudy window into the courtyard where the wagons are parked, at a ceremonious chicken, bowing mechanically to the straw, a dog weighed down with years and melancholy, sighing on the threshold, its nose between its paws. The sky is gray, and slate-colored clouds hang over the roof of a barn. The peat fire gives off wisps of smoke. A man comes in, another goes out, loud voices fill the public room. He will forget the name of this village; he will not forget this moment on the soil of Holland.

A street in one of those small ivy-covered towns, and black or green gates opening onto noiseless courtyards. Bridges made of beams and stone, built for stopping to watch the thoughtful reflection of the sky. He goes from town to town. He has nothing pressing to do. Sometimes evening catches him while the sharp lines of the next town are still on the broad horizon. Copper or golden suns, or glowing suns like coals in the mist. Windy days, stormy days when the wind whistles through the oaks and willows. He is fond of this land that is not wholly his, the light so typical of Friesland and Holland, their art of windmills and locks.

As though here the division of the waters from the dry land that first day had been left to the industry of man, as though here the flood still lapped at our feet, water gurgles in the ground. The traveler passes through these villages where the sea—but that was a hundred years ago—once sprawled across pastures, swamping houses and churches as well as boats and tall ships. Of the entire now verdant hollow, which at one time boasted fifty steeples, only a little girl and her cat, asleep in a cradle, were saved; they say the cradle was found nesting in the crotch of an oak left standing by the flood. These men, Bruegel thought to himself, have worked as hard as those at Babel, but their work melts into the horizon. They have won their gardens from the maw of the deep. They have pushed back the voracious walls of the sea, and this misty plain is their Promised Land. Sometimes he would bend down and tenderly pick up a lump of earth, then put it back again.

The countryside through which Bruegel is walking was highly praised by the Italian traveler, Ludovico Guicciardini. "All Holland," he writes,

is wonderfully populated, and the men are generally tall, well made, good humored and brave, very civil, humane, agreeable, entertaining, clever, and shrewd. When you enter these towns and contemplate the people and the buildings, both public and private, you are struck by the civility and the order you see. But then, upon entering the houses and considering the wealth of household furnishings and all manner of utensils, the order and the cleanliness of every thing, one finds them most pleasant and even more wonderful. There may be nothing like it in the world; so I have heard said by the furriers of the Emperor Charles V, who accompanied His Majesty throughout nearly the whole of Europe; and, as everyone knows, those who have entry to all houses in every town and locality they visit are better able than others to speak. Next, go into the shops, visit the public places where people labor, go aboard their boats and, lastly, consider the dikes and fortifications these people build, not only for the preservation of their island, but also in order to preserve a number of cities and particular sites; consider the many canals and ditches at every turn, dug by hand not only for the sake of necessity, but for every kind of small convenience; consider the manner of tending the meadows and pastures and how, from one canal into the next and so on to the sea, so much water is evacuated, which abounds on all sides because of the tides and the low-lying lands; and, when all is said and done, you will clearly see how every thing is done with such dexterity of instrument and hand that it is a wonderful and incredible thing from which one can learn a thousand fine and worthy things. Indeed, Holland is a little country, but full of great and noteworthy things; there are a good many large towns and pretty villages, very tall men and women, big cattle, great wealth and great strength.

And he goes on:

The women are stout-hearted, fair and most intelligent; and are generally so active and independent of mind that they occupy most of the masculine functions and principally in the handling of trade.

4

In the century of Ruysdael, who depicted them in his paintings, numerous water coaches plied Holland's rivers and canals, sometimes
driven by the wind, but more often warped by horse. Most were
rather humble craft capable of carrying comfortably some sixty passengers. Some, however, were luxurious embarkations of state, floating palaces of velvet and wood. They even sailed by night, guided by
lanterns and bells. The wealthiest passengers would take a cabin;
from the portholes and hatches they could watch the countryside
coast by in the moonlight. They would drink wine from the Meuse
in affectionate company, then sleep between linen sheets, while, past
the silent hull slipped cottages and fields, the earth recumbent beneath the stars and the high-heaped clouds blown in from the sea.
The handsome fur hat and the cloak swayed imperceptibly from the
oak peg on the wall. One could embark in the evening at Amsterdam,
read Virgil by lamplight, be rocked to sleep, and wake in the morning
to see the sun rising through the sails, over the rooftops and turquoise
turrets of The Hague.

Were there as many coaches in Bruegel's time? I do not know. But
it is possible to imagine him sometimes leaving the dusty ruts for the
canal or river. The trip is smooth; the world opens up to the passerby
like a book whose pages are turned by the wind. Even with his eyes
lowered, book or drawing pen in hand, the traveler senses the countryside go by, changing with the hour and the angle of the light or,
suddenly because the sun has broken through, shining with a straw-
bright brilliance, a piece of glory beamed to earth amid the windmills
and the fields still cloaked in mundane light, a presage of another
light, a taste of honey, an angelic fault, before our eyes, here below.
The great clock of the world and the flow of time, like the passing of
clouds, reminds him that his own life's time, which he would believe
immobile, is dripping away, each drop recorded for all eternity.

The water laps gently as though in confidence. The boat glides between the seasons. Like Ulysses and Jason, like everyman, thinking
he is far at sea, having left the world behind, returns to his native
land and, once again seeing his fields and meadow, the logs stacked
under the bench, the clothesline, the sky the color of childhood and
melancholy, and the narrow muddy path overhung with bushes, his
heart aches and melts.

Is he thinking of the voyage of Lucas of Leiden—on a boat he had
equipped, decorated, and stocked with everything needed to work
and dream—to visit the painters of Zeeland, Flanders, and Brabant,

some forty years before? In Middleburg Lucas met John of Mabuse and gave a sumptuous banquet for him and the artists of the town. John of Mabuse accompanied him to Ghent, Mechelen, Antwerp: and in each town, a banquet! Lucas of Leiden was no less curious about the artists themselves than about their paintings and engravings. John of Mabuse, who had been on familiar terms with both the emperor and the pope, conducted himself in lordly style and went about in a robe of gold brocade. Lucas wore a suit of fine yellow camlet, which glittered like pure gold. Was there no jealousy between the two luminaries? It must have been amusing to see them dazzling society, each trying to outdo the other. Was Lucas's boat gilded, like a doge's gondola, from stem to stern, down to the tassels and fallals of the tent and dais? The crystal clinked with each roll of the deck, the wine and the sun lent each glass its hues, the conversations murmured through the locks. And these self-appointed ambassadors exchanged primers and varnishes like veteran cooks.

But his finest encounter was with Albrecht Dürer, who had come personally to see his fellow artists of Flanders and Holland, and particularly Lucas of Leiden, whom he had long admired, as Lucas him. They wrote, they set the time and the place, they saw each other from afar and they quickened their step. Dürer was so moved that, for a moment, he could not speak. Then, clasping Lucas to him, with a smile he expressed his surprise at such a small person for such a great name. If this quip has come down to us, it is no doubt for lack of something else to repeat, for no one was privy to the conversation that followed. They spent long days together. Each drew the other's portrait. Bruegel imagines their silence, the looks exchanged. Each observing his friend with an eagle eye, the masterly hand hovering over the plate or sheet. But they also talked: of Italy, which Dürer knew and Lucas had never visited. They shared their secrets, not all about burins or acid. They confided their dreams of the night, their fear of dying, despite their belief in an afterlife. Lucas recounted his youth, his desire even as a young child to draw and paint, and his apprenticeships: to an engraver of coats of arms and then to a goldsmith; then Dürer spoke of his father, he, too, a goldsmith, son of a goldsmith and who had made him a goldsmith as well: and so the arts migrate from one shop to another; from inlaid armor to the horsemen of the Apocalypse in missals; and the painter, with his intricate Tuscan marquetry, his checkerboards, diamonds, tooth ornaments, and sea shells, learns about perspective and in his mind already improves a medley of rooftops and ripe, sloping fields. They spoke of perspective and proportion, of the heavenly music of volumes and the concert of the stars that accompanies our lives. They spoke of metals that age in the earth and of comets and wise men. They spoke of Venice. They spoke of fellow artists. Dürer was kinder and more indulgent than Lucas: of a mediocre engraver he would almost always say: "He did what he could, he did his best"; he would always find something to praise in a piece: a moment, a passage where, at last, the artist had begun to enjoy his work, and inspiration had come—a spark, a bright spot, a promise. And this uncalculating moderation earned him the right to live in peace with that prickly race.

Had he been born a few years earlier, the child Bruegel, skipping stones on the canal or fishing for frogs, would have seen the boat carrying Lucas and Dürer glide along between moon and sun. Today, in his watercoach, he muses on their meeting. He imagines a dialogue, which he fleshes out with all the engravings he has seen and which have been his joy and his classroom. Would he have drawn the Alps and those vast landscapes he did so well without Dürer's lessons? And his peasants and apostles without Lucas of Leiden? The masters speak to him from the other side. (Who will hear his own voice one day?) They are there in his boat, beneath the sky with its clouds that gather and clear—a precise moment here and now—and he with them, attentive, aboard that craft bearing them away. What had Lucas called her? No one knows. Perhaps, simply, the *Saint Luke*. Bruegel can see the engraver in his wooden workshop, his gaze level with the shore; night falls; the slapping of the water shapes something close to words; the lips of the water caress the wood of the boats; night falls; the moon sheds its clouds; by candlelight Lucas works on, then slumbers, still full of his vision, cradled in the sleeping waters. How is it, Bruegel wonders, that every painter, every engraver, does not choose to work from a boat. I was sailing in a nutshell along the waterways, along the rainways, and, in the cup of my hand, I drew the map, the shape of the world.

Snowflake sheep graze in the fields afar. The day moves on like a ewe in lamb. Snowy flake and virgin wool. The wind comes bearing a bell from afar. Between the winter and the spring, between the autumn and the winter, a silvery sky, a snowy sky, often. Light the color of sun and wind. And we go, as boats go, to their fate. And our heart is like the brown or russet sail that the red sun soaks purple as it sets, or rises. A friendly hand waves from the shore; one must guess the smile; a phrase drifts to us on the wind. Urchins bundled against the cold race our boat along the bank, and I see a man on his way home to his fire. He pulls the door shut. I will not see him again until

Judgment Day, perhaps. Will we remember that moment, when a light shone on the world, when you were going home to dinner and I toward the rainy horizon. Big black-and-white cows, brown ones like boulders or reefs, raise their munching muzzle toward the clouds, or lower it. Superb animals! Fountains, rivers of milk the likes of which can be found nowhere in all of Europe. Productive herds. This land, rescued from the waters, brims with vigor and life. And sometimes a horse, foam-and-snow white, stands gazing thoughtfully over the water. The sound of the wind in the oak leaves, the willow leaves, the reeds on the banks and in the hollows; the sound of the water, of the waters, the watery path of our boat, the gurgling water drunk by dry land. And the rustle of our thoughts.

5

Bruegel's diary of this trip has been lost. Perhaps it was burned with the papers and drawings destroyed after his death. *Naar het Leven,* which can be translated as "from the life," indicates the genre of the collection. Sometimes Bruegel would jot next to a drawing a proverb or familiar expression, the name of an object or tool. Sometimes a passing thought as he drew. Elsewhere he would indicate the color of a field, a village, a piece of clothing, a hat, a pitcher on a table. There were many drawings: people at the inn, boats on a canal, a team of oxen on the bank, the dome of a church, a horse being shod in a circle of curious children, a young birdnester his hat askew, a rooster, a sheaf of wheat, a fox, a woman sitting under a tree, a basket in her lap (with detail of the embroidery on the hem of her dress and the weave of the basket). There were farmhouses in the middle of a field, a village street, step-gabled houses with a sign out front. The struts of a bridge. We now know that the *Naar het Leven* drawings traditionally attributed to Bruegel are the work of a Northern Lowlands painter born seven years after Bruegel's death; but they no doubt resemble the *Holland Sketchbook,* and perhaps this kinship explains the error. First sketched in sepia or charcoal, the studies were gone over in ink, and comments added. It is easy to imagine Bruegel, standing in the wind or drizzle, in the meagre shelter of a shed, drawing those beggars, peddlers, woodsmen with their axe planted in a stump; then in the evening by the yellow light of the candle or the glow of the coals, thinking back on the day and writing a leisurely letter to an absent friend, or to Mary, and, with scratchy pen and nocturnal ink, redrawing the figures of his travels and dreams.

This country is like a leaky boat at sea. It was a stroke of genius to have used sail and wheel to turn the force of the winds, which drive the waves inland, against the sea itself. The winds rush in from open sea, wild winds, free winds, grand lords of the sky, to be captured by canvas and wood, become as tame as oxen at their plow. Page after page of the *Holland Sketchbook* is filled with these polder windmills, *wipmolens.* Paddle wheels could raise water only to shoulder height; therefore several ponds had to be connected in stairstep fashion, with the last emptying into a canal that returned the water to the sea. There were sometimes as many as sixty windmills, working together in "gangs," all turning to empty a lake or a marsh.

Had he seen the Archimedes mills, which used a long, sloping screw instead of a wheel, so that a single mill could lift water to the height of a house? *Tjaskers* were small devices that sat on the ground, the slanted shaft entering the water like a spade the ground: the upper part was equipped with vanes, the submerged portion with a wheel. It was impossible to cross this winged landscape amid the sounds of wind and sails, whose arms cast turning shadows on the ground, and not rejoice in these conquered, tamed forces, wind bound to water by the industry of man; it was impossible to see the earth come forth from this relentless turning, this perpetual harnessing of the winds, as golden butter rises to the surface of churned milk, and not feel a profound joy akin to pride, a Dædalus-like pleasure.

Bruegel, who was soon to paint the winches and treadmills of the tower of Babel (had the men of that time only thought of using wings and sails to harness the winds and breezes from the sky, what heavenly terraces they would have reached with their scaffoldings—only to have them overturned and dismantled by unnamed winds from the stars and the sun and the moon, by the lashing mane of a shaggy, oblivious comet! Those first brickmakers, those boasters of Sennar, who stopped them inventing—if only on the job, up on the third level, for example—a winch turned by the wind as the donkey turns the grindstone, or the stream its mossy millstone? Or is the inventing of machines, like truth, the Daughter of Time, one thing after another, like one word after another, until the end of the book. One step after another . . .) Bruegel the engineer watched the windmills of Friesland and Holland. He observed the various ways they turned. In the case of the squat *standerd-molen,* the whole mill pivots; outside the mill, attached to a winch firmly anchored in the ground, a long tiller, like that of a boat, is used to set the sails to catch the wind. In the stonework windmills, only the head turns; and the cap, which glides on a rail wheel, is worked from a circular stage situated near the top; when this stage sits atop a knoll, the mill is called a *bergmo-*

len. Sometimes the miller can shift the sails without going outside. Sometimes the set is governed by the wind: in this case, the mill is a smaller model called a *weidemolentje.* In a landscape that the city visible on the horizon designates as lying hear Haarlem, Bruegel has drawn a *spinnekop,* a windmill having neither base nor tripod, whose revolving vanes brush the grasstops, drenching the canvas in dew.

The last drawing shows a miller busying himself before the storm: like a sailor, he is tying down the "storm jibs," those panels that form the narrowest surface of each vane. The lowering sky asks the familiar question: "Ken ye catch the wind?" In the distance, boats hasten to port. A steeple guides them in. Seagulls have settled on the canal and gone to sleep with head under wing.

I shall tell you about the Ocean Sea, which is, not only by its proximity and conjunction, the main member or rather the head of the province. I tell you then that the face of the Ocean is great, infinite and superb, but awesome and most perilous when it swells up in anger. It stirs with such fury and such tempests, that at times the countryside and whole districts are covered and drowned. In this province, especially along the shores of Zeeland, the sea has often caused heavy damage. Nevertheless, with the help of the skill and industry of the inhabitants who have raised dikes and built walls, the dangerous portions have been little by little arranged so that, if no terrible winds blow up and combine with the Maistral, the highest waters can hardly cause any noticeable disorder. It would be superfluous to speak of the damaging and sinking of ships occasioned by its unleashed fury, for this can easily be imagined; nevertheless, when ships are well out to sea, as on the Sea of Spain, they incur fewer risks, for they have room to run and heave without colliding. But in narrows like the long English Channel, and near here, they are in grave danger and often undergo serious damage, and even more beyond Calais along the coast of Zeeland and Holland, in such stormy seas: for, displacing from time to time its bed stirred up by the winds and the waves or tides, it builds up here and there mounds of sand, called bars, which cause much damage, upon which ships often run aground and perish.

Bruegel left no letters, and perhaps he was no writer. A traveler he may have encountered, in Delft, Leiden, Rotterdam, or Bochum, could have written this one, decorated with its sails and waves, and a wandering whale, to a friend in France or Italy.

2

HOME TO ANTWERP

1

It was the custom of the great families of Florence to establish their sons in Antwerp—Dozzi, Portinari, Deodati, Salviati, names that lent an Italian cast to the town. The name of Ludovico Guicciardini has become inseparable from that of Antwerp. This young man could have lived like a Florentine in exile: he learned Flemish, bought land, and, at the end of his life, was honored with a pension. He could have kept his distance from public misfortunes: he was arrested by the duke of Alba and thrown into prison. He could have devoted himself to banking and business, his trade: he wrote a *Description of All the Lowlands.* This is a valuable book for anyone trying to picture Peter Bruegel's time, his daily routine, and all those things that were familiar to him. Letters, chronicles, memoirs, journals are so many shells that resound with everyday speech now extinct.

The capacity to imagine voices, inflections, timbers, the figures and cadences of conversation, no less important than the ability to visualize clothing, fabrics, objects, places, and settings, is a rarer gift. I can dimly see Peter Bruegel, as the end of his Holland trip draws near, standing in the silver morning light; but how did his Flemish sound?

It is, in Guicciardini's words, "a full language, with a capacious vocabulary and most capable of conceiving, expressing, and shaping all possible words or phrases; but it is most difficult to learn and even more vexing to pronounce; so that even children born to it are already well advanced in years before they can shape and utter it properly." I can hear the throaty roll—as he tells of Rome, or his mountain encounter (as he was descending into Italy) with a bear, its nose glistening with honey, going about its business like a colleague who, heaven only knows why, that day feigns not to see you and crosses the street—the boiling of his fine Flemish, rising like the sea, like ripe fields in the sun, the wind, and the stormy light. I can hear this tongue that has traveled the world and yet not conquered it, the tongue of sailors and peasants; but also the tongue of Erasmus, of

Ruysbroek, of Mercator, fit for the furrow, fit for the sails, and fit for
the stern, for making merry and for raising the cry, for proclaiming
freedoms, a tongue for harangues and for cradle songs, a tongue with
a gift for the proverb.

No doubt Bruegel could speak French and Italian, Spanish, German, perhaps a little English, when the occasion demanded, since he
lived in this veritable Babel of a port, had traveled across France and
as far as Sicily, was living under the rule of Spain, and rubbed elbows,
at the Sign of the Four Winds, with people from all over Europe. He
knew a few words of Turkish: he had learned them from his master
and second father, Pieter van Aalst, who had been to Constantinople.

"Most people," Guicciardini writes in his *Description*, "have a few
notions of grammar, and nearly all of them, even the villagers, can
read and write. Even more have such an intimate knowledge of languages that it is remarkable and a source of wonder, for there are
countless numbers who, besides their mother tongue and notwithstanding that they have never been abroad, speak various other languages, and principally French, which they know well; and many
who speak German, English, Italian, Spanish, and several other
tongues which are more distant." In his *Table Talk*, Luther quotes a
proverb that says, if you carry a Fleming tied up in a sack the length
of France and Italy, he will still find a way to learn the language of
the country.

Peter Bruegel was often taciturn. But he was fond of a practical
joke and used to frighten his apprentices by playing at ghosts. It is
said that he often went to fairs, weddings, and banquets. And it is
impossible to remain silent at a long harvest or wedding table. At the
end of the meal, everyone must tell a story or sing a song, and all join
in the refrain: it would have been unthinkable for him, who claimed
kinship with the bride and came bearing the proper gifts, to have
refused a song or a tale. He would never have dreamed of it. This he
enjoyed.

He must have spoken well, smartly (and smartingly at times). He
must have had the gift of the *mot juste*. He must have wielded popular
wit and the scholarly saw. Someone whose painting shows such a
keen taste for proverbs must have had a collection on the tip of his
tongue, inventing, at times, when the need arose. He was never at a
loss for a story—stories that went on and on, like a snake biting its
tail, or that branched and branched never losing the teller, or stories
like those wonderful boxes within boxes within boxes—and short,
sweet quips that can be repeated down the table for whoever did not
hear, over almost before they have begun, and the teller can sit back

down to his meal, showered with laughter. He knew how to amuse tables of *rhetoriqueurs* and guild banquets as well as rustic wedding guests—but did he change his tone for each? He was at ease with prince and merchant, at ease with the farm hand. He followed the image that came to him and was the first to be surprised by the turn of his phrase, now noble now comic. His speech flowed and carved its path, like a stream, like a dream, like those pictures that paint themselves in the workshop of our nights.

2

Sailor. Now that would have been a life. Not a sail nor a rope he could not name, in several languages. He gladly lent the crew a hand, even when the weather was fair. He was not very different from those taciturn fraternal men (they called each other, even those they did not know, "brother"). He had only to set foot on the deck of a ship and feel the roll, and the years dropped away. To pack his kit in a canvas bag, sleep in cramped quarters, write and draw on his knees, take in the old smell of well-traveled wood, the sound of the waves and the wind, swept him back to the joys of childhood. It was a good feeling to be carried solidly along by the vigorous surge of the sea.

He embarked on the Zuiderzee (or on the Walcheren dike), one morning, in the snow and the crying of gray-and-white birds: nippy enough to turn up his jacket collar, but oh, joy of the flickering dawn, and he returned to Antwerp by sea. Directly? The coast of England was a few hours from Amsterdam; Ireland or Scotland, a couple of days. From Holland to Denmark or Norway was less than a week. Perhaps he went as far as London, to Goteborg, or Trondheim? Nothing is known of this trip. He alone knew his whereabouts and he savored the pleasure. A few steps, a few hours and we are hidden from all who know us. We burrow into distance, even a short distance, as into the oldest of deaths—but we live, and we know we are alive and feel it. He was now, for every man he met, just another man, another traveler, a stranger, someone, anyone. People took him for a merchant. When he appeared at those barn doors, at those weddings, he was always greeted as an uncle or the cousin of the bride. Most of those who crossed his path, unaware of who he was, took him for an ordinary man. And he was an *ordinary man*, wasn't he?

One boat and then another. They headed out to sea; they hugged the shore. It was a galiot or a fishing boat. They sailed down to Antwerp or headed up north. And they often kept in sight of land. He liked to see, in the distance, the towns and villages, the steeples, the fields, the little flock of roofs. He watched this land and the quiet earth as we watch someone who sleeps. A man at sea is more alert than those who go between the hedges and reeds, along fences, through pastures. He told himself that, when it came time to die— and he advanced in that new realm—the new mere invisible spirit must see the earth and those who dwell in it in their ordinary light; yes, surely, the dead man must, as he takes his leave, see all that is left below as does the man carried and rocked by the swell. The Ancients were right to distinguish three kinds of men: the living, the dead, and those at sea. But those at sea are more akin to travelers of invisible realms than to those who tread the earthen paths. They also say that sleep is the brother of death; but the life of the sea is far more awake, more attuned, a far vaster dream than the other. Sailors on watch sometimes see things in the dawns, in the nights, during the night watches, in the banners of lightning on a stormy day. What do those who sleep beneath the roofs of city and town know of this? The face of the stars is starker at sea, and life illuminated as in momentous dreams.

One boat, then another. And sometimes, even, via the launch between two ships, he would change routes. He was wandering, and working: Cock had asked for a series of prints to celebrate the great men-of-war. Not fishing boats or simple merchant vessels? No, warships, with cannon protruding from the gun ports, and even firing, with flame and smoke, battles, a ship afire and going down. That is what the customers will like. We will sell them by the sheaf, by the ream, in Lyons and Switzerland. So let cannon roar. After all, perhaps it was he who gave Cock the idea and the taste, when he showed him the Burning of Reggio di Calabria by the Turks, and the sea-green battle off the coast of Messina (madness and hell on his way to heaven and the light of Sicily, that petal-soft pollen-hued light, that hallelujah light bathing the hills). We will not omit a single ill-tempered cannon on its mounting, mastiffs, round, bronze, Cyclops'-eye mouths, not even the one pointed at the pursuers, on the poop deck, next to a bell (that the slightest breeze sets ringing like a knell). Men-of-war, merchant-men: they are one and the same; what present-day ship of a certain tonnage does not carry a rampart of artillery? The sea routes have their brigands like the others; and what are empires and kingdoms, as the petty thief said to Alexander, but a gang of crooks, a gigantic, piratical enterprise.

> L'empereur si l'arraisonna:
> "Pourquoi es tu larron en mer?"
> L'autre reponce lui donna:
> "Pourquoi larron me faiz nommer?
> Pour ce qu'on me voit escumer

En une petiote fuste?
Se comme toy me peusse armer
Comme toy empereur je feusse."

A landlord must a warlord be, and all war is the work of Cain.

Bruegel draws galleys with their mussel-shell sails. He draws them as they look in the distance, oars raised, ready to dip and strike the gray sea; at a distance, but he sees, he imagines, the galley slaves bare chested, heads shaved, sweating and swearing and groaning as they bend to the enormous oar. Bruegel draws their hardship, or rather he draws that insectlike thing that is a galley seen from afar. Without those thieves would princes have the force to vie as they do for seas and trade? Bruegel draws the wretchedness and ferocity of man, but we do not see them unless we reflect. What we see are graceful sails and hulls, like swallows, rapacity on the wing and the scourge of flies, as graceful as gulls, whose every flourish spells the death of a fish (which fish perhaps was opening his mouth to swallow a smaller one, which . . .). He draws in the cooling breeze and the sighing of sails and knows his drawing will bring him compliments and a fee. He draws ships about to fire on a brother ship and those creaking galleys, in which petty thieves and prisoners of war or dubious Christians slave and row like damned souls by the grace of those who could have hung them. And this hell keeps the holy pot of empires boiling. Glory to the most Christian prince who strides the seas, dreaming of girding the world about his belly! Surrounded by these tall ships, galleys, and galley slaves, Breugel draws. Who decided that it should be he who sat in the shade while others labor in hell? Who gave Judas his role, each of the thieves his, and the inheritance to Peter?

The sea is not always deserted. In some places, at times, ships come and go like Sunday promenaders on the boulevard or in the church square, or like chickens and pigeons and sparrows busy in the yard with a handful of grain. Sails dip in passing, and sometimes men cry from deck to deck, shouting news of the other world, or simply of the village next door. Silk and spices pass salt fish. The things that go by sea! Some of these tall chests are even packed with paintings and tapestries, bound for Spain, Italy, and the New World. And they all look as free as birds. But Bruegel sees the strings attached. Each ship sailing there, in the gray mists of sea and foam, or the celestial blue, running before the tireless bellows of the wind, is also sailing in the thoughts and calculations of men who never leave port or pier. Each ship looks as tight as an egg, but he who has eyes can see the pieces, like slices of a cake. All this merchandise boils down to gold in some

chest, and gold is but paper in its visible form, for banks, stock exchanges, moneylenders in their dens. If only one could show, beneath the waves, the bowels of the sea and, piercing the hulls, not
only the contents of these trunks from the world over, but the subtle
usury at work. Bills of exchange are swifter and safer than all the
visible vessels entrusted to the perils of wave and wind.

Vitruvius writes eloquently on trees, but too little on building from
wood. For Bruegel, with due respect to all masons, stonecutters, and
bricklayers since Babel, the most beautiful building, or at least the
dearest to his heart, was first of all that of carpenters, originally a
peasant trade: builders of houses and churches, joiners of beams and
rafters, not with nails, but with glue, pegs, spiles, tenons and mor-
tises. And the first wooden structures were not sheds and huts, but
boats. It is because he built these floating homes, or rather these superb, deep palaces, that man began to invent true dwellings and,
sometimes for lack of timber, unless it was from overweening pride,
finally built in stone that which he erected in wood on the rivers and
seas; but the columns and cornices recall the shafts and beams of old.
As Vitruvius writes: like swallows, masons filled the hollows between
the beams projecting from the walls; they cut the ends flush, affixed
small blocks carved in the manner of the triglyphs we now see and,
to hide the offending cut, covered it with blue wax; whence the ar-
rangement of triglyphs, metopes, and spaces between the beams of
Doric buildings. And just as the hut was born of the weaving and
interlacing of branches, so all boats come from the straddled log, from
a few logs lashed into a raft, the hollow trunk already a boat, then
the barrel, and from the pole, the oar and then the sail. Until finally,
the goblet-shaped tall ships.

In Holland and Friesland, Bruegel went from shipyard to shipyard;
there are more shipyards than churches in those countries. He was at
home around the tapping, the banging, regular, irregular, now dull,
now sharp, of hammers and mallets on wood; and the braying and
panting of the saws. He enjoyed this bustle, but was it even possible
to draw ships faithfully without understanding them, and to understand them without knowing their inner form and everything that
can be seen only during construction? And was it enough to take
pleasure in the tumblerlike aspect of these northern ships without
grasping the engineers' reasons, which are those of the sea and her
sudden high swells? He took it all in, as he sat there among the carcasses, the bones, the church roofs—here inverted—the cradle of
ships to come, the gathering of skeletons receiving the flesh and skin
of the ship that tomorrow would roam the seas, five years, ten,

twenty perhaps, until the sea ate it away or swallowed it up, or fire consumed it like straw, while other ships flying new banners in the morning wind set out to run in its stead. He knew the pleasure of Noah and his children; as they hammered, astride the ribs of the ark, they could already see themselves closing the last shutter on the soot-black sky, rent by lightning and waterspouts, making their chest fast against the wild rain. And Bruegel dreamed of Solomon. He thought about his temple, his palace, the palace of the Egyptian king's daughter, whom he had married. He dreamed of the beautiful friendship of Hiram and Solomon, king of Tyre and king of Israel. The temple was built entirely in silence, without as much as the sound of a mallet or saw, for the stones had been quarried and dressed in the mountains; and the cedars and junipers from Lebanon had been cut far from the temple ground; only the joining remained. And the temple, Hiram (Hiram the builder) had covered the inside with wood, like a chest, covered in juniper and cedar, fragrant before any incense had been burned. And all these vessels sailed to meet the Messiah. Solomon's ship, the wise man's ship, give us shelter, we who, refugees from that ship of fools, still paddle about in a most acrid tide, and the bitter wash of our past. And our heart, like the oracle and the inner temple, yes, let the purple wood of our heart be plated with gold, with Thy light, 0 Lord!

The engravings done from Bruegel's drawings were published by Cock somewhere around 1565. Some of them show Dædelus, Icarus, and Phæton, flying and driving above the ships of the time. Astride a dolphin, Arion plays his lyre. Sometimes a monster raises his bald head among the hulls and fixes us with a gloomy eye. Perhaps, as he sat among the carracks drawing the poet cast away by Sicilian sailors, as Herodotus tells it, Bruegel dreamed of his own youthful trip, of the sun over Taormina, of Ætna smoldering in the blue haze. Perhaps he dreamed of Dædelus, harbored by the Sicilian king, Coclos, named for a seashell. Phæton and Icarus: two heavenly castaways. Did he dream of the fleets, swallowed and forgotten, submarine gardens of seaweed and oysters, with neither sun nor moon? He liked ghost stories: did he know the one about the ghost ship and the Flying Dutchman, that Wandering Jew of the seas?

He drew ships whose fate we now know. When we see those proud vessels, we cannot forget that they are sailing for the glory of Lepanto, and we see the winds of death rising over the king's would-be invincible Armada. We hear the first cheers of the Sea-beggars. And we know that Bruegel will not have time to learn of the Spanish and Venetian victory over the Turks, nor that of the English and

Dutch over proud Spain. Into the immense sails he drew the power of the North winds, and we tell ourselves the story, which perhaps he foresaw. He watched the sails work in the wind, like organ valves, or the tongue and teeth, and he quivered to this language of travel. He saw the angels of silver and rain flying beside the ship, one foot poised on the ropes. Gazing into the distance, suddenly alone, his hood pulled low, he strained his ears for the hushed murmur of the ship, like that of a forest, and he felt, as we all do at times, wholly alive and unknown. The sun affixed its red seal to the end of each day and left like a lamp being carried away. It sometimes happened that the feather from a seabird would light, like a snowflake, on the ship. The traveler flew over the sea and the foam, enveloped in the vast whiteness of the sails, like the fabled child borne day and night on the regal wings of the wild goose. And the voyage over the seas, through the darkness, in the bright beams of suns, was the image of his life.

3

Guicciardini, like Bruegel, was drawn to the sea and those who go down to it in ships. And, of course, he admired the lowlanders for their navigational art.

They are expert in maritime matters, for they constantly travel the world in their ships, of which they have a great number, and they are so confident at sea, because of their experience and the stability of their vessels, that not only do they sail the year round, but they never run to port, even in the worst tempest, until the end of their voyage, courageously withstanding all winds and storms; because of which they lose no time and complete their voyage more rapidly than all others.

He regarded the sea and its ships with the eye of a shareholder (which, no doubt, he was):

But to return to our principal subject, having recounted the damages inflicted by the Ocean when, in its fury, it wages war on part of this land, it is now time to relate the advantages and benefits it affords the entire province when it is at rest, without which benefits (so great and varied are they) there is no doubting that the country could not provide for half of the people who dwell there today. For however fertile the soil may be, it would still not suffice to feed them all, nor the industry of men to keep them in the other necessities. Every day the advantages of the sea supply all manner of goods from all over, edibles as well as every other item useful to man, not only for this land, but for the provision of several other provinces as well. Which advantage has caused the said country to become what can be called the port, fairground, and marketplace of all Europe, because of which there is a coming and going, a loading and unloading, a chaos insomuch as an infinite number of persons, outsiders as well as those from the locality, come together here and work.

He looked upon the sea—that Lenten realm—with the gaze of an epicurean, but faithful, steward:

The benefit and rightful fruit of the Ocean, besides being such an ample advantage, is such that it is truly worthy of its grandeur, and consists, as one might think, of the countless fish of all sorts that are to be taken; which fish not only satisfy and content the delicate appetites of the wealthy, but also feed the poor and provide not only for these people, but in part for their purse, for so much is left over that they can supply part of France, Spain, Germany, England and other countries; and several sorts—principally salmon and cod—are salted and sent as far as Italy.

The ways of the herring delight him:

The *herring*, which the Latins call *halec*, is not found in any river or sea, not the Mediterranean or the Spanish Sea, or any other (if my memory serves me), except this septentrional ocean: its size, shape and excellence, when salted and dried, is already widely known; but now let us leave this aside and say a few words of its nature and great quantity. This type of fish comes out of the furthest reaches of the northern sea and, rushing towards land in awesome and unbelievable quantities, makes its first appearance in the Germanic seas of Scotland and England towards autumn. And should the cold set in earlier than usual, they appear all the earlier and in incomparably greater abundance, from which one must suppose that they are fleeing those icy seas, and consequently, according to the time of arrival of the cold or hot weather, one knows whether the year will be good or bad, or late or early. Thus the herring come to dwell and sow their seed in these more clement seas until Christmas is past. The route followed by those that come into this quarter (leaving aside those that keep to the more northerly waters of Norway and Sweden) takes them once around the island of Scotland and England and then back out to sea. But it truly seems that nature sends these fish to feed man, for they come right up to the shore and throng there where they see any fire, a light or human creatures, as though to say: "Take me, take me!" They no doubt have kings, as do bees; but these kings are the same shape and size as the others, not bigger, like those of the honey bee, but they have a sign on their heads resembling a crown and are a reddish color, especially about the head. These kings swim ahead and are followed and accompanied wherever they go by fry and an awesome multitude of other fish, and at night they resemble a streak of lightning, so like shining lights are their eyes; it is for this reason that they are called, in common parlance, "night lightning."

The sea is the true Land of Milk and Honey:

The quantity and number of fishermen and ships, principally from these countries and France and a few from England, along these shores in fishing season, is nearly infinite. . . . Having diligently ascertained in Friesland, Holland, Zeeland, and Flanders (for the rest do not send much worthy of note) how many boats ordinarily fish these waters in times of peace, I find (others estimate more) seven hundred vessels. . . . Each of which going out three times, as they do, nets and brings back (when all is said and done) at least seventy *lasts* a piece.

A *last* was twelve barrels, and each barrel held a thousand herrings tightly packed.

But the best place to savor the pleasures of this land is under a tree full of birds. Having written of herring, cod, and salmon, Guicciardini begins to dream:

one can imagine, if these three fish, to mention only the salted variety, less the cost of the salt, earn these countries more than two million *ecus* a year, the wealth that the other fish bring in, in general. But it is vain to pass the time in such calculations, for the phenomenon is infinite, awesome, and ineffable. And so let us go on and take our rest in the shade of these fine trees that greet our eyes.

Men of Guicciardini's ilk knew how to appreciate those fair ships even as they reckoned their profits. We can see them at their desk, now raising their head to look out at their ships entering port or weighing anchor, now noting in the red-and-white ledger the sum represented by those stacks of gold. And, on the desk in front of them, the gleaming scales. But these men, with the calculating eyes of a notary or horse trader, also believed in fairies and mermaids.

Guicciardini, writing on Haarlem, says:

In the year 1403 (according to Le Meyer and the affirmations of the annals of Holland and public rumor), a naked, mute mermaid was brought to this town; she had been caught in one of the lakes of Holland, into which she had been cast by a seastorm. They dressed the woman and accustomed her to eating bread, milk and other foods; later she learned to spin and carry out other duties, honoring and bowing before the Crucifix and other rituals that she saw her mistress perform; she lived for several years but never spoke. They also claim that, around the year 1526, a merman was taken in the Frisian sea, formed in every way like the rest of us; they say that he had a beard, hair on his head and other hairs that we have, but quite setulose (that is, resembling the bristles of a pig), and harsh, and that they accustomed him to eating bread and other ordinary foods; they say that in the beginning the man was very wild, but that later he became gentle, though not totally tame, and he was mute. He lived for several years and finally, having once escaped the same illness, died of the plague in the year 1531. In the Sea of Norway, near the town of Elepoch, another merman was caught whose aspect was such that he resembled a bishop in habit; he was given to the king of Poland, but only lived (having refused to eat) for three days, without uttering any sound other than deep sighs; and I have a true-to-life portrait of him by my side. These are certainly strange novelties; but whoever considers what Pliny and other credible authors write of the mermen found in the past will not be amazed by this; and he will be all the less amazed in view of what they write of tritons and other sea monsters and likewise of satyrs and fauns on dry land, which satyrs Saint Jerome refers to as being real.

Did Dürer really believe he had seen the bones of a giant like those living in Noah's time? He wrote in his diary:

In Antwerp, I saw the enormous bones of the giant. The thighbone is five and a half feet long. It is extraordinarily heavy and quite thick. Similarly, his shoulder blade is the width of a stocky man, the same being true of other bones as well. This man stood eighteen feet tall, he held sway in Antwerp and he performed many marvellous deeds, as the Gentlemen of the town have described at length in an old book.

We think that what he saw was the skeleton of a grampus, unearthed by workers digging at the foot of the Castle Steen, which guards the port. An engraving from 1515, showing the Scheldt and the road-stead, bears the inscription: "Dits de burch daer Antigonne de reuse te wonen plach" (this is the castle in which the giant Antigone lived). Wooden or cardboard busts of the giant were placed upon triumphal arches to welcome princes or were carried in processions. Peter van Aalst made and painted the one that still exists. Visitors to the bones are told that Druon Antigonus, who was so big that he bestrode the river, exacted a ransom from the boats passing on the Scheldt, failing which, he would sink them. He would cut off the right hand of river-men who refused to pay tribute and throw it into the water. Cæsar himself was unable to dislodge him and kept his distance. One day, a young fisherman by the name of Silvius Brabo challenged the giant, killed him, cut off his hand, and threw it into the river, which turned red as though at sunset.

When Dürer learned that a combination of high tide and severe storm had beached a whale at Zierikzee, in Zeeland, he set out at once. The whale measured more than one hundred feet, and no-body on that stretch of shore had ever seen one even a third the size. They were unable to refloat the animal, and people said that it would take more than six months to cut it up and extract the oil. He em-barked and spent the first night anchored at sea in the icy cold. On his trip, he saw submerged villages with only the rooftops projecting from the waters. Upon arriving on Arnemuiden, one of Zeeland's seven islands, he nearly perished:

Just as we were coming alongside and the cables were being thrown ashore, a large boat rammed us. People were disembarking and, in the crush, I let everyone ahead of me, so that, besides myself, only George Közler, two elderly women, the boatman, and a little boy remained aboard. As the other boat hit us again, these persons and myself still being on board and unable to make ourselves fast, the big cable broke and, at the same time, a violent wind came up and drove our craft back out to sea. We all cried for help, but no one dared risk himself, and the wind drove us further from shore. I spoke to the boatman and told him to be brave, to hope in God and to see what could be done. He replied that, if he could hoist the small sail, we could once more try to land. With great difficulty, we managed to arrange matters, we raised the sail to half-mast, and we landed.

So much trouble and peril for naught: "Early Monday morning we embarked and left for Zierikzee. I wanted to see the great fish, but the tide had already carried it out." Reading this account, one is reminded of a painting, perhaps Bruegel's last; it is in the Vienna Kunsthistorische museum: entitled *The Tempest*, it represents the whale that saved Jonah. In the distance, through the slanting downpour, one can just make out the shore with its Flemish spires. Perhaps Bruegel was once that little boy gone to see the beached monster, which the storm had carried out to sea, or the painter benumbed with the cold from which he was soon to die and who lost neither his faith nor his courage. He had but to embark beneath an inky sky to find himself, only a few leagues from the spires, face to face with the Leviathan. The tempest opened an awesome bible. The winds' sermon lashed his face: "Remember, you too are passing! You too must die!" Suddenly the familiar sea vomited at his feet the huge beast of the depths. He was engulfed in the entrails of the night. Look closely: in nearly all of Bruegel's pictures, and so often in Flemish painting, there is a ship passing near the village with its inn, a ship is sinking or about to, a crew is perishing, men are passing from this world to their judgment.

In 1525, shortly after the Feast of Pentecost, Dürer dreamed that he saw columns of water falling from the sky from such a height that they seemed to descend in slow motion and strike the earth. He felt these waterspouts shake the ground, accelerating as they fell. The entire region was flooded. The hurricane, the noise, and the buffeting were terrific. He awoke trembling. In the middle of the night he made a drawing, a sepia, dark blue and green wash, of this fearsome pentecostal deluge. He gave no interpretation of the dream, he did not look for one. He simply wrote: "May God make everything for the better." That year, throughout Germany, people expected another flood.

4

Happy is the man who regains Antwerp by boat. He passes slowly from sea to fields, to farms and pathways, to villages, roads, and wagons. Windmills stand on mounds at the base of which shimmer rare puddles of river. The broad sky with its disorderly clouds heading out to sea, the high sea, cloud ships, and migrating geese. More and more numerous, the little boats dart recklessly among the big ships, which turn, heave to, catch the wind and sail away. Once again the gray nervous straw-strewn waters of the Scheldt, where gulls dive more restless yet and shrill. Calls and cries, the sound of sour trumpets on the wind. City smells and warehouse smells, of cattle on the piers, of fish, of exotic animals being unloaded. Leaning on the rails, Bruegel could name, for the first-time visitor to Antwerp, the sights along the shore: the Kronenburg Gate, Saint Michael's Abbey, the towers of Saint George's Gate, Notre Dame and Saint James churches, the town hall, Saint Walburge's church, the Kipdorp Gate, the Red Gate, the gray and green ramparts, stocky Castle Steen. Each place holds a living memory from his childhood. The ship enters the city of sails and masts, of paunchy hulls—the rocking harbor city. Here is the wharf, the *Werf,* a smoothly paved promenade, also called the *Craene,* after that marvellous crane that looks like some sort of catapult. "A truly pleasing and admirable view," wrote Guicciardini, "to take in at a glance the broad expanse of such a river, with its perpetual tides, to see coming and going at all hours, in all parts, ships from every nation and country, with all manner of men and merchandise, to see so many kinds of ship, so many instruments and means for maneuvering them that there is always something new to see."

Here is the labyrinth of wharves and unloading docks, crowded with tall, round vessels. And here the six-sided fishmongers' tower; red and white, topped with a small belvedere. Just beyond the wharves and warehouses, lies the beginning of the brick and stone city—and, for the newcomer fresh off the boat, step-gabled roofs, pinions, towers, steeples, all those spikes and shells mingling briefly with the sails and banners of the ships. How many ships? Ordinarily, more than two thousand, perhaps, on the eight major canals criss-

crossing Antwerp, spanned by seventy-four bridges, not counting
Meirbrugghe. Twenty-two squares, large and small, nestle in the
tight tangle of streets. Twice a year, the fair. Parades of boats—five
hundred a day enter and leave—and convoys of carts. For a week
or more the children of Babel come, in their varied dress, speaking
their tongues, they do their business. By way of the *vlieten*—the inner
canals—barges, galiots, small craft pile merchandise onto the warehouse wharf, the Hanseatic House pier, at the Portuguese, Norwe-
gian, and English docks. An enormous commerce and manufacture
of every object imaginable! Antwerp, like a mirror, reflects the world
in miniature.

"Antwerp produces everything one could ever want," wrote Guicciardini.

For here not only do they make woollens, all manner of linens, tapestries,
turkish rugs, fustian, armor and other munitions of war, leathers, colors,
Venetian earthenware, gold plate, silver plate, all kinds of trimmings of gold,
silver, and other metals, silk, cotton, wool, and countless other items; they
also produce all kinds of silken fabrics, such as velvets, satins, damascs, and
others; but in addition they use its worms, quasi contrary to nature and the
climate, to produce the very silk itself, however little it may be, and that
coming from abroad which is in great quantity. And finally they refine with
art and industry metals, wax, sugar and other products and produce to per-
fection the vermilion that we call cinnabar.

How many painters were living in Antwerp that year, those years?
How many sculptors, engravers? Several hundreds. In 1535, three
hundred painters left Antwerp for Italy, a good third under commission to the duke of Mantua. The *Schilderpand*—the picture exchange—was a permanent exhibition held beneath the arcades,
nearly spilling into the street. Vasari said that there was not a shop in
Italy that did not have a Flemish landscape hanging on the wall.

Not only was Bruegel in the habit of going to the *Schilderpand* to
sharpen his eye, gleaning lessons from admirable as well as mediocre
works; he learned from and enjoyed going to the *Tapesierspand*, the
tapestry warehouse; even at a distance he could tell the production
of Brussels from Sint-Truiden or Oudenaarde. He often mixed with
the crowds that flocked to the Dominican cloister: there all the precious objects produced or sold by Antwerp were displayed—books
by Plantin, chased and inlaid arms, helmets and breastplates, diamonds, jewelry, gold and silver cups and vessels, Nuremberg watches
set with rubies, looking glasses and rosaries, perfumes, laces, Venetian ceramic and crystal.

"The town," says Guicciardini,

grows and flourishes amazingly day by day. People live for the present (although some of the lower classes, as well as some of the more austere, observe the old custom of sobriety in food and drink) most sumptuously and perhaps more than is fitting. Likewise, men and women of all ages dress well according to their ability and state, and always in the newest and finest fashions, but many much more richly and ostentatiously than civility and decency require. And then one can see weddings, banquets, dancing at all hours; on all sides one hears the sound of musical instruments, singing and merrymaking: in short, the wealth, ostentation, and splendor of the town is everywhere to be seen.

Twice a day, morning and evening, the merchants would march in procession to the Stock Exchange, and the Hanseatic delegation would be preceded by a fanfare whose instruments were wider and taller than the musicians themselves.

Dürer preferred living in Antwerp to any other town of the Lowlands. He felt like he stood on the shore of America and at the heart of the world. He paid three florins for two ivory saltcellars. Laurent Sterk, the city treasurer, presented him with a wooden shield from the Indies. Erasmus gave him a short Spanish cloak and three portraits from his collection. He visited the burgomaster Arnold van Liere's new house in the Prinsenstraat and found it very well laid out, extraordinarily spacious with a great number of splendid, large rooms, a richly ornamented tower, an immense garden. *Summa summarum,* he notes in his diary, "such a magnificent house that I have not seen its equal in all of Germany." He made a silverpoint drawing of the tower, rising behind the shoulder of Lazarus Ravensburger, an Augsburg businessman, determined looking in his large hat with downturned flaps (the tower is almost oriental in its delicate detail). He did not regret the pourboire he gave to climb the tower, which must have been higher than the one in Strassbourg. He enjoyed the wind and the rain, and the gulls and crows playing around him; he enjoyed conquering his fear of heights and looking down into the secret recesses of the city. He let his gaze plunge into the narrow courtyards, scan red-scaled roofs, pick its way through the maze of narrow streets and canals, slip among the casks and bales on the piers, light on a boat, the deck of a ship, follow the stately river out to the mist and clouds of the sea. He could sense Germany, invisible in the gray distance. He prayed for Luther, whom he knew to be in danger. He observed that the cathedral was so vast that several masses could be sung without hindering each other. He marvelled at the liturgical furniture and its sculptures; he admired the stalls, the choir,

the carved stone triforium in Saint Michael's Abbey. "In Antwerp,"
he wrote, "they do not stint on things of that sort, for they have more
than money enough." Those who received him gave him a royal welcome: reverences, rows of dignitaries, gifts and gracious speeches,
banquets and presents of little casks. The Sunday following Assumption Day, he sought the best spot from which to watch the procession
of Our Lady. The entire city turned out, all the guilds and corporations, everyone dressed to the hilt, each according to his station. The
corporations and guilds had their individual characters, and he
sketched them as they passed. There were also, after the German
fashion, a great many fifes and drums. The brass bands blew for all
they were worth, and it made an enormous row.

Had he planned to go to Charles's triumphal entry when he went
to receive the imperial crown at Aachen? His host, Peter Gilles, the
chief secretary of the city, Erasmus's publisher, the friend to whom
Thomas More dedicated his *Utopia,* was one of the masters of ceremonies. He conducted Dürer to the workshop where the artists were
building the triumphal arches, the stages and scenery, the proces-
sional floats. He had personally drawn up the plans and designed this
wood-and-canvas city which would rise in the middle of the everyday town and which would be etched deeper in memory than all
those thousands of houses that time would destroy by the following
century. Dürer bought the program of the festivities and wonders to
come: "Hypotheses sive argumenta spectaculorum quae sereniis. et
invict. Caes. Carolo Pio sunt editori" (price: one denier). But what
he saw surpassed everything the brochure had led him to expect. Five
hundred young burghers from the best families, dressed alike in velvet and satin, mounted on flawless horses, led the procession. Then,
mounted on wagons or ships, scenes representing the Prophets, the
Annunciation, the Wisemen, the Flight into Egypt, and Saint George
slaying the Dragon. Was it the Scheldt float, or the one with the
Muses, that so dazzled Dürer? A knot of the most beautiful patrician
girls, their hair flowing, or bound up with pearls, dressed in light,
transparent linen, their breasts bared like Nymphs, curtsied before
Charles, who lowered his eyes. Dürer did not blink. He would later
even confess his delectation to his straight-laced friend, Melanch-
thon: "I have rarely seen such loveliness. I looked at them carefully,
I even stared, because I am a painter." Did he dream, watching Cæsar
in the throes of his theatrical apotheosis and his subjugation of the
city, that he was seeing a man whose one thought, in the midst of all
the "Vivats" and Spanish and Flemish music, was to end the life of

Luther, the Just. Cornelius Grapheus, Antwerp's other secretary and
the man who had worked with Peter Gilles to create the triumphal
decor, had presented Dürer with one of Luther's pieces: *Das Babylo-
nisches Gefängnis der Kirche* (The Babylonian Captivity of the Church).
Perhaps Dürer had slipped it inside his shirt as he watched the beautiful girls of Antwerp and their bare breasts, serene as though allegory
had the power to transform them into pure images. *O God, if Luther
is dead, if they have killed him, who will make the Holy Gospel so clear
to us?* It is for your faith that you are persecuted, and because you
attack the papacy which is no longer Christian and which opposes
our liberation in the name of human justice, and because we are
robbed, drained of our blood and sweat, yes, because of all this, you
risk your life.

And Dürer paid five pfennings silver for a pamphlet by Luther.
And he paid a pfenning for *Condemnatio doctrinæ librorum Martini Luther per quodam magistror Lovanienses et colonienses facta, cum respon-
sione Lutheri*. Would he have bought these pages had they not
contained the persecuted man's reply? Luther had many friends in
Antwerp. The police preferred to turn a blind eye. Such a port could
not survive without freedom and license. If they did not want the
foreign population to move to London or Germany, they must tolerate that which, elsewhere, was tracked down and burned. And it
would be tolerated as long as possible. What would have become of
the empire, Spain, their armies and fleets without the wealth of Antwerp? Charles resigned himself to the impious books, the heretical
conversations, the wild, rebellious thoughts as one sets aside a district
for brothels. Dürer could have ended his voyage there. Antwerp, like
Venice at one time, had offered him three hundred florins a year, a
house, and exemption from taxes. But he returned to Nuremberg.

Had I been born a few years earlier, Bruegel mused, I would have
seen Dürer walking these streets, along this pier. I would have met
Thomas More when he came as an emissary to Bruges and, while the
Spanish had retired to Brussels to deliberate, decided to go to Antwerp. Would it have been better to have lived then? The Island of
Utopia caught his fancy less than the first pages of the famous book.
"No friendship was sweeter than that of Peter Gilles. It eased my
longing for my homeland, my home, my wife and children. One day
I had gone to Notre Dame, one of the most revered churches and one
of our finest buildings. After mass, I was making my way back to the
hotel when I noticed Peter talking to a stranger who was past middle
age. His tanned face, long beard, simple cloak, the way he looked,
stood, gazed about him, marked him as a shipowner . . ." And then he

began the account of his travels. But he spent less time on the mores
of Amaurote than on the portrait of a sailor on the docks of Antwerp.

5

The history of art sometimes invents painters who have no name.
Whence the designations: The Master of the Virgin among virgins,
the Master of Augsburg and the Master of Flemalle, the Master of the
Shuttle, the Master of the Altenkirsche Cornflower, the Brunswick
Monogrammist. Some believe the last to be Jan van Amstel, Pieter
Coeck's brother-in-law from his first marriage. Others think it might
be Mayken Bessemers Verhulst. Could they have thought this if the
anonymous artist behind the monogram had not seemed to announce Bruegel? In either case, Bruegel could easily have seen his
work in the course of his apprenticeship. But the similarities between
his own work and the Monogrammist's appear only after the trip to
Holland. Was the painter whose work he saw at Coornhert's the artist
historians call the Brunswick Monogrammist?

It was at the end of his visit that, almost as an afterthought, Coornhert showed him his latest acquisition, which he had barely looked
at himself: a group of paintings put up for auction, a legacy without
an heir. Nothing was known about the owner—he had died or disap-
peared—nor about the painter (perhaps the traveler himself). Bruegel had seen them in dim light, set on the stairs, held up by Coornhert
and Cornelia, propped on the harpsichord, the largest one standing
on an easel. He had held up a candle to see them better. And what
he saw touched him as no other painting had done before. It was not
the genius of the works that struck him, but the the path to which
they pointed; they bespoke the possibility of a new work: it would be
his own.

We see him as he disembarks in Antwerp; he crosses the port and
the city without slacking his stride. Here he is in the still-shuttered,
dark room. He is glad to be back in his house, in his workshop with
its paper-strewn table. Of the whole trip, it is not the towns or the
skies that stand out, nor is it the phrases and the faces, the squalls at
sea and the exhilaration of the waves and the roar of the wind, but
that night in Haarlem and those candle-lit paintings.

At first he had thought that one was the parable of the Wedding
Feast as told by Luke: a man gives a banquet, but the guests make
excuses: one has to marry his daughter, another must try out a new
pair of oxen; and so the master of the house tells his servants: "Go

through the town and the villages and find me all those who are poor, even the dirtiest, the most wretched, and have them come; I am waiting, and everything is ready." In the courtyard of a farm-house—as high as a castle with turrets and even battlements—stood long tressel tables covered with embroidered white tablecloths and heaped to overflowing with piles of fruit, platters of meat, and baskets of cakes. A crowd of peasants in their Sunday best was eating and drinking. They were telling stories and laughing. A few couples were dancing to a small band playing atop some barrels or on a platform. At the gate, hat in hand, could be seen a line of beggars and cripples, perhaps even a few brigands, and they were being urged to come in, to sit down and eat. They were making an orderly entrance on crutches. To one side, or under the tables, some dogs were gnawing on bones. Forming a backdrop well to the rear was a smaller table. Seated under a green-and-gold canopy against a wall hanging was an old man, the master of the estate, and a white-robed young man, who resembled him. This, then, was not Saint Luke's feast, but the Prodigal Son. Behind the castle and tables lay the fields and stables, the herds, the ripe fields, then the distance; the gaze left the estate and its vicinity to follow roads, lake- and seashores, lose itself in blue-black forests, scale mountains and cross their snowfields to ocean shores where fleets, their penants flying like festive ribbons, did battle. There lay the wide world where the Son had strayed, the wide, inviting world, inviting every odyssey. In one town, with its sugar-candy turrets, through an open window (a bay window orna-mented with arches and lanterns) one could see velvet-gowned pros-titutes adorned with gold coins: these were the women who had devoured the Son's inheritance. In the lower town, where plague and famine now held sway, was the courtyard where he had served, the pig-trough hewn from a log, and the pigs the wretched child had tended. When the gaze had embraced the entire scene, it followed a line from the hellish courtyard to the father's heavenly court. Anyone contemplating the painting made the same journey, from the life of vice to the peaceful glory of home, like wise Ulysses. But it was not merely the picture's uplifting subject that touched Bruegel so. It was what the painter had invented: here was no longer, as in Patinir's work, a vast landscape setting for a biblical subject, the Flight into Egypt or Job's Sorrow, but a wedding of landscape and scene; he painted the world as he saw it, and with it, life. And the candle cast shadows over the plowed fields, the tablecloths, the snowy peaks in the far distance of the tale.

The candle cast daylight and dawn, snow, nighttime over the

plowed land, the roofs, the herds and ships, the boats on the lakes, the white peaks at the ends of the world. And Bruegel told himself that the world in which these parable characters dwell is not merely a setting. It is part of the parable. The world is a parable. I am passing through the visible world and its profusion of mountains and seas, its towns, its forests and fields, but this passing reminds me above all of my true passing: from the invisible to the invisible. I am a man on his way. Every man is on his way. Some are walking in their sleep, like soldiers who march with one hand on the cart rolling through the night. Some go through this world with their eyes on the ground, without a glance into themselves, seeing nothing of the world about them. Some go from birth to death with no sense of awe. I want to wake to this life and to the life invisible. I know that my journey through the world I see is a parable of the soul's own journey. And I will paint, to know this better. I will paint what I see to awaken myself to what I cannot see.

6

Van Mander writes that, in Middelburg, the home of Melchior Wintgis, master of the Zeeland Mint, contained three most remarkable paintings by Patinir, one of which, peopled with tiny figures, showed a battle executed in such minute detail that it had no equal among miniatures. Perhaps Bruegel saw it, if he came to Middelburg in the footsteps of Dürer, who was invited to Patinir's wedding, did one or two silverpoint portraits of him, was lent his host's apprentice and given free use of his colors and who, the day of his departure, left four Saint Christophers on gray paper highlighted in pink and white. What was that immense miniature battle whose armor and lances so gleamed in the luxurious home of Melchior of Middelburg? Was it the battle of Joshua, who seized the sun's chariot by the reins and held back the moon until he had won? Was it Moses' battle with Og, the king of Bashan? Or was it the battle Saul lost to the Philistines? The Bible is full of battles, there are even more battles than harvests or lovemaking in the shade of haystacks. War sweeps through the Book to the last pages of the apocalyptic Revelations.

The first dawn broke on the fratricidal knife in Abel's throat. The last sun will set on the chariots of Gog and Magog, jolting over the bodies and blood of the dead. Even our most peaceful days are wreathed in clouds of massacre. Not a valley but has seen a passing squadron or army. In Egypt the sea still eats at Pharaoh's arsenal, rusting it away. In the fields of Brabant, the plowman sometimes

chips his blade on the helmet of one of Cæsar's sergeants. Our grandchildren will pick up the helmet lost at the foot of an embankment
by some brute from Estremadura. The Bible, like the world, is a wheel
of blood. God became man and the lance pierced his bare side seeking
the heart. The seething savagery of mankind surges around the de-
fenseless God.

Bruegel painted Saul's last battle and his death. Were there a fir
tree growing at the left edge of the picture, no one would see the
dying king, for Saul ended his life alone, on a rocky ledge. If a narrow
strip were cut from the panel, we would see only an ordinary battle
in the midst of a vast mountainscape with a river. One must look
closely to discern the fighting: archers on the bluff, crossbowmen,
troops crossing the river, and, in the hollow in the foreground, a
mesh of helmets, horses, and lances so tightly packed that it looks
like a gray shower of needles and pins, but they are lances, halberds,
pikes so dense that one cannot tell the Philistines from the Israelites,
nor the direction of the battle. Both sides are locked in strife like so
many beetles, so many swarming locusts. Amid this host of wingcases
and shells, a horse stands out from the human herd, more deserving
of pity. But who can look on these massed helmets and lances milling
about in the gorge beside a river flowing toward illustrious towns and
on these flags, banners, and pennons, which, from that height and
distance, could be taken for a flurry of leaves falling in the gray light
of a rainy day? Who is watching this show of ludicrous wrath, this
fistful of fury in the hollow of a superb landscape, our games and
insectly savagery in a serene world bathed in the light of a beautiful
day? Who sees the grasses of war mowed down by death? Who
paints these absurd ears that harvest themselves to feed hungry
crows? Think of a spectator standing on a mountain high above the
mountains and the rocky prow depicted here, so like islands in the
expanse of plain and river. But such a mountain is unimaginable. It
must be an eagle or angels or the spirit of God, briefly contemplating
the story of our lives, or the spirit of man, or the painter who, casting
a swift glance over the valley of the Book containing the tale of Saul's
carnage and his suicide atop an isolated crag, sees things as the
chronicle tells them. And still the landscape unfolds, opening before
our eyes. The armored melee borrows its form from a seashell.

Samuel poured the oil onto Saul's head, and King Saul marched
toward madness and into the night of death. His jealousy of the
young shepherd who played for him and drove the Philistines from
his borders was like a poison. Three times he raised his spear to pin
David to the wall; with his men he pursued him into the mountains.

He withheld the offerings he owed to God and lied like a horsetrader. And when God fell silent and refused to speak by oracle, dream, or prophet, and when the prophet Samuel was dead, Saul, who had sentenced all soothsayers to death, donned a disguise and paid a nighttime visit to a necromancer's cave at Endor, and asked her to summon Samuel's ghost. Wrapped in a cloak, the old man rose from the depths of the earth and predicted that the king would be crushed like a nut between two stones, himself, his army, and his sons, by the Philistines. The end has come. His army has taken flight. Philistine arrows have cut down Jonathan, Abinadab, and Malchishua, his sons. And now Saul is the hunted man. He has taken refuge on a hill, to die, and not fall into the hands of idol worshippers, nor on the path or in public for others to gloat and blaspheme. He is wounded. Blood pours down his breastplate and covers his hands. His breath fails him. The crown on his gray head slips over his brow. He looks like an old jester dressed up as the king of Israel. And yet God chose him to rule over this people. He lifts a blind face to the sky. Is he thinking that David would close his eyes gently, tenderly, with respect?

Now he understands the breadth and the depth of his sin, his wretchedness; and the sob in his chest is round and hard like a stone; the grace of tears is not for him; he lacks the strength to hope that, in his eternal dawn, God will raise him up and bless him. The wind whipping the cheerful Philistine banners at the other end of the world brings him the panicky neighing of his horsemen's mounts, but the clamor is far away, like the laughter of his childhood and the hour of his consecration. What dark pennon has he followed all his life? He knows that his three sons lie bleeding in the stream, that they are already being stripped of their arms. He calls to his armor-bearer whom he sees red-stained nearby. He asks him to take pity and deal the final blow, but the boy recoils at the sacrilege, and lacks the courage to shorten the agony of his aged king. What if night were to come before the Philistines found them? Then Saul places his sword against his breast and lets himself fall. At the sight, the armor-bearer throws himself on his own sword; the painter shows him buckling beside the king. The night of death is about to descend on the army of Israel. The Israelites are fleeing their towns to the plains along the Jordan; the Philistines lose no time, they occupy, they plunder. Tomorrow those come to strip the dead will find Saul and his sons lying in the dew of Mount Gilboa. They will sever the king's head and take his armor. They will sound horns and proclaim the news throughout the land, in the temples of their false gods and to their people. They will place Saul's armor in the temple of Astarte and fasten his body to the wall of Beth-Shan. By the grace of God, faithful warriors from Jabes will come, under cover of night, and take away the remains, the relics; they will burn the bodies of Saul and his sons and bury their bones in the shade of a tamarisk.

Was the king mad? But what of the people? It was madness for the Israelites to ask for a king. They feared the Philistines. They wanted a leader, to be like other peoples. God's promise and protection were not enough. They went to Samuel, the prophet-judge. "What do you want with a king!" said Samuel. "He will take your sons and assign them to his chariotry and his cavalry, he will turn them into horsemen and bearers, he will make them run before his chariot or litter, blowing horns and waving fly-whisks! He will make them plow his fields and harvest his crops, make armor and gear for his cavalry. He will take your daughters for perfumers, cooks, and bakers. He will take the best of your fields, gardens, vineyards, and olive groves and give them to those who serve him. If you have manservants and maidservants, he will take them for himself. He will need your cattle and your donkeys for his own work. He will tithe what remains of your flocks. And you yourselves will become his slaves. When the day comes, you will cry out on account of your king, and God will not answer you." But the people would not listen, and, taking the sacred oil, Samuel anointed the head of a certain Saul, who was taller and more handsome than all the other young men of Israel, and who was God's chosen one.

A dead tree, shattered by a storm or old age, stands in the center of the picture. One might easily think that this is the end of Israel, that God has turned away from man. But we know that Samuel has anointed David, the hidden king. Just as Saul's body is hidden from the tangle of soldiers in the valley, young David is absent from the picture, but we feel his presence. One day Saul was pursuing David, seeking to kill him. David was on the other side of the mountain. They followed each other as day follows night. Saul's hatred and madness never dimmed David's love for the unhappy king. But David was forced to flee. He who once sang for the king, and whom the people acclaimed for his victories in battle, was now hunted, on the road, in the desert, with his band of soldiers. Who today gives any thought to David the resistance fighter? Did the painter perhaps have in mind Charles's imperial hand resting on the shoulder of young William of Orange as he walked to the throne he was about to abdicate? Did he have a premonition of William as the prince and liberator of the Seventeen Provinces? In the lower left-hand corner of the picture he wrote not only the date and his name, but the exact reference to the Book of Samuel, the last chapter of the story: SAUL XXXI CAPIT. BRVEGEL M.CCCCC.LXII. This is perhaps the only time he was to specify the text that his work commented upon. It meant: "Read it." Read the last chapter, which makes sense only if you have read the whole story of Saul and David. David was not a perfect king, but he was the ancestor of Christ, the only prince of peace in this tumultuous world. The subject of the painting is not the Death of Saul, but the Coming of King David, and the promise of the Coming of the Word in our Flesh. One must see past the disarray and the fury of combat, beyond the madness and wretchedness of kings and peoples to glimpse new life rising with its promise. One must see the unseen David. One must see him as the foreshadow and the root of Christ. Above the weeping and wailing, above the din of the fighting in the gorge, Bruegel heard the sound of the brook and the wind of the harp, the sound of King David's Psalms.

7

In the Valenciennes Prison, a twenty-year-old man, Gratien Wyart, was being held on suspicion of heresy. The burghers of Hainault were accustomed to sending their sons to study with bankers in France and England; from them they learned the art of bookkeeping and the latest refinements of the letter of exchange; that was why they were eager to send them to London, Nuremberg, and Frankfurt, despite placards declaring this a crime. Gratien Wyart may well have been one of the young burghers who had lost much of his Roman faith in one of these "suspicious countries or towns." No one could frequent the disciples of Luther and Calvin and not be obliged to think. Sometimes, on returning home, these young men even refused to go into business, but became preachers, converting whole districts and hamlets. When arrested, the new converts seemed to want nothing more than to die for all to see, that their blood and their blazing pyre announce the Gospel and the descent of the Holy Spirit—a taste for "rash vainglory," the judges called it. At times, it became expedient—despite a repugnance for breaking the rules, and because the crowd sometimes scattered the firewood, stamped out the flames, broke into the prisons, and delivered the prisoners who were singing one last psalm—at times it became expedient to forgo public punishment and strangle the rebels in their cell or hold their heads in a trough for a time. That way they died a natural, or a supernatural, death.

The daughter of the Valenciennes Prison warden was not yet eighteen. She loved this boy who was about to die, perhaps tomorrow, drowned in a vat or hanged by his linen. She was Irene mourning Sebastian—but she did not want him to die! She loved Gratien, and not with a sudden love born of desperation: they had known each other since childhood and every Sunday had exchanged endearments after church. And now, they spoke through the bars and the heavy door, they whispered that they loved each other, that they would love each other forever. In one corner of the kitchen, out of sight, she pressed her lips to the hard bread they took to his cell; the thought that she was kissing not the warm lips that would touch the bread, but the already cold brow of a deadman was too much to bear: her heart broke, and she knew they would run away, they must not wait, for she could already hear the heavy boots of the strangler, a big man who, it seems, was unaware of what he was doing, coming up the stairs from the cell. That very night, certainly by some divine miracle, her father, who never went out, left the house to answer a neighbor's call. She seized the keys and opened the doors. An angel of mercy guided her trembling hand. Night had fallen; they ran as far as the ramparts and the muddy stream; they had to plunge and swim. The girl lacked the strength. She begged Gratien to go on alone. God would protect her. And so Gratien made his way to Antwerp, while the child hid with the widow Michielle Deledale. Some days later, however, a neighbor, looking out his window, thought he saw her in the garden. Directly, soldiers circled the house and searched it. The girl woke and heard noises downstairs; she jumped out of bed and slid down the hen-house roof, but did not dare take to the street, for she was nearly naked. She crouched beneath a rosebush. It was almost winter, she was shivering, and few leaves remained on the shrubs. The soldiers, who were now beating the garden bushes, flashing their lanterns into every nook and corner, seized their pretty prey, bound her—barely pausing to throw down her dress and cloak—and took her to the judge. For her father's sake, Jacqueline summoned her courage and said that Gratien had asked her to do what she had done. The gray-bearded judge, the wise Catholic judge muttered that her shameless conduct had gravely endangered her father. But was Gratien merely a suspect? His flight proved he was guilty (at least of running away), and the girl, that wanton girl, his accomplice, deserved, at any rate, to die. Which she did that very day. Tied to a stake in the marketplace, she was simply strangled. Gratien learned of her death two nights later, in Antwerp; news traveled fast in that dark, troubled land under the heel of judges and torturers, under the heel of prelates.

The account adds that "Gratien managed to bring the girl's younger sister to Antwerp and marry her, thus doing his best to keep his promise to the elder." Personally, I think that Gratien Wyart was on board one of the vessels that, in the end, delivered Flanders from its devils.

3

OF GARDENS AND OF WARS

There are few flowers in Bruegel's painting. I am not forgetting the purple or the red iris growing in the ditch into which *The Blind Men* of Naples fall. Nor the blue iris beside the lumpish young peasant, about to tumble into a stream as he points to a birdnester in the crotch of a tree. I am not forgetting a bowl of daisies hanging on a tree beneath a picture of the Virgin in one country dance scene. I would never forgive myself if I forgot the Christmas roses peeking through the snow in the narrow garden by the leper's hut in *The Tithe*. I can still see the clump of red flowers in *The Hay Harvest*, and some flowers and a tall thistle on the slope leading up to Calvary. The thistle and the iris: perhaps these are symbols, like the iris in Annunciation scenes. If iris evoke Iris, the messenger of the gods, a sort of female Hermes, is this to remind us that we must seek the right path, be on the lookout? It is possible that, in early paintings, each flower was a message, a lesson, a proverb, a prayer. The forget-me-not still speaks to us. And we still ask our fortune of daisy petals. But is it certain that we hear everything the old paintings and tapestries—the millefleurs tapestries of the old Low Countries—are trying to tell us with their plants, with their flowers and bouquets? Van Eyck's *Apocalypse* is a garden. Hugo van der Goes has placed two bouquets of wildflowers next to the straw in his Nativity scene, one in a delicate vase, the other in a crystal glass. Peter Bruegel has not followed them on this point. Neither did he pause, like Dürer, before the mystery of a clump of grass or an earthy, damp cluster of lily of the valley, fresh as a late-spring rain, rich black earth still clinging to the roots, as though all that is candid and verdant was destined to come forth from the night that slumbers beneath our footsteps, forgotten. He did not show himself with an emblematic wild carrot or thistle in one hand. Like each of us, he enjoyed a morning walk through dewy meadow grass, past willows and elders, past poplars rustling in the wind; but I do not remember a single small daisy or buttercup, not a dandelion

in the meadows around Babel or on the banks of the building site.
No poppies in *The Harvesters'* wheat fields (I see a flicker of bachelor
buttons, though). Neither violet nor primrose under the trees of his
kermises. This painter who never omitted the birds, in his landscapes
or his scenes of daily life, hardly gives a thought to simple plants:
his love of greenery is reserved for trees, big trees, and knee-high
brambles. Perhaps to all our gardens he preferred snow and the fire
of icicles hanging from the eaves. The flowers would fall to his son
John, nicknamed Velvet, or Flower, or Paradise Brueghel, who would
revel in garlands and bouquets. A single bouquet, like the one in
Milan's Ambrosian Library, would occupy him from spring to fall.

Even in the days of Bruegel the Elder, Holland and Flanders had a
passion for flowers. People ruined themselves for a single bulb. Was
this a legacy of the cloisters and beguinages? Did it come from the
dyers with their gardens at the foot of the ramparts, where their
many-colored wools lay drying on frames—*rames;* where, among the
squares of wool, the weld, madder and woad grew for their dyes?
And if so many roses adorned house fronts, was it, as a poet of Bruegel's time suggests, because, in a country where the sun is all too
rarely seen, flowers are the stars that stand in its stead.

In the middle of the sixteenth century, Pieter Caudenberg, an Antwerp pharmacist, imported four hundred plants from America and the
East and acclimated them in his garden. He spent even more time on
the waterfront than in his greenhouses and borders. All the captains
he knew had instructions to bring back, in the large boxes he had
invented and built to withstand any weather during the voyage, the
plants God sows at the ends of the earth. Under the patronage of Saint
Dorothy, leagues of flower lovers and brotherhoods of gardeners
would meet and vie with each other. In a sonnet entitled *Happiness
in This World,* Plantin wrote of: "A garden lined with sweet-scented
espaliers." No doubt he found no less pleasure or profit in publishing
books of plants than collections of maps. Even war enriched the gardens. From Tunis, which the Flemish had besieged on behalf of the
emperor, they brought back the carnation.

No doubt Bruegel knew Auger Ghiselin de Bousbecques, who was
about the same age and who had been ambassador of the Holy Roman Empire to the court of Suleiman, had spent seven years in Constantinople in a house he had bought on one of the hills overlooking
the Bosphorus, surrounded by monkeys, birds, a brown bear or two—
in his letters he called his villa "my Noah's Ark." Returning home, he
brought with him not only ancient coins and Greek manuscripts,
among which, one by the botanist Dioscoridus, but lilacs, horse-

chestnuts, gladiolas, and tulips—which still bear the Turkish name, *tulbend,* 'turban'. He brought with him a promise of eight years' peace between the Turks and ourselves and that glory for the gardens of Europe. Wars between peoples, massacres halt neither trade, nor exchange, nor the commerce of beauty and wisdom: books, thoughts, images, music, and flowers. So, at times one hears above the din of battle, in the heart of the killing grove, the laughing song of a blackbird. Our hellfires cannot consume every thread of the heavenly memory or promise. While some devote their time and genius to the art of torture and slaughter, others dedicate their lives to the coloring of a corolla.

2

At that time the Turks were the terror of Europe. In Italy or Spain one could be walking along the seashore, even at some distance from the water, and turbaned pirates could spring out: this spelled the chain gang, the galley, or the harem in Tunis, Algiers, or Constantinople. Barbary pirates plundered villages, ports, and castles. Every four years, the sultan's troops would descend upon the Balkans and take their boys for bodyguards and servants. In 1529, the Turks occupied Hungary. In 1533, they laid siege to Vienna: an army of three hundred thousand, whose white tents formed a canvas city all about the stone city defended by a scant twenty thousand men, camped on either bank of the Danube. The siege lasted three months. At last winter, the rain, and the mud discouraged the Turks. But Barbarossa, the admiral of their fleet, was ravaging the Italian coast. In April 1534, he occupied Tunis; Sicily lay before him. Between the winter of 1534 and the following spring, Mediterranean Christendom was shaken by thirty-five general alerts. At last, at the behest of the emperor, Genoa sent galleys and carracks; Naples, galleons; Portugal, caravels; the pope and the knights of Rhodes dispatched fleets to form an armada of three hundred ships which assembled in Barcelona, then set sail for Tunis. It was during these bloody times that Pieter Coeck van Aalst was making his way to Constantinople. Coeck had learned to draw under Bernard van Orley, a painter and designer of tapestries. And then van Mander goes on,

he had visited Italy and Rome, the great school of the arts; he had spent day and night studying the statues and monuments. After his return to the Lowlands and the death of his wife, he was sought out by a Brussels' tapestry firm by the name of van der Maeyen to travel to Constantinople, where they hoped to create a sensation by the manufacture of fine, rich wall-hangings for the Grand Turk. To this end, they commissioned Pieter to produce several paintings for presentation to the Sultan. According to the Law of Mohammed, however, the Sultan could not accept images of man or beast. The venture had for unique outcome the voyage and the great expense it occasioned.

It may be that Coeck did not take the actual cartoons worked up for his client, but tempera paintings that simulated tapestry, done in distemper like the cartoons themselves but on canvas, which was less costly than either tapestry or oil painting. This industry made the fortune of Mechelen: Mayken Verhulst, Pieter Coeck's second wife, excelled in the technique, and no doubt Bruegel employed it. This could explain a certain way he had of using bold strokes, and the fact that he chose tempera for *The Blind Leading the Blind* and what, for me, is his finest and most touching work, *The Adoration of the Magi,* which is little more than a drawing with a light color wash. The unbleached canvas shows through the snow and stubble in place of the hills, and one cannot tell whether the fragility, the tenuous, soothing impression of this barely visible painting is due to the skill of the painter or to the prodigious work of time on that fragile medium of tempera on canvas.

I find it hard to believe the reasons van Mander gives for this journey and its failure. How could the Flemish be unaware of the Islamic prohibitions on images. And were there not Turkish paintings portraying the sultan with his wives, his deer, battle and hunting scenes, the palace musicians and dancing girls? Had not Gentile Bellini painted Mehmet II? Perhaps the purpose of Coeck's voyage had been to bring back the secret of oriental dying: the crimson of Damascus silk, the drapery of Alep or Acra, or Ispahan carpets.

I do not know if he returned with any such secrets, or plants and seeds, as did Bousbecques. But he did bring back pictures.

"Having spent nearly a year in this country," van Mander goes on,

Pieter learned the Turkish language and, incapable of remaining idle, took pleasure in drawing scenes of Constantinople and its vicinity. His drawings have been reproduced on seven wood panels showing various Turkish customs. First of all, one sees how the emperor of the Turks is in the habit of riding out with his bodyguard and retinue. Second, a Turkish wedding and the manner in which the bride is preceded and escorted by musicians. Third, the way in which the Turks go about burying their dead on the outskirts of the town. Fourth, the festival of the new moon. Fifth, the way in which Turks take their meals. Sixth, how they travel. Seventh, their manner of waging war. In all the panels we see beautiful backgrounds and the curious behavior of the figures, their manner of carrying loads and other burdens, skillfully rendered attitudes and poses, tiny figures of women prettily dressed and veiled, a great variety of costumes, all of which provide a very advantageous idea of Master Pieter's intelligence. In the seventh panel, he has drawn himself in Turkish costume and holding a bow. He is pointing to a figure beside him holding a long lance with a flame.

These engravings were published three years after Pieter Coeck's death by Mayken Verhulst, whom he had married shortly after his return. The plates bore the inscription: *Les moeurs et fachons de faire des Turcz, avecq les regions et appartenantes, ont este au vif contrefaictez par Pierre Coeck d'Alost, lui estant en Turquie l'an de Jesus Christ* M.D. *33* ("The customs and manners of Turkey, drawn from life by Pieter Coeck van Aalst, himself having been in Turkey in the year of Our Lord M.D. 33").

Bruegel apprenticed himself to Pieter van Aalst several years after the latter's return from Turkey. How old could Bruegel have been? Ten, thirteen maybe. Van Aalst's tales entertained him, and he listened avidly, trying to separate what had truly happened from what had been improved upon. He was for ever asking van Aalst about what he had seen, his adventures en route, the wonders of the world. Pieter van Aalst seemed to have forgotten it all. He seemed oblivious of the aura of travel and distant lands that young Peter perceived about him. His mind was on what he was doing now, on what he was going to do. The house was aswirl with as much activity as any waterfront concern: tapestries, paintings, designs for facades and gardens, stained-glass windows; all these projects and commissions came and went, along with the clients and travelers, and they were always behind. If he thought about it, Constantinople seemed scarcely any further than Nuremberg or Basel. Day by day, you get there, that's all there is to it; and then you come back. You see the sun set on the Bosphorus a hundred times and today here you are, back in this light, like someone who has never left Brussels. When he met a traveler, young Peter felt very like he did when he touched a Roman coin: Cæsar or one of his men might have held it between thumb and forefinger, as he was doing now. The world lay before him, and he felt slightly intoxicated as he took his first step. What held him back? He would go to Italy. He would go by way of the mountains. He would go to Rome and see all that Coeck had seen. Would he come back? Beyond Rome, he could glimpse Jerusalem. Or perhaps he would go to Venice, and from there strike out for China? He could picture himself traveling over those cloud-covered snowy mountains, crossing hog-backed bridges, following the shoreline of those great lakes, embarking for some transparent isle or taking shel-

ter from the wind beneath an umbrella, as in the silk paintings from
that country. Would he return? He would. And he would be older.
He would visit Antwerp's waterfront and the shops of his childhood.
No one would recognize him. He would have forgotten certain everyday words, or would pronounce them in a curious way.

Along with the Turkish drawings, Mayken Verhulst Bessemers
published her husband's books on architecture. This was not the least
part of his work. Guicciardini pays him this homage: "He has the
particular praise of bringing back from Italy the canon of architecture, and furthermore translating the fine and excellent work of Sebastian Serlio, of Bologna, into Flemish, to the great advantage of the
Netherlands."

And van Mander writes:

He wrote books on architecture, geometry and perspective. As he was a man
of letters and well versed in Italian, he translated the books of Sebastian
Serlio into our language; such that, through his efforts, he enlightened the
Low Countries and brought back to the straight and narrow the art of architecture, which had gone astray. We owe it to him that the obscure passages
of Vitruvius can now be read with ease, and there is hardly any need to read
this author on the orders. It is Pieter Coeck, then, who is the source of knowledge on the true manner of constructing and the adoption of the modern
style.

Coeck's book was entitled: *The Making of Columns with Their Capitals
and Their Proportions, after Vitruvius and Other Authors, abridged for the
use of painters, engravers and stonecutters, published at the urging of his
friends.* It came out in 1539, some twelve years after Pieter van Aalst's
stay in Rome. Printing and engraving were instrumental in acquain-
ting the Low Countries with Antique and Italian models. In 1546,
Hieronymus Cock opened his Four Winds printshop, for which Bruegel worked until his death. Almost immediately Cock published several treatises on architecture, among which the *Præcipia romanæ
antiquitas monumenta,* accompanied by fifty-nine copper-plate engravings, and the *Operum romanorum per diversas Europæ regionis,*
which included twenty plates. These collections were no less precious
to painters than to those whose trade it was to build. Pieter Coeck
lost no time: Serlio's Fifth Book had just come out in Venice; he began translating the work in its entirety—and Serlio, who was in Fon-
tainbleau at the time, looked forward to the result.

But in matters of architecture Coeck was not content with mere
books. Prince Philip's joyous entry into Antwerp in 1549 gave him
the occasion to design and build a superb series of stage sets. A
wooden theater suggested Florentine palaces in the heart of the old

town. The ornamentation, executed *en grisaille,* announced the stone ornaments. Two thousand workers labored at this town of allegories and dreams. Coeck was not alone in the undertaking: Hieronymus Cock, Frans Floris, and perhaps Vredeman van Vries also had a hand. It was the custom that each country represented in Antwerp should present the prince with a triumphal gate. With its pylons and four obelisks, the Spanish gate added to the Roman monument an Eastern flavor.

3

Many historians doubt Bruegel ever studied with Pieter Coeck. Indeed his work bears little resemblance to Coeck's, which is highly Italianate. It is said that van Mander invented this apprenticeship, thinking of Peter's marriage with Mary: "He learned his craft from Pieter Coeck van Aalst, whose daughter he later married. When he lived with van Aalst, she was a little girl whom he often carried about in his arms." It may also be that he confused Pieter Coeck and Matthias Cock, Hieronymus's elder brother. Matthias Cock was an excellent landscape artist: "He was the first to give to this genre of painting the variety it lacked, taking his inspiration from the Italian or the Ancient manners, and he showed much imagination in the composition of his vistas. He painted many excellent pictures in oils as well as tempera." He was the son of Jan Willens van Cock, of Leiden, who was also a landscape artist. It is said that he was one of the first, if not the first, to use a wash over his drawings. Could Bruegel have been trained by Matthias Cock? It is not unthinkable. Cock's drawing *Landscape with Village Surrounded by Trees at the Foot of a Range of Hills,* or *Boulders in a Bay,* both at the Louvre, and even the *Rape of Europa,* despite some Italianate figures, are reminiscent of Patinir or Herri met de Bles, but they could also be forerunners of Bruegel's windmills and trees, his water-worn boulders standing in the sea, and his distances. One *Nocturnal Landscape,* once thought to be by Bruegel, is now attributed to Matthias Cock. And the apprenticeship under Matthias would also explain how he came to know Hieronymus, of whom van Mander thinks less well:

Of his brother, I have little to say except that he gave up cultivating art early in life to devote himself to business. He commissioned and purchased paintings in oils and tempera, published engravings and etchings, especially after his brother's work. There is particularly a series of twelve landscapes that is much in demand. Hieronymus became a wealthy man and bought up houses, one after the other. He married a girl from Holland by the name of

Volck or Volcktgen, who gave him no children. As he was a wit and a versifier, he was in the habit of repeating and sometimes inscribing on his prints his motto: "The cock [cook] cooks for the good of the people," or *Hout die Cock in eeren*, "Hold the cook in esteem," and other such puns. On certain plates he inscribed, after the fashion of the Rhetoriqueurs: "The cook owes his public dishes most varied / Roast meats and boiled / If the dish does not please / It can be rejected / But do not blame the people or the cook."

In effect, Cock's shop carried something for everyone and for every bent of mind.

It is unfortunate that one cannot visit the Four Winds salesroom and workshop as one does Christopher Plantin's house and printshop. One can only dream. The engravers in the back room, working by the windows, the daylight setting the copper ablaze; the presses with their star-shaped wheel, like the wheel on a poop deck; the black of the inks, the carefully coaxed proofs; the shop with the comings and goings of clients and browsers, prints drying on lines, tapestry cartoons, packages to be carted away to a ship or down some road. The shop printed pictures—all kinds of pictures: Raphael and Hieronymus Bosch, Titian and Michelangelo, saints and patriarchs, the Virtues and Vices, gods and goddesses, all manner of animal, maps of earth and sky, city maps and bird's-eye views, customs and costumes, the theater of proverbs, landscapes of America or Brabant, examples of architectural styles, street scenes, peasant scenes, crowds skating on the frozen Scheldt, seagoing men and their vessels, wartime disasters and sufferings, the splendor of the emperor, a monster fish beached at Gröningen. Imagery both scholarly and popular; often the two. One collection of landscapes of Kempen and Brabant bore the title: *Multifarium casularum ruriumque lineamenta curiosa ad vivum expressa;* another: *Prædorium villarum et rusticorum icones.* Sometimes the same engravers could be found working for Plantin and for Cock. The two houses were more allies than rivals.

It was not the need to earn his living that kept Bruegel at the Four Winds; it was happiness. He was happy to be a member of this crew, this family, happy in the midst of so many inventions and exchanges, happy to be able to say things the way simple folk like and understand. Icarus and Dædalus beat their wings high above the Scheldt: that is Ovid speaking of fairs and farms. *Big Fish Eat Little Fish* and the *Battle of the Strong Boxes and the Money Bags* are pictures for all times. But their message is more pointed when a single brewer can own twenty-four breweries in Antwerp or when a bankruptcy can break the city again. This taciturn man took pleasure in the silent lesson which was no sooner conceived than engraved and spread across the land and throughout Europe like leaves swept before the wind. It gave him pleasure, sitting poised before his drawingboard and paper, to imagine the thousands of theaters he would open in homes, the landscapes he would roll out for all those who would never see more than these inked shadows. His art of the simple form and unforgettable proverbial image were acquired during his years at the Four Winds. We know the painter he was to become, and we think he was dawdling along the way, too long unknown to himself; but he was aborning! He was honing his skill by practicing on this nearly anonymous art; everyone of these drawings might have been lost. One pen-and-ink drawing from 1550—or perhaps 1559—is a seascape with rising storm and slanting rain, just off the coast of Antwerp, which appears on the horizon. A small island harbors a wheel and gallows leaning in the wind. The huge swells are those of *The Tempest,* which he was to paint at the end of his life.

4

"The women," writes Guicciardini,

besides being (as I said above) beautifully and excellently formed, have a fine and gracious demeanor, for they begin in childhood, according to the custom of the country, to converse freely with all and sundry, because of which, in their ways, speech and in all other things, they become quick and adroit; but notwithstanding their great liberty, behave with most recommendable decency and decorum, often going about their business alone, not only in town, but as often from one town to another, with a very small retinue, giving no cause for blame. Indeed they are most sober and active, dealing not only with household matters, in which the men take very little part, but also concerning themselves with buying and selling merchandise and goods and turning hand and tongue to every other sort of masculine matter, all with such skill and diligence that in several parts of the province, as in Holland and Zeeland, the men leave almost everything to them, which manner of proceeding, together with the natural female appetite for dominating, no doubt makes them too imperious and at times too troublesome and proud. But let us move on.

In the Netherlands, women were sometimes "paintresses," as Guicciardini calls them: "Anne Smijters of Ghent, a truly excellent and worthy paintress."

Anne Smijters married Jan van Heere and was to become the mother of the painter Lucas van Heere. Before taking up Lucas, van

Mander speaks of his mother: "Dame Anne Smijters was an excellent illuminator, author of rare works executed with an exquisitely delicate brush. Among other things, she painted a windmill with vanes, the miller carrying a sack up the ladder and, on the mound, a horse and cart, and finally some passers-by, and the whole scene could be covered by half a grain of wheat." In his *Description,* Guicciardini mentions other women painters: Levinia Bening, Catherine van Hemessen, and Mayken Bessemers.

It is said that Anne Smijters challenged Mayken Bessemers to a contest of miniatures. Mayken accepted and is supposed to have added to the painting of the windmill the size of half a grain of wheat, a clearly identifiable child holding a toy pinwheel. There are other stories about Parrahsios's curtain or Zeuxis's birds, and the like. The truth is, however, that her talent lay less in tours de force, like the flea circus or wonders that could be seen only through a jeweler's glass, than in her imagination and gift for composition. If I were writing a scholarly (but imaginary) biography, I would pass over Pieter Coeck as Bruegel's painting master. Mayken Verhulst would have this role. She would train young Peter as she trained her grandson, John, thirty years later. She would instruct him in the art of the miniature as well as in tempera on canvas. And Bruegel would combine the monumental composition of tapestry with the detail of miniatures. And miniaturist he was: the Italian painter of miniatures, Giulio Clovio, owned a little *Tower of Babel* on ivory, now lost; and, in a *Last Judgment* by his own hand, a medallion by Bruegel depicting Ships in a Storm (perhaps an End of the World: "Un quadretto di miniatura la metà fatto per mano sua et altra da Mᶜ Pietro Brugole"). For Clovio to ask his collaboration, this *piccolo e nuovo* Michelangelo, as Vasari terms him, thirty years his junior, must have been more than a beginner. It was as a miniaturist, too, that he painted the teeming armies of Saul's last battle. It was again the miniaturist drawing the rivers and valleys from his mountaintop vantage, capturing the tip of a spire, the corners of a roof half hidden in the distance, the rabbit about to be killed by a hunter. Often he was to unite the immense and the minute. He would juxtapose two scales, and thus embrace the world. And might he not have cherished the subject of Babel so because Babel is a giant miniature? More vast than anything under the sun, or within the compass of land and sea; so vast that the mountain seems a mere mound at the foot of the spiraling wall; and yet high in the scaffolding I can see the yellow bird, and the stone-cutter pausing for his break and holding out a crumb in his fingers.

Below, in the distance, shimmering in the haze, the blue roofs of the town stand out so sharply that I can distinguish and name the tangle of little streets where the builders ran about as children.

Pieter Coeck introduced him to the art of tapestry. When he set out to besiege Tunis, the emperor had taken with him Jan Cornelis Vermeyen to witness and record the exploits of the Christian army. This was a year after Coeck's voyage to Constantinople. It was a great adventure, of which not the least exalting episode was the uprising of the Spanish prisoners who, having escaped from their cells by ruse, lit fires to signal the liberating fleet and proceeded to attack the garrison. Did Vermeyen actually see the blood, the severed limbs, the death throes, the wounds and abscesses? Or did he see only the marine light, the magnificent deploying of the troops, and the future beauty of the twelve tapestries glowing softly with a yellow cast: *Reviewing the Troops at Barcelona, The Landing of the Imperial Troops, The Attack on the Goulette, Combat on Horseback, The Taking of the Goulette, The End of the Siege, The Issuing Forth of the Besieged,* et cetera? A dizzying monument of ships and boats, oars and sails, prancing and galloping squadrons, canon, soldiers and captains, pikes and halberds, morions, crests, muskets, waves, walls, and foliage. Maria of Hungary, then regent of the Low Countries, commissioned their weaving. It has been said that Pieter Coeck collaborated with Vermeyen. And that Bruegel assisted. If this is true, he would have known Vermeyen and remembered his lesson in bird's-eye views, ships in the foreground, the harbor barely visible in the distance, and the artist himself on the edge of the landscape, sketching the battle. All this brings to mind *Ships off the Coast of Naples,* one of Bruegel's first paintings; several Alpine landscapes in which he includes himself beneath a tree, pen or paintbrush in hand. Were tapestry-making not customarily regarded as one of the minor arts, it would no doubt be easier to see all Bruegel owed it: his vision of the world, his use of solid, broad masses, and not only in the imitations of him painted at Mechelen. *The Seasons,* which he composed for Jonghelinck's house, in all likelihood for a rotunda, Jonghelinck could have commissioned from a master tapestry-maker. As he worked, Bruegel may have had in mind van Orley's tapestries of Maximilian's hunts or *The Months,* produced in the workshops of Brussels. Perhaps he recalled the *Tower of Babel* tapestries, now hanging in Cracow, as he set about to paint the same subject.

Pieter Coeck was to introduce him to architecture. The artist who painted Towers of Babel—the big tower, in Vienna, an enormous construction site; and the small tower, in Rotterdam, which shows two lines of dust running up the wall beneath the hoist rope, one red, left by the bricks, the other white, from the lime—this painter was an architect. He dreamed of the edifice to end all edifices, but he knew how to reckon as well. He assessed the power of the cranes and machines. He observed the movement of the trolleys on the slopes, the carts as they crossed: he planned, he organized. He thought out the carrying capacities and the buttresses. He combined the orders and the lighting. With keen pleasure, and precision, he ornamented the openings, arches, moldings, cornices. He constructed an image that had the force of a dream, the truth of a memory, the precision of a plan. He took as much pleasure in showing the undertaking and the site as the levels and stages of a work as yet inhabited only by masons and birds.

"Some of his best works are today in the possession of the emperor," writes van Mander, "to wit: one large panel representing the Tower of Babel seen from above with numerous highly colored details, and the same subject in a small format." The Tower of Babel *as seen from above!* Indeed, to provide a glimpse of the inside, its construction, to give an idea of its plan and, along with the circular facade and spiral ramps, a cross-section as though he were addressing less the art lover or the theologian than a contractor or an archaeologist. But such an eye for architecture does not come from a simple reading of Vitruvius or Serlio or Palladio. One must have looked up through scaffoldings, forded trenches on muddy planks and supervised several sites. One must have learned from experience how to balance loads, how to pursue that sort of peaceable struggle by means of which materials are assembled into those shells and nests that enfold our humanity. If Coeck introduced Bruegel to the art of building, it was through practicing the skills.

In Antwerp, Pieter Coeck built a mansion that was to be the epitome of all he liked in architecture. Years earlier, he had bought some land in the district where van Schoonbeke would set up his pump outside the old ramparts. Van Schoonbeke was the brewer who owned twenty-four breweries and who drove his competitors, the small brewers in the Cammerstraat, to bankruptcy because his invention—a water tower affair in what would become the Brewers' house, down near the waterfront—could pump water cheaply from the Herentals Canal and distribute it throughout the town to his breweries, while the rumor circulated that the brewers using water from Meier Pond were poisoning their customers. When the aldermen would try to stop their brewing, they would reply that the water from

van Schoonbeke's *Waterhuis* was infested with vermin. A battle of
strong boxes and money bags, right up to the riot that would force
van Schoonbeke to flee to Brussels to recoup his fortune there. But
for the time being, the city of Antwerp had financial worries, and
they ceded him a block of empty lots. Was it for love of beer that van
Schoonbeke turned brewer and invented his water pump and the
network of hollow logs that carried tons of water until the present
century? Or did he want to fill the housing he built with workers and
waggoners? His father was already bitten with this passion. He had
begun the construction of the Koningstraat; Gilbert finished it. Then
he laid out the Grain Exchange, surrounding it with a maze of
streets—Bloemenstraat, Orgelstraat, Ketelstraat, Kelderstraat, Arme
Duivelstraat, to which he added others still. In one of these streets,
perhaps on Coeck's advice, he built the *Tapesierspand,* the Tapestry
Exchange, which would not open until two years after Coeck's death,
in 1552. Ten years earlier, Antwerp had begun the construction of a
new town hall. What with the ramparts and the moats, the final bill
would amount to a million gold crowns. But work had come to a
halt. Van Schoonbeke offered his services. He was in a position to
win the commission. He owned lime kilns on the banks of the Meuse,
near Namur, and boats to ferry the lime to Antwerp. He enjoyed the
right to cut oaks in the Forest of Buggenhout: those were his beams,
girders, and scaffoldings. In order to save on outlay for bricks, he
made his own: thirty brickworks at Kallebeke, on the Scheldt; and
transportation by raft to the foot of the wall. To heat the lime and
brick kilns, he bought heathland at Zevenbergen and extracted the
peat. Bruegel had strolled about the site, he had walked in the road
dust, the brick dust, the lime dust. This he enjoyed much as he did
the waterfront. He trod the slippery ground, the hardened ruts, looking and listening. He leaned against the walls of the houses van
Schoonbeke had built for his workers, like the camp of a besieging
army, so they might be ready to hand, work in relentless shifts, never
losing sight of their task. Leaning back, his drawingboard balanced
on his forearm, he sketched the wheelbarrow and the hoist, the la-
borer propped on his shovel handle, the wall made even redder by
the rain, the rickety shed and the flower, which had already taken
root between two bricks, nodding in the wind, and perhaps longer
lived in its seeds to come than all our buildings and thoughts.

Antwerp was bursting with new buildings. It was not only van
Schoonbeke, but his rivals and colleagues, Grammaye, Boelman, or
van Hencxthooven, who were punching through the labyrinth of old
streets and alleys, imposing their straight, airy throughfares. They

tore down the wood and thatch houses that caught fire at the first spark and stood in foul water. A Venetian, Marino Caralli, sighed, "Antwerp causes me pain, for I see Venice surpassed." But Guicciardini, whose heart belonged to Antwerp, rejoiced:

And besides being encompassed by such beautiful and strong city walls, garnished and ornamented with all manner of handsome artillery and perfected munitions of war, and all manner of other bellicose instruments and apparatuses. . . . Antwerp now has, counting big and small, two hundred and twelve broad streets, for the most part straight and fair. . . . In Antwerp there are now more than thirteen thousand five hundred houses, and space designated for one thousand five hundred more. Such that, if the town continues to prosper as it has for the last several years and as it continues to do, it is estimated that, within a short time, this space must be filled with dwellings; which will make, all told, fifteen thousand houses, together with some beautiful gardens. . . . Besides the private homes, there are several magnificent public buildings, such as the *Tapesierspand,* the Butchers' House, the New Weigh House, the superb dwelling leased to the English, called Thof van Liere, or Ivy Court, because of Aert of the most noble House of Liere, who designed it after the fashion of a royal palace for the court of Emperor Charles V, and had it built; the sumptuary *pachus,* or warehouses, that the town had built to order for the same English; the dwelling that is lent to Portugal's transport agent; the new building at which the overland merchandise will be unloaded. But the Osterlins mansion will stand over and above all these by its size, beauty and magnificence, set nobly in the new town, between two canals, which, as I was finishing the present work, was going up with a most stately show and appearance. In short, all that was lacking was a palace for the nobles of the town, fitting and worthy of such a republic and corresponding to its other parts, which they have since built; and it is most sumptuous, capacious and truly stately, so that, when all is said and done, it will cost nearly one hundred thousand ecus.

The Coeck mansion would delight the eye with its alternating blue and white stones and brick. The front of the house would be reminiscent of the facades of Florentine palaces. The inward-facing facades would open onto a succession of courtyards and gardens and porticos. Corinthian columns would mix with Tuscan pilasters, and pointed with curved pediments. Long halls would be provided for rainy-day strolls and drawingrooms in which to converse in comfort. The mantelpieces would be decorated with profusions of grotesqueries and sculpted with the most moving scenes from the *Æneid.* Snowy marble staircases would lead to the upper floors. The galleries would be there, lighted by wide bay windows, in which tapestries and paintings could be exposed. The library would be hexagonal, and the music room round: the floor design would be a wheel of gold and azure mosaic with grapevine garlands; Apollo would lead the procession of muses winding among the columns along the wall. The friezes of the main courtyard would feature the Tiber and the Arno hailing the distant Scheldt, king of the rivers, receiving his crown from the hand of Mercury. Jonghelinck would cast in bronze the Seven Planets encircling a fountain with a sleeping Bacchus. The gardens would be lined with arbors. A summer house amid carnations and tulips would recall the master's journey. Antiques would dot the labyrinth. The rising sun would flush the noble facade, and the setting sun would stain the courtyard windows and the Fountain of the Planets crimson and Turkey red.

This is what Bruegel sees in the lot that is being cleared. He helps the workmen with the chalkline. He snaps the line on the ground. The steps he takes over the flayed earth have already led him along the garden paths or about the dining room with its glinting porcelain ware. He frequently makes trips, down the Meuse to Namur or Dinant, in search of marble, and sometimes to the waterfront for other materials, or for Italian marble. Coeck drew the plans, but he is not doing the building. Bruegel plies between the architect and the builder. He assists the overseer. From time to time he works the winch or lays bricks with the bricklayers. In the evening, Coeck asks to see the notes of the day, his sketch pad: ornaments, tools, equipment, installations, scaffolding, workers at their job. If Bruegel mentions a visitor or workman whose name he does not know, Coeck says: "I don't see who you mean. Draw him." He asks him the exact term for everything, not only in Flemish, but in French, Italian, Spanish, and whenever possible, in Latin, according to Vitruvius. It is all a game. But Bruegel's appetite for knowledge is insatiable. He is always about his business, on the go, barely sleeping. He loves to see the day break over the site. Even as he strolls, his eye is alert, as active as a drawing hand. His nights are peopled with pulleys and ladders. "It's not enough to see things as everyone else sees them," Coeck tells him. "You've got to understand them. That's why you draw. You have to imagine building everything you see. Even the ornaments on the alabaster. Look at how they are constructed. Do you know what Alberti says? 'A true architect begins by mentally taking to pieces whatever he contemplates.' When you see a boat, watch the wind work the sails, appraise the cargo, follow it to its destination as though your whole fortune were riding in the hold. You need to understand, to reckon!"

Coeck celebrated the birthday of his daughter, Mary, by inviting a host of friends to inaugurate his new home: painters, sculptors, clients, aldermen from Antwerp and other towns, Spaniards, Germans, and, of course, Italians, who could well imagine themselves in some *palazzo* magically transported to the banks of the Scheldt. The guests flocked into the halls, the courtyards, the torch-studded gardens. In the glow of candelabra and chandelier, some paintings were unveiled for the first time, like the immense work by Floris, representing a feast of the sea gods: naked Tritons and Nereids entwined as wave enfolds wave, and shell- and pearl-crowned goddesses banqueting on fishes and crabs, crayfish and lobster; their table was a basin of mother-of-pearl such as is never seen outside Neptune's halls. On the sideboards and by the fire, guests had laid their gifts. And then Mary came down, gently descending the stair, one hand on the dark wood banister, a maid of Flanders amid the triumphal splendors of Italy and Antiquity. She wore a traditional dress of green velvet worked with gold. Peter looked at her long blond hair falling onto her shoulders. He gave her a secret name, "the young Sibyl." Her mother led her to the music room, and the girl laid her hands on the keys of the clavichord. A hush fell and the silence extended from the gathering to the garden.

Some time later, Peter Bruegel left the house. Looking back, he saw the windows lit like lanterns and the new stone of the facade. He heard the sound of laughter, conversation, and snatches of music. He was at loose ends. His work was done. The wonderful worksite closed upon that faultless shell. What now? He felt an outsider in this wealthy crowd. He sensed that a part of his life was over. He thought about his destiny: from his village to this princely mansion, where Coeck and his wife had received him like a son. He could just as well have been one of those peering through the garden fence to catch a glimpse of the festivities. But Coeck had passed, a splendid, jovial grand lord; perhaps one of his carriage wheels had needed rehooping and this was the reason for his unplanned stop at the inn. He sat down. He ordered food and drink. He got up again and went out. On one of the doors in the backyard he saw a faded charcoal-and-chalk sketch of a rearing horse with flowing mane, black hooves, spots like islands on the rump and chest, and a tail like a comet. The life in that horse—and the eyes! Coeck stopped short in front of this shed beyond which lay the countryside. Back in the public room he asked:

"Who did that horse?"

"What horse?"

"On the door out back."

"Oh, it must have been the boy."

The boy was listening, a pitcher in one hand.

"Is that yours?"

"The horse? Yes."

"Do you like to draw? Are you happy here?"

"It's all right. I'm happy anywhere."

"Would you like to come to Antwerp and learn to paint?"

"Yes."

"I need an apprentice. How about coming along? Go get your things."

Outside, there was an open door, a blue and gray sky, a fine rain falling in the sunshine, the smell of lilacs: he remembered it all. He made his way through the crowd of wretched onlookers. Among them, beggars and cripples; they were hoping for a handout, and what was left to eat and drink when the tables were cleared. There were also simple people, waiting for nothing of the sort, but watching the festivities of the rich. Many of these worked in the new manufactures: the salt or sugar refineries, the soapworks or the dyeworks. Some did not earn half the pay of a carpenter, a bricklayer, or a butcher's boy. Bruegel wandered in the dark side streets, away from the faces at the fence, from the merry burghers of Antwerp laughing and drinking. A few years later, very few, these same poor creatures, or their children, on a night like this would rise up and lay waste to the cathedral and churches. They would break into the *signoren*'s palaces and set them ablaze. A river of flames would join the *Banquet of the Gods and Goddesses,* and little by little, the rains and grasses would cover the broken, deserted dwellings.

5

> I, whose grandeur once reached the sky
> I, once known in lands unknown,
> I, so rich in peoples and goods
> I, once so swelled and pleasing to the eye
> I, who before these civil wars wore me down,
> I was first among all the towns
> Who, from Europe first crossed the world's great hump
> Or rather held the world fast in my embrace
> What am I now, what have I become?
>
> Leo van Meyere, Prosopopoeia for Antwerp, 1594

Leaving the train station in Antwerp, the traveler finds himself a stone's throw from the zoo. I can never look at the posters without thinking that in Bruegel's time the city already had a wealth of strange animals. The waterfront was both Babel, because of the populations that converged there, and Mount Ararat, where the animals left the ark. The lion that Dürer saw in Ghent and drew most certainly came from Antwerp, as did the rhinoceros, which he also portrayed. In Antwerp he bought, or was given, a branch of white coral, a buffalo horn, a moose foot, seashells, a large fish scale, a tortoise, dried fish, a little green parrot, and a monkey. Children would hang about the docks waiting for the strong smelling animals to be unloaded, for dockers to appear warily carrying cages full of rare birds.

In 1562, Bruegel drew for Cock *A Peddler Pillaged by Apes,* which sold well. It shows a Flemish landscape with a peddler blissfully asleep at the foot of a tree, while a band of small monkeys ransacks his wares and capers about. The subject was popular. It appears in a painting by Herri met de Bles, but the farce, or the allegory, occupies only a small corner in a vast landscape à la Patinir. The picture now hangs in Dresden. But van Mander saw it in Amsterdam, in the Warmoestraat:

In the house of Martin Papenbroek, there is a grand landscape by Herri met de Bles, which shows a peddler napping at the foot of a tree while a band of monkeys ransacks his wares, hangs them from the trees, disporting them-selves at his expense. Certain persons maintain that this is a satire on the pa-pacy, the monkeys being Martins, Martinists or Followers of Luther discover-ing the source of the Popes' income, which they describe as "peddlers wares." In my opinion this interpretation is highly questionable. No doubt Herri meant nothing of the sort, since art ought not to be an instrument of satire.

Perhaps it was the name Martin Papenbroek that suggested the mon-keys as figures of Martin Luther's followers and the peddler, the pope.

Bruegel's drawing may have been only a joke. But it may also con-tain a grain of wisdom. Is not this man, who has fallen asleep on his way and who now dreams while being robbed, the human spirit caught off guard? Is this not the soul, which does not wake and watch, but gives over its possessions to the antics of the world? The monkeys are the image of dissipation. The peddler is a sort of Saint Anthony unable to resist temptation. Stupor and monkeyshines: the opposite of true man.

The same year, Bruegel painted two monkeys crouching in the opening of a wall. They are chained, and the chain is fastened to a large ring in the wall. Some nutshells are strewn over the stones. One of the monkeys faces us; the other is looking out over the city of Antwerp in the distance, the sails on the gilded Scheldt, the pale sky and the passing birds. The painting is very small. One never tires of looking at it. The gaze is held by the curved embrasure of the window. It is carried outwards in the direction of the city, over the river, to the sky with its birds. Then it returns to the pitiful captives, to the mask of the monkey turned our way, the red hair on its head, the white-ringed eyes, the blue-black face, the sadness of the slave. Do these creatures stand for servitude and captivity? Do they signify enslaved populations? Are they the soul, chained to its passions and errors when it could be soaring like the birds? It is possible that Bruegel painted these two monkeys as Dürer the Ghent lion: *chose vue,* something he had seen. The picture could be set into a wall rather than hung, to give the impression of a window with two bored monkeys looking over the waterfront. It could hang in a wealthy home, in the house of a ship's owner.

But I like to think that it crossed Bruegel's mind that this window, placed at such a height, higher than all the houses in Antwerp, and set in such a thick wall, was one of the openings in the Tower of Babel. It was from the tower that one could look out over the harbor and the city. Bruegel tucked himself into one of Babel's thousand nooks. And from there he saw the tower rising, at first transparent, like a column of cloud, on the shore of the Scheldt, overlooking the sea and the plain. He saw its every detail. He painted it. He painted the blue rooftops. In his mind, he painted them. Later, the following year, he would really paint it all. But now he was engrossed in the vision that had just filled his mind. Antwerp was Babel. Antwerp was the image of the world. Like a huge seashell, the world had become a tower whose shadow revolved and scaled the sky. Babel. One of the finest triumphal carts of the 1561 *ommegang*—Pride—represented the tower. Surrounded by his stonecutters, the architect was bowing before Nimrod, who had come to visit the site. The tower already pierced the clouds. Everyone saw this as an allegory of Antwerp. Perhaps somewhere along the route of the procession Christopher Plantin knew that, one day, he would publish his *Bible Polyglotte*—a Bible for Babel.

Did Bruegel think of Babel as he walked around the Coliseum and picked his way through its bleachered crater? The Babel rising in the winds of Antwerp is the same shape. But beside this veritable colossus, the Roman coliseum seems a scale model. The girth of Babel is to all walls what the age of the world is to the age of one man. And its height reduces any mountain to a mound.

All the while he was painting this picture, it can be said that Bruegel inhabited the Tower of Babel—he dreamed of it. Or rather, it was in his dreams that he saw it most clearly. He saw the rampart walls

along which rumbled stone- and lime-laden carts. He saw the huge
ramp rising like an apple peel from the plain to the clouds, the high
scaffolds shuddering in the wind, where masons were always catching cold. He heard the pulleys squeal and the birds cry out in their
dizzy flight. He rested in the wooden sheds built at long intervals on
each level, in the shelter of a buttress. The builders he met were not
those who had dug the foundations, nor even their sons or grand-
sons. The idea of building was so old! Villages had grown up nestlike
in the insets of ramparts and galleries. There Bruegel shared the
bricklayer's homely soup and bread. Below in the haze, the gothic
roofs gleamed, but the town had grown unfamiliar. It was simply
where they came from. They would not go back. It was too far, now.
Bruegel savored the accents that changed from one village to the
next; and tiny fractures in the coloration of the different speeches
already heralded the birth of tongues, which would clash against the
deaf ears of men born on the other side of the world. Yes, of the
world, for this tower was the world: it was just as round, as high, as
old, and they shared the same future. Bruegel paced the roads and
paths of Babel, its side streets, beneath its arcades as he had wandered
the mountains of Italy, from one valley to another, from one village
to the next. He leaned from the windows. He saw the Scheldt, the
spires of Antwerp, and ships, the waterfront. He looked for his house,
the hoistbeam of the loft, the workshop where a painter by the same
name was brushing an immense picture of Babel. He let his gaze
dwell on the boats and rafts ferrying bricks and beams. He saw them
sail past a postern gate, draw alongside at the foot of the tower, close
by the horses and carts. He leaned out over the inner sills of the city.
He examined the caverns and chasms of the edifice. All Babel rang
with the whorl of the winds and the noisy flood of waters beneath
the vaults. Far below the foundations he could hear a river. He imagined the shadowy docks and the warehouses behind iron doors, behind iron bars. He imagined the cloaca. At times he was afraid of
becoming lost in the labyrinth of vaults and tunnels. Babel echoed
like a stone seashell. As high as the masons went, they still took care
with details. They invented small columns to ornament each bay.
When Bruegel looked up, he saw the scaffoldings, new walls that
looked like ruins, and the sky still out of reach.

The tower was like an enormous Vanitas. All this would pass.
However solid and well built it might be, the entire construction
would one day be as sand smoothed by the sea. The rigid forms of
arch and pillar were no more solid than the clouds that drifted
through the gaps in the structure. All the reckonings of the masters

and the product of so much hoisting were as a dream banished by waking. Death and ruin were eating at this epic of tar and stone. Like Troy, Babylon would be but a memory and a poem, an image for the never-ending childhood of Man. The image of our vanity chasing the wind, the image of our life. We know the vanity of Babel, Bruegel told himself, but are our labors and desires less vain? We listen to Ecclesiastes, but we do not hear. Why this circumnavigating of ships, this tramping of paths, this conquering of the globe. The tower is never finished. We are building still. Like dreams and the matter of our nights that the open eye never sees; but these are our roots, the tower is the shape of our lives. I spy you in the rigging, little man, working the sails, oblivious of the whole ship' s running, of its tacking in the winds; how could you know that the ship is carrying its load to the port of Babel? You do not see the giant city, nor its shadow; and yet, you are building with the rest. You, stonemason, smoothing the mortar with a swallow's care, sitting there, legs dangling, breathing in the sharp morning air: what wall do you think you are bracing? You, stonecutter, with your jug handy for the next thirst, working in the dust and noise, will you never look at the colossus you serve? The king comes, the emperor comes to inspect the marvel. He dreams of conquering and ruling the globe. Then he dies. Like the dying emperor in the corner of *The Triumph of Death,* Assur, Nineveh, Babylon have fallen, a few ruins survive, such as Ciceronian Rome. The tower is History, and the cycle of its centuries. It is like the tree, whose age can be read in its concentric rings, and each level is the work of a time in the history of mankind; but despite the perpetual building, it is ever necessary to repair and re-do what time has already weakened or destroyed.

The day went by. Days went by. Was not he the vainest of men, so carefully painting the image of those vain labors? So carefully but so pleasurably! His was the pleasure of the stonemason, the stonecutter, the raftsman sleeping beside his cargo of beams for the last levels of the tower. Each of those he picked out on the face of the edifice was ignorant or oblivious of Babel and its empire, basking only in the simple pleasure of being about his task. It is true that the world is but a vapor, that nothing is worth the while, but nothing is less vain than to apply oneself thus to the work at hand.

4

BRUSSELS

1

Today the rue Haute and the rue Blaes bound the district known as Les Marolles. It is only a short distance between the two, and they are connected or paralleled by a few streets with grand-sounding names: rue Notre Seigneur, rue du Miroir, rue des Renards, rue aux Laines (formerly rue de l'Enfer), rue des Tanneurs, rue des Orfèvres, rue des Brodeurs, rue des Chaisiers and rue des Tonneliers, rue des Charpentiers, rue des Ramonneurs. If you imagine them as when Ghelderode was writing of long, gin-sodden evenings spent with the last puppeteers trying to save some long-forgotten Passion, if you are expecting a quarter teeming with popular images, fast talkers, and a kind of fervor and laughter rising from the cobbles; if you think you glimpse a labyrinth of crowded side streets, courtyards, and alleyways, resembling a slightly sordid theater, perhaps, but punctuated by the strain of something like a very old comic song, a tender typically Brabantine streak, if you feature a step-gabled squadron of roofs standing guard at the foot of the sky and the burgherish hill; if you imagine a district of french-fry-and-beer stalls, a bustling quarter but one for strolling; or the dimly lit spot where Verlaine fired upon Rimbaud, and which might still serve as a hideout for the *voyous de velours* of George Eekhoud, Ghelderode's old master and Virgil, who once led him through this little hell of *faits divers* and bloody trunks, of pink and black alleyways; if you are looking for *Casque d'Or* and old Belgium, it is no use going to Les Marolles.

Ensconced between the ramps and cliffs of that vertiginous and surrealistic castle, the Monster of Justice, and the Hal Gate, a medieval traffic-battered reef, Les Marolles is a broken-down, deserted-looking quarter, foresaken by its former joy. It is not the slums, it is not the city. It is an out-of-the way place, even though the center of Brussels, with its stores, old gold and noble house fronts, and its luxuries is only steps away and almost visible from deep inside these warrens. Perhaps old Marolles, the real one, still lives in the back-rooms of the little bars. I did not find, in those dark shops, the *curieux bric-a-brac* promised me in a no doubt dated book, but I do remember gloomy hardware stores. And those puppet theaters housed in vaulted, enchanted cellars, where puppeteers put on *The Temptation of Saint Anthony* or *Jason's Voyage*. Did Ghelderode see these as a child? I think he must have descended the cellar steps in his dreams, like Aladdin in the orchard, and that they must possess that kind of truth.

On the corner of the rue Haute and the rue de la Porte Rouge, a quiet, steep street, there is a plaque identifying Bruegel's house. Is that where he lived? It is said that the house belonged to Mayken Bessemers Verhulst, his mother-in-law, and that his last descendants inherited it. It is a smallish, brown-brick house with a walled garden and old-fashioned windows. Visits are by appointment only. If my memory serves me, from there one can see the dark, blackish Mongol-cap dome of Notre-Dame de la Chapelle. It seems to me that the church is almost always closed. I saw Bruegel's tomb one winter evening in the dim chapel. We tried to read the epitaph by candle light. In the shadows, I took an ordinary Virgin for Notre-Dame de la Solitude, a tragic dark Spanish Virgin, celebrated by Baudelaire and Ghelderode, and perhaps known to Bruegel.

The men of yesteryear, those we love, are not to be found in the places where they lived. We must follow the path of dreams, of friendship if we want to enter their dwellings and see them live. It is by the faintest of signs that they make their presence known. On one of my early visits, as I walked up the rue de la Porte Rouge as far as I could to catch a glimpse of Bruegel's garden, I saw a little girl coasting down the steep street on her skateboard at break-neck speed. And in this child I saw those in the rings of the *Children's Games* that hangs in Vienna. Another time, not far from there, a young boy had laid down on a low, sloping wall and was dreamily contemplating his foot against the clouds. As though perennial child-hood, the sky over the city, the clouds in the wind were Bruegel's deathless country, and not the shape of a quarter where he had, per-haps, lived, or that of a house on a city map. Thinking back on Les Marolles, I see little bands of playful, dreamy children; and their presence there, below that Babylonian monument of a courthouse, amid the brick clefts and the backstreet breaches, redeems the dis-grace of the spot—as a lone clump of tenacious yellow flowers in the ruins and rusty scrap heaps suddenly reminds us of the faithful glory of the earth.

2

On the twenty-second of October 1555, before the assembly of crimson-mantled knights of the Golden Fleece, the emperor laid down his title of Grand Master of the Order: his son Philip would take it up the following day. On the twenty-fifth, around three in the afternoon, at the Coudenberg Palace in the Grand Salon of the dukes of Brabant, hung with a gold-worked tapestry representing the story of Gideon, he abdicated. He was dressed in black, and his only decoration was the small pendant of the Golden Fleece. He was fifty-five. His beard had gone white. He walked with difficulty, and everyone could see that his fingers were stiff from gout. He advanced with a cane in one hand, the other rested on the shoulder of William of Nassau, prince of Orange, who was his page. Standing beneath the canopy, he recalled the accomplishments of his reign: the wars, the voyages, the conquests. He spoke of his fatigue and the weakness that had come over him. He bequeathed Flanders to his son. He exhorted him always to defend the Catholic faith and to reign lovingly over the land. Of all, he begged forgiveness for any wrong he might have done. One witness reports that there was not a single man in the assembly, foreigner or native, who did not shed abundant tears during a great part of the address. Charles himself could not keep back his tears. "Do not think that I weep for the sovereignty that I lay down. I weep for the country of my birth and for taking leave of such vassals as yourselves." Then he invested Philip with powers to rule the Low Countries. Philip II said a few words, apologizing for speaking neither French nor Flemish, and it was the bishop of Arras, the future Cardinal Granvelle, who read his speech, while the king seemed far away.

On the sixteenth of January 1556, in his little house by the Leuven Gate, which for some time he had preferred to the Coudenberg Palace, Charles renounced his kingdoms of Castille, Leon, Navarre, and Granada; he renounced his office of grand master of the orders of Compostello, Alcantara, and Calatrava; he renounced the kingdoms of Aragon, Valencia, Cerdagne, and Sardinia; Catalonia, Roussillon, Majorca, and Sicily; he renounced the earldom of Barcelona. Philip II became the master of these. For himself, Charles kept only the Franche-Comté: he was to relinquish it within five months. As for the title of emperor, if the Diet was agreeable, it would go to his brother Ferdinand. On the twenty-eighth of August, Charles left Ghent for Flushing. Two fleets, one Spanish, the other Flemish, escorted him to Spain.

He wanted to end his days in the Estremadura monastery of San Jeronimo de Yuste, among the Hieronymites, in the little house they were building for him. It was a long journey and a painful one, with goodbyes at each port of call. On the third of February 1557, the halberdiers of his procession stood their pikes before the threshold, signifying that all worldly honors ended there.

He prepared himself to die. On the thirtieth of August 1558, he had the Office of the Dead and a Requiem mass celebrated in his name. He attended, accompanied by his retinue, all dressed in mourning. In the evening, feeling feverish, he took to his bed never to leave it. Near dawn on the twenty-first of September, while it was still night and only the tapers lit the room, he clasped his crucifix to his chest and murmured: "Ya es tiempo" (The hour is come) "Ay! Jesus!"

Throughout the lands of the empire ceremonies were held, the most striking of which took place in Brussels. On a frosty windswept twenty-ninth of December, a procession left the palace and made its way to Saint Agatha's church. The clergy opened the march, robed in black and silver; then came the royal chapel musicians, the aldermen and notables and two hundred paupers carrying torches: the silence was such that one could hear the flames. Behind the paupers marched the throng of officers of the imperial house. The torchbearers wore long robes with the hoods pulled down, like the sculpted mourners at the tomb of the dukes of Burgundy. After the standards came a large triton-drawn wagon bearing the allegory of the emperor's reign. Dignitaries and captains led the emperor's horse, carried his helmet, his golden mantle, his scepter and sword, his globe, crown, pendant of the Golden Fleece. Each of his majesty's peoples and kingdoms was represented by a delegation of nobles in mourning and a black-plumed, riderless horse. Followed by the knights of the order, Philip II walked slowly, dressed in a long, black-hooded robe, like that worn by the paupers, the Golden Fleece on his breast.

Beneath a four-tiered catafalque lighted by tapers, the emperor's coffin rested, draped in gold cloth worked with a red cross. The attributes and insignia of his power would be laid upon it. In this way, writes the author of one *Description des obsèques*, published by Christopher Plantin: "We came to know in how little esteem we should hold these earthly things which are so frail, fleeting, and vain."

In another *Descrittione della pompa funerale fatta in Brussele,* an Italian poet places these words in the mouth of Charles, who has gone to heaven:

> Non sete mai, ne sacra fame d'oro,
> Non di gloria ambition, o desidero
> D'accrecer Regni, o d'ampliar l'Impero,
> M'armo contra Christiano, o Scita, o Moro;
>
> Ma posponendo l'util' al decoro
> M'accesi d'esaltar la Fè di Piero,
> In questo antice e nel novo Emisfero
> Sol per gistitia, e amor di Quel, ch'io adoro;
>
> E dando un picciol segno del mio zelo
> Con raro essempio il Mondo renunciai,
> Per acquistar' al fin' ancor' il Cielo;
>
> Lieto à l'Empireo Ciel dunque volai,
> Mercè del mio Fattor, che senza velo
> Veggi' hor godendo, e vuedro sempre mai.

3

In 1563, Bruegel left Antwerp for Brussels. He would be married, not in the city of his youth, in the city where he had been made a master and from which he had left for Rome ten years earlier, but in Notre-Dame de la Chapelle, between Sablon and Les Marolles, in the upper town; in the register of his new parish was written: "Peeter Brugel, Mayken Cocks—solmt," which stands for *solemniter*, 'solemnly' (unless it should be read *solvit*). Were it not for the *liggien* of Saint Luke's Guild in Antwerp (the name "Peeter Brueghels, schilder," appears in 1551 on the same page as "Hieronymus Cock and Joorge Mantewen, corporen plaetsnyders," that is, Giorgio Ghisi, also known as George of Mantua, "engravers on copperplate"), and the parish register, we would know almost nothing certain about his life. A letter from Bologna, in April 1564, sent by the geographer Scipio Fabrius to his colleague Ortelius, entrusts him with greetings for Martin de Vos and Peter Bruegel, whom Fabrius had met in Italy. And this is nearly all the *written evidence* of Bruegel's passage.

The most important traces have been left by Bruegel himself, for he nearly always dated his pictures. Together, they form the pages of a sort of diary—like a Book of Dreams. But a date on a painting tells us at best the day it was finished: it says nothing of when it began. And yet, as the night dream springs sometimes from the far reaches of our lives and, who knows, from beyond our birth, and as the last step of a journey is inseparable from the first, which we have perhaps forgotten, the day that marks the full-blown image is but the last of an ocean of days. The day that at last sets its seal on the image contains a treasure of hours whose age, antiquity, origin, the painter himself ignores. You know that, beneath the visible surface, the layers of size and color interact with the light and play their part—as Mother Night nurtures the days—in what we see. But beneath the hidden layers, and beneath the effaced layers, and beneath those layers merely contemplated and which never became matter, how many pure movements of the painter's mind! Who can tell the depth of an image, and see, in the night from which it issues, its subterranean limbs and the hair roots of its reasons, from which it draws its substance and form. In a true painting, the invisible part is always the greater. So the frost on the windowpane and that garden brushed and dispersed by our breath is borne to us in the vessels of Icelandic winds. The whiteness of this morning's grass comes from a kingdom that does not know us, from a far side of the world. And forehead to the windowpane, I feel someone within me dreaming, someone deeper than myself, dreaming, his brow against the pane, enchanted by the hoar-white garden—enchanted to be alive.

Bruegel liked to stamp his paintings with the imprint of time: his way of marking out life and placing his finished work in conjunction with the stars, along the course of human events. He often wrote the year of his work, and his signature: BRVEGEL; as one day he began to write his name, and we cannot say why he abandoned the H (or kept it for himself). Is it worth pausing over this change of spelling, made in 1559? That which affects one's name often affects one's being. One day Abram became Abraham. Perhaps Bruegel wanted to rid his name of a hint of hell. Or forget the hieronyme—the sacred name—of Hieronymus Bosch, his father in imagery? Or mask Hermes's initial, and by this disappearing act paradoxically, but *hermetically,* bespeak Hermes's presence in his work? Or perhaps, for the sake of the eye and the flow of the signature, he merely wanted to simplify his name?

It is not known whether this name, which his sons were to write in its original form, was taken from his father, or from a village, as a surname: the village of Brogel, near Bree in Kampen in the region of Limburg which is today in Belgium; or near Breda, in northern Brabant, today in Holland? "Peter Bruegel . . . was born not far from Breda in a village named Brueghel, a name he took for himself . . . ," writes van Mander. So begins, in his *Book of Painters,* the chapter on Bruegel.

Nature found and laid hold of the man who in his turn was destined to lay hold of Nature so magnificently, when in an obscure village in Brabant she chose from among the peasants, as the delineator of peasants, the witty and gifted Peter Bruegel, and made of him a painter to the lasting glory of our Netherlands. He was born not far from Breda in a village named Bruegel, a name he took for himself and handed on to his descendants.

But van Mander may have confused Bree in Kampen, then called Breedes or Brida, and in Latin, Breda, with the Breda of Brabant. As for the Kampen village of Brueghel or Brogel, it was divided into Grote Brogel and Kleine Brogel. "Brogel" designates a scrubland.

I can easily imagine young Bruegel in this twin village, a world of its own. On one bank of the stream, Lesser Brogel, on the other Greater, like the Fat and the Lean. It must be a boon to be born in a village that goes by a single but two-part name: like the magpie, black and white; and I am tempted to mention other couples, too: to say the snow and the crow; the bare branch, winter, and the sun through the trees showing red on the horizon like a pan of glowing coals; December frostbite and July noon torpor, awash in the golden smell of harvest. It is good to be born in a place whose name speaks of thickets and brush. A childhood of building dens and rambling deliciously in filbert groves, among the alders and willows; smeared with blackberries from the brambles; cutting elderberry twigs for whistles, fifes and flutes, and *clacquebeuses* (a kind of peashooter), stripping sticky hazel branches for bows; lying in wait, in the branches and brush, for the enemy to come over the hill; marvelling at eggs, sky-blue and snow or rust spotted, in the cup of a nest. To go by the name of a forest must be a boon. But perhaps this childhood village is a figment of my imagination. Perhaps Bruegel grew up in a town? If van Mander saw him coming into a peasant world, perhaps it was because he painted their patronal feasts, their plowed fields, their herds. We know nothing of his birth. Bruegel starts from his name as a bird from cover. He chose it to reflect the force of this inner image: a round village, tilled fields, bordered by brambles, brush and woods.

Bruegel left Antwerp. He left his habits, his meanderings in the windy city and along the wharves, his walks along the seashore with gulls screaming overhead, his reveries. He would no longer sit in *Rhetoriqueurs'* chambers at the long covered tables (the fabric casts a greenish light on the room). He would no longer sit in taverns with sailors and dockers. He was giving up his closest friends: Franckert, Ortelius. He was leaving the Four Winds and its warm but excessive hubbub. True, many of those he used to encounter daily had already left. They had gone to Leiden, Amsterdam, London. Plantin had not returned from Paris. Was it out of caution that Bruegel left Antwerp? Brussels was scarcely any safer for a free-thinking mind. Hedge sermons were being preached in the countryside near by. And people were becoming used to the increasingly frequent street patrols and house-to-house searches. Nevertheless, Bruegel ran fewer risks by distancing himself from his circle of liberal friends in Antwerp. And then, the governor and cardinal, Perrenot de Granvelle, was one of his clients.

"As long as he lived in Antwerp," writes van Mander,

he kept house with a servant girl. He would have married her but for the fact that she was in the habit of lying. He made an agreement or contract with her: he would procure a stick and cut a notch in it for every lie she told, for which purpose he deliberately chose a fairly long one. Should the stick become covered with notches in the course of time, the marriage would be off. And indeed, this came to pass after a short while. In the end, when the widow of Pieter Coeck was living in Brussels, he courted his daughter whom he had often carried about in his arms, and married her. The mother, however, demanded that Bruegel should leave Antwerp and take up residence in Brussels, so as to give up and put away all thoughts of his former girl.

But how could the man who is presented to us as fleeing a lying woman lead a double life? The story of the notched stick is told only to show Bruegel as a truth-loving man. Perhaps it also means that, by taking a wife and changing cities, Bruegel intended to lead a life that was nearer the truth. He was leaving his old life and the city of his youth, and setting out in search of a more retiring, productive life. He was leaving a waterfront and the seaside, the winds that swept the town and the vast voice of the world echoing in this shell for a landlocked city, quiet, somewhat austere behind its double wall, surrounded by plowed fields and woods, built on a hill—and he would live in the rue Haute.

I can hear their conversation, grave, friendly, joyful. Mary was not far away, in the next room, perhaps, barely separated by a pale oak door. She was dreaming, smiling, waiting. Between the lace flowers on her bodice, her finger traced "Peter and Mary," or simply "yes." The door was going to open, she would stand up, the following step would take her from maidenhood to wifehood. The proposal had come as no surprise to her mother. But respectful of custom and in order to settle that which must be settled, the tête-à-tête had to be. Peter and the woman he had known since he was almost a boy had seated themselves in high-backed armchairs. They faced each other in the wan light of the day. The thick table gleamed between them. Did they speak of the past? No doubt little: Mary was waiting in the kitchen by the fire. They thought of her. Peter saw the clouds skudding past on the wind. He saw a slender tree in the garden. At the back of the house, a servant was scrubbing the black-and-white tiles, with a wooden bucket beside her.

Mayken Verhulst wanted her daughter near by: she had no close friends, she said. She did not say that she had been lonely since Pieter's death, ten years before. She said that she needed Mary to help her with the tapestry shop, that she wanted to complete her daughter's business education.

"You won't spend the rest of your life at the Four Winds, Peter. You earn your living (not very well) and your drawings are good. I have nothing to say on that account. But your real task is to become a painter. And you're a philosopher and need to take your time. If Mary works, you will have the freedom you need. And we have a house in Brussels that will make a fine workshop. It isn't big, but it's big enough. You can engage two or three apprentices: that will be a help."

Peter says nothing. It is always the same: he feels like a poor child adopted by a family and made into some kind of prince; and yet one is supposed to make one's own way in the world.

"These scruples are unfair. The wealth is not ours. You must learn to receive or lose it, in accordance with God's will. Since he has beckoned to you and has wanted this love to be, continue to accept his Providence, and lay down your pride. Why are we here but to partake in God's plan, and to serve one another. But it's not even for you that I'm doing this, I'm thinking of my grandchildren to come."

And so he would leave Antwerp. And the city of Brussels would be pleased, having asked him many times to compose a series of cartoons or paintings to celebrate the digging and inauguration of the canal. The work was well paid and a great honor. If he desired, he could become not only Brussel's favorite artist, but a pillar of society, a figure of the city. "I'll talk even less," Bruegel said to himself. "I'll become known for my silence, I'll keep to my house, to my workshop; I'll walk in the woods, through the fall colors and the fragile frosty paradises, to the sound of distant bells in the snow. I'll work.

I'll shorten my nights. I'll keep to myself for long stretches of time, like a hermit. When I think of it, when I think of the work to come, of the work that is so near, I feel something like the beating of great wings in my chest and I see something like my heart glowing and burning in the night, like a lantern on the mast of a ship about to set sail for the ends of the earth."

He leaves Antwerp. He takes up residence in Brussels, in the rue Haute.

4

The Brussels of that time was a beautiful city. The imperial court had left Mechelen and taken up residence there. The great lords were building their houses: Nassau, Culemberg, Brederode and many others. Guicciardini marvels:

> In general the houses are well built, but in particular there are several very handsome mansions, the foremost being the Town Hall which has a very beautiful, tall tower; and then the mansions of several principal nobles of the land, who come to take care of their business and administration and pay court to the king or his governor. Similarly, there are several extraordinarily handsome buildings belonging to some of the prince's ministers and officers and other gentlemen and burghers of the town, with ample orchards well provided, as is the whole town, with beautiful clear fountains which send up the purest and most perfect of waters. There is also the royal palace, which, though not at all completed and furnished according to the original plans, is still ample and comfortable and worthy of the court and above all situated in a beautiful setting. Adjoining the palace is a most noble and spacious park which is entirely walled and stretches to the second of the town walls. Inside the park are dwellings for the prince and others, fields for jousting and for private and public disport, handball courts and other royal amenities: garden, maze, fishpond with several swans and dainty fish in great abundance. In addition, the park has several small hills and dales with vineyards and several kinds of fruit, as well as pretty little woods and meadows full of several species of wild animal, which can be seen from several parts of the palace, and one can see them grazing, playing, and breeding.

Brussels, he adds, is shaped like a heart. And he tells of his walks in the verdant gardens between the double walls, the "beautiful gardens, meadows, and shrubs, which make it a cool, healthy pleasant spot with a very pretty view and appearance."

Rue Haute, where Bruegel was to live, was once a country lane. It had become a street of nobles and burghers. The city officials were busy tearing down the wattle-and-daub houses. They had ordered the thatch replaced by tiles. Only the district at the foot of Saint

Gudule's Cathedral escaped the renovation; set in the middle of town, it still had the look of a village with its waterholes, its streets turned to mud at the first drop of rain, its greenery, fences, trees, "its little houses and mud huts." In order to prevent fires, the aldermen did not merely forbid the use of straw and wood, they installed wells in various locations around the town.

This was a prosperous town. The temporary or permanent presence of ambassadors, officers, Church dignitaries, and courtiers attracted artists from all over Brabant, the neighboring provinces, even Germany, Spain, and Italy. "Brussels," writes Guicciardini, "is home to fifty-two trades, divided into nine bodies called nations; among these trades, that of the armorors is beneficial and of great importance, for, besides the beauty of the many sorts and makes of armor, they so perfectly temper it that it resists the fire of the harquebus. But above all, the tapestry-making trade is remarkable and of great utility: you will see works in silk, gold and silver wonderfully expensive and ingenious." All Europe buys or copies the tapestries of Brussels.

The drawback of Brussels was that it communicated with Antwerp and the sea that opens onto the wide world only by road or by the Senne, a river that was sometimes high, sometimes low, hardly favored navigation, and was silting up. An imperial privilege decided the digging of a canal. And, as there was a sharp drop between Brussels and Antwerp, four locks would be needed. The canal would flow toward Vilvorde, then Willebroek, before emptying into the Rupel. Mechelen pleaded its right to a lock. But Locquenghien, the engineer, and two cloth merchants successfully pressed the case for Brussels.

Work began in June 1550. The canal was to be inaugurated on October 12, 1561. There was a prodigious celebration. Antwerp's official painter, Jan Leys, had decorated the boats and barges, and for several days they plied between Brussels and the sea for their pleasure. The old waterfront on the right bank of the Senne had given way to interior docks for loading and unloading merchandise. Soon two other inner basins were to be dug, the bassin des Barques and the bassin des Marchands, and unloading docks were to be built. In 1565, the bassin de Sainte-Catherine was laid out perpendicular to the first two. The bassin de l'Entrepôt and the bassin de la Ferme des Boues were to follow. Bruegel, who was fond of the hamlet of Saint Gudule and the shade of the tall trees around the city, also liked all the commotion and the construction. He no doubt sensed that the Willebroeck canal linked the most important cities of his life: the city of his youth, and that of the period just beginning. He must also have felt something like the contemporaries of the Brooklyn Bridge.

5

ANDREÆ VESALII BRUXELLENSIS: the first page of *Fabrica corporis humani*, in seven books, associates the name of the illustrious anatomist with his place of birth. Jan van Calcar, a Fleming whom Vesalius had met while in Venice, a man of such forceful and admirable talent that his engravings were long attributed to Titian, of whom he was an obscure disciple—Jan van Calcar must have taken a patriotic pleasure in linking these two names on the title plate: a lesson in dissection in which a group crowds into a rotunda lined with antique-style columns to see an eviscerated model over which stands, grasping the handle of his scythe like his harbinger, a skeletal Triumph; but this is no Triumph of Death, it is the Triumph of young Vesalius, one finger raised and a professorial hand touching the entrails. This glory adds to that of his native town. Is one, plate after plate, in the scenery and landscapes dropping away in the background before which are posed a strange, flayed, skeletal people (to say nothing of the branch and root manikins, the morning glory and hart's tongue arteries and veins, these man-shaped wild plants like the mandragore, hovering in midair, their only setting or scenery the whiteness of the paper, and that look like creatures from another world; and yet we harbor these leafy rhizomatic monsters within ourselves as we would never shelter a loved one; this embroidery and lace are the stuff of our being, this dark shrub is the garden of our blood, the hidden servant of our life, our indwelling angel, and our inner shade, and yet, if we look upon it, the dreamlike vision turns us to stone). But let us return to our phrase that this fascinating apparition has distracted from its course: Is one, in this scenery before which these skeletal and flayed manikins primp and pose, as though unaware of their present state and believing themselves graceful artist's models still, heroes, leaders, admirable orators, ladies, perfumed princesses (whereas they are more than naked, and their fibers dangle didactically like so many scarves, and a quadrant of their cranium has been doffed like a hat so that each may see how the brain is made)—is one in these ramparts and pediments, these ruins and rivers, these arcades, thickets, hills, and despite a pyramid here and an obelisk there, to recognize a certain place in the vicinity of Padua, perhaps Petrarch's home, which van Calcar left Campagnola to draw? Is one at times to imagine it is Brussels? Or to see, in these worlds and landscapes, any moderately prosperous town of the time, and of other times, a mere pedestal for these bodies, a backdrop for the macabre medical comedy? Despite the skeleton leaning on his spade, Holbein is already far away! It is Vitruvius viewing and analyzing a flayed temple. (But this ruined, ragged temple is our body, I was about to say our person. You open this splendid learned book and you enter the dens of death, you see yourself in sections and slices, in sets of little bones: this looking glass shows you as you will never see yourself, man with your eyes on the end of their thread. And you know, dear Reader, that time will decompose the knowledge you hoard, everything you know, as it does all things, these members, these filters, this thinking box. The worm reigns over these wonders, and nonbeing over the worm. Who can believe that a body glorious watches from beyond this disaster, and waits, faithfully, like our shadow on earth?)

Before he became Vesalius, his name was van Wesele (which means "weasel"), whence the family coat of arms: three weasels courant on a field of sable, as on the frontispiece of the *Fabrica corporis humani*. He was born to a long line of medical men. His great-great-grandfather, Pieter, had written a commentary on Avicenna and begun putting together the fabulous library that would be young Andreas's childhood attic and dream castle, his port of embarcation for knowledge. His great-grandfather, Jan, studied at the newly opened University of Leuven and went on to become the most important doctor in Brussels and the duke of Burgundy's personal physician. His grandfather, Everard, who wrote commentaries on an Arabic author and on Hippocrates's *Aphorisms*, had been physician to the Emperor Maximilian. His father, Andreas, was pharmacist to Margaret of Austria and then to her nephew, Charles V. Andreas himself, if a horoscope drawn up by Gerolamo Cardano, the Milanese mathematician and physician, is to be believed, was born on the thirty-first of December 1514, at 5:45 in the morning; this was in Brussels, near the Minim Convent, rue du Manège (later called the rue d'Enfer and today the rue aux Laines).

One must imagine young Vesalius among the jars, the ointments, the scales, the dried herbs and flowers, the roots, marble mortars, blue-and-white ceramic pots, the poisons in their iron box next to the theriac. One must also imagine him perched on a stool with a dog at his feet, between the counter and the wall, listening, watching the pageant of bodily woes. One must imagine him as a young child upstairs in the circular library, surrounded by books on medicine and surgery, astronomy and mathematics, advancing through plagues and carbuncles, pus and scrofula, like some Saint George through the dragon's fiery breath. But how could these images and tales discourage him or turn his stomach? Had he not always had before his eyes, in the distance, yet visible from his window, those justly hanged victims, rotting in the wind on Galgenberg, and, whenever the wind turned, breathed their violent sweet smell?

He saw the hanged men not only from a distance. At night he would slip out of the house and climb the hill to the gallows and the wheels, picking his way through the rats and the will-o'-the wisps. Men condemned to death were denied burial; left to rot until they fell to pieces. Rats and dogs scattered the remains. And Vesalius walked that desert of rotting flesh and bones, carrying a shuttered lantern—and when he raised his head, he could see the flicker of the city, the moonlit mist of the countryside, the farms where sometimes a cock or an uneasy dog could be heard, a distant cough—searching the ground for an undamaged skull as other children hunt four-leaf clovers or rare shells in the sand. Where did he get the complete skeleton that, as a young master, he gave to his colleagues in Padua, or the one he presented in Leuven, if not from the gallows of Brussels (or those of Montfaucon, since he would continue his gleaning as a student in Paris)? I see him, not as a sorcerer gathering herbs in the Val d'Enfer, nor as a prospector of mandrake or mandragore, nor even a beachcomber on these isles of Death, but as the long-haired young man in the extravagantly plumed hat depicted in an engraving by Lucas of Leiden: thoughtful, cradling in a fold of his cloak a skull to which bits of earth still cling, a broken pitcher that once held the thoughts time has now dispersed as it dispels the morning dew. Just as, dear Vesalius, it has dispersed your Latin, your Greek, your smattering of Arabic or Hebrew, along with your keen longing to see and to grasp how the Great Architect—as you call him in your letters—built and hewed this temple of the Spirit that is our mortal body, promised to Resurrection and the Last Judgment. (But that Adam be made of clay will always be less inconceivable than Lazarus, *who already smells,* once more taking up his human form, a face and speech, and conversing as he comes forth from his tomb as of late from his own doorway: but it is the same Spirit that blows and mocks our stupefaction. We find it so natural to be born and to live, and so unnatural to die.) And I imagine Vesalius, the familiar of ossuaries and catacombs, wrapping his scarf around a begrimed skull, already polished by hail and rain, a rock that yesterday embraced the mud and lush grass—that riot of wild carrot and burdock, on Galgenberg!—and placing it on his table

among the books. Outside it is still dark. The candle illuminates the
sullied ivory. Dawn will soon be at the window. A small purple flower
grows in one of the sockets. But Vesalius is already scouring the in-
structive object.

At the time Bruegel moved to Brussels, Vesalius was contemplating
leaving Madrid for Jerusalem. He could no longer suffer the jealousy
of his Spanish colleagues, the glassy eye of the Inquisition fixed on
his works, the impossibility of laying his hands on a cadaver, the
bitterness of being Flemish at this court where loathing and contempt
for the Low Countries grew more palpable each day. It is said that he
had the following misadventure: one day as he was dissecting a
woman, the cadaver awoke with an abominable scream. The pilgrimage is said to have been imposed as a penance.

But perhaps it was nothing more than lassitude. And perhaps the
illness of the crown prince, Don Carlos, had precipitated events.
Don Carlos had found a cache from which he could watch a young
servant girl at her toilet. One night, as he descended a steep stair in
the dark, he missed a step and struck his temple on the stones. He
was found partially paralyzed, with blood running from his head.
Eleven Spanish physicians were summoned to his side. They bled
him, they purged him, they enlarged the wound: the patient grew
worse. At last Vesalius arrived. He was the king's physician, but the
others obstinately blocked his path. They sent for a Moor from
Valencia, Pinterete by name, with his unholy unguents: even that
was better than Vesalius. The young man was still out of his head.
For days on end and many nights, the duke of Alba did not undress
but stood by his bedside, tenderly bending his long harsh face over
the panic-filled visage already beaded with what resembled the sweat
of agony. Prayers filled the room with a relentless hum. All Spain
was in prayer and procession. The crown prince is dying! In haste
the dry, sainted body of a convent cook who had died in ecstasy (it
is he that Murillo later painted in his *Angels' Kitchen* which hangs in
the Louvre) was called for. The most holy mummy was carried into
the room of the dying prince. Tapers sputtered, and incense masked
the putrid smell. The body of the dead monk was laid—the whole
and terrifying relic was laid—in the boy's bed, body on body, and
God help him! In the end Vesalius performed a trepanation. And a
little later the young man regained his senses; he rose from his bed
and attended a bullfight in his honor. But did they congratulate Vesalius, did they thank him? If the crown prince was well, it was because of the heavenly cook (the king demanded that Rome canonize

him). Those who had their doubts cried that it was Our Lady of This and Our Lady of That—every chapel in which Spain had prayed. Only the most stubborn of physicians maintained that he alone had worked the cure (his colleagues saved him from the Inquisition by shutting away his memoir—and his pride—in the obscurity of a chest).

But Vesalius was tired. Let that band of fakes doctor the king, his family and retinue. Treatment for treatment, he would care for the poor as he had already done in Venice; after all, he had made a fortune since then. But above all, he wanted to continue to learn, to gain a better insight into the gears and fluids of our machine. And he wanted to teach: Padua wanted him, as in former times. He was not yet thirty when he began following the Emperor Charles from town to town and battle to battle. Now he was nearly fifty. He wanted to enjoy the handsome mansion he had built on the site of his birthplace (the old house was too small and threatened to fall down), with its orchard, kitchen garden, medicinal garden on the hill with such a fine view, facing away from the gibbets. Then he said he would make a pilgrimage. He embarked for the Holy Land. He set sail for Jerusalem. It was a pretext for leaving the royal court, but no Escorial could outshine the Holy Sepulchre! Perhaps it was not a pretext after all. Perhaps Vesalius, who finally admitted his horror and fear of death and his yearning to live in the hereafter, went with all his heart to pray to Christ, in the places where he had lived, died and been buried, appeared as a gardener to Mary Magdalene, the contemplative of skull and lamp, appeared to Saint Thomas who placed his hand in the wound and knew that death was not victorious—knew it, like Andreas Vesalius knew death to be inexorable, knew the silence and the rictus of the bare-boned jaws.

No one knows whether the ship foundered on the return from Jerusalem, and Vesalius's body rolled up on the shores of Zante— a goldsmith is reported to have recognized the body and given it a burial—or whether Vesalius fell ill and, fearing the plague and on the point of throwing him into the sea, the sailors left him on the first island they saw. Some say that he walked from the beach to the gates of the town, where he died. An isolated tombstone bears the inscription: "Tomb of Andreas Vesalius of Brussels, died on the fifteenth of October in the year 1546 at the age of fifty, returning from Jerusalem." From Venice the news of his death reached Brussels by successive waves, and masses were said for his soul, the number diminishing with the years like the tolling of a bell when the cord is released, each knell fainter, further from the last, until silence, like the stillness of death.

6

From a distance, it looks like a village, in the middle of its fields, by the side of the sea. But on drawing closer, you see that everyone is doing the opposite of what he should be: here a man is banging his head against the wall, and there a woman feeds roses to a piglet. I did not invent this farce, this village of proverbs: peddlars have been selling prints of *The World Upside-Down* for a long time. But it was my pleasure to paint it. Others paint Mars and Venus smothered in garlands. I prefer almanac humor. I never tire of seeing our figures of speech, once you really *see* them, turn into so many images that, strung together, form the summum and the pageant of human folly. I painted a dozen proverbs on a set of plates: discovering what the neighbor has drawn puts the guests in a merry mood—Who is carrying coals to Newcastle? Who is casting his pearls before swine? Who is acting like a dog in a manger? Who is banging his head against the wall? Who is seated between two stools? Who is closing the barn door after the horse has been stolen? But this time I have brought together a hundred at least! Is this a village square or a stage? As you will: the stage is a mirror in which all the world seems a stage.

In my childhood, when the stage was being built, I was hardly the last to turn up in the front row. The first blows of the sledgehammer pounding in the stakes were already part of the festivities: I liked the sound of the canvas being stretched; it was the sound of ships and sailing. Others pushed and shoved us from behind, but we stood fast so as not to be crushed against the boards. I could hear the carter's laugh above the others. I watched the antics of Greed, Malice, and Anger. It surprised me that people did not recognize themselves on stage; that they did not see this theater where every man descends, one step at a time, into his waiting tomb. Those asleep on their feet, who must be prodded along, how could they see that this world is a stage? They cannot tell the reflected image or the body from its future glory—or its everlasting night. They cannot tell their thoughts from their dreams, or their dreams from their daydreams. Nor their thoughts from their humors, nor their mind from their bile, nor their soul from their role on the road of this life. Sleepwalkers that they are, how could they know? And should I too awake, what tree should I climb to watch the scene I play in, the instant here below, its movement, the parade, the crush, the crowd of those who, like ants, go bearing straw or flour, loves and labors, the going out and the coming in of fleets and armies? Where is this character, this unique individual, myself, the person that every man is for himself, who goes by my name, whom I have known from a child, better than the hand knows the glove, and who wears my features, my face?

I can imagine myself on the road, playing in *The Battle of the Strong Boxes and the Money Bags, Orson and Valentine, The Wedding of Mopsus and Nisa.* Happily would I have carried the mirror of human comedy. Once the backdrop is rolled away, nothing remains. Sometimes I prompt the Chamber of Rhetoric with a *mot* or a pun, but that is not my trade. My stage is my sheet of paper, my canvas, my panel. My role here is to draw and to paint.

I have drawn the stage of the world, stripped bare. Am I a playwright, then? No, rather a geographer. I have drawn the mountains, valleys, rivers, the whole panorama. This is not only the place of our past: I saw the history of the earth played out. I saw the earth in the grip of time, which transforms us all. Those who see my drawings as mere scenery are mistaken: the still river flows and is never the same; there before our eyes, it is the son and father of itself. And all that folding and crumpling of mountains over time! Geographer, scribe, archivist, I record the earth's passing from one form to the next, which others will see in my stead, for I, too, am passing, even as I am that traveler seated under the tree, on the stone, gazing at the river glistening among the distant hills, so like a still lane.

A moment ago my paper was blank, a simple field of snow; now ink or chalk transform it into this motionless mirror of the moving world. Who appointed me chronicler of landscapes? Slowly, like some far-off flock, like the shadow of a cloud on the vales, the forest now climbs, now descends, changes, thickens, or thins. So a drop of water or ink on paper pauses and gives a small shudder before stopping and being absorbed. And so the dog turns round in the straw before lying down to sleep. This stone seat: the sun in its course turns it pink, then gray; and the patches of moss and the rain and the hail relentlessly wear it away. Here I draw and listen to the world flow by. I see the windstreams twine into leafings and tresses. I hear the season roll and slip by. Beneath the canopy of branches, I draw the listening landscape. I draw myself, leaning against the chapped trunk. My hand, too, is aging, that traces the flight of young birds through the greenery and the wind.

I draw mountains, like coliseums beneath the calling crows. The diluvial rain reduces them to ruins, and still it chisels on. How many lesser floods since that first dawn? And how many more brew beneath the wings of time? How many Atlantises slumber beneath our feet, beneath our oars? For the people of ants, dwelling amongst the roots, the slightest shower, or the contents of my tankard are a deluge; is there such a thing as a flood for the stars? I have drawn the world's slow shudder, its tremor. "One day a bronze anchor was found on the mountain. A road once led from Naples to Messina. And should you seek Helice and Buris, once cities of proud Achaea, you will find them beneath the waters; the sailors still point out their drowned walls," writes Ovid.

I have painted time.

I have painted jousts and the Battle of Carnival and Lent. I have painted their twin processions between the church and inn. Driven by masks to the sound of a *rommelpot,* the fat figure of Carnival, a bloated butcher with one foot in a stirrup made from a cooking pot, rides a beer barrel: he is armed with a spit on which are skewered roast chickens and a pig's head. From the other direction, drawn along on her rolling stool to the grating of rattles, comes the desiccated figure of Abstinence: she is holding a baker's paddle with two pickled herrings. Scarlet face meets pale face in mock battle: Fasting and Feasting are about to pass courteously, as night, yawning its way to bed greets drowsy dawn rubbing her eyes. But the year goes round, and day follows day. And yet I have shown Carnival season and Lenten season approaching each other and soon face to face: like two jacks-o'-the-clock mounted on discs turning in opposite directions. Do not the future and the past move toward one another until they meet in the present? Does my death come out of the future to meet me as I emerge from time gone by? Or is it I who advance to meet my death? We are walking toward each other, in step, in time. Like Penelope weaving and unraveling her work, the thread of day and the thread of night unendingly cross and mingle; for to be born is to die, as Heraclitus says, and the uphill and downhill roads are one and the same.

The village square is a calendar. Various locations are the days of the year. Here is where Shrove Tuesday pancakes are flipped; there the Feast of the Three Kings is held. On the upstairs window ledge of a yellow house perches the Fool, the hub of this wheel: he alone sees Time turning and spinning its days. He bespeaks our own folly, we who are careful or careless of time and believe it is our whole life. But he recalls, too, the wise folly of those who celebrate the true

Easter: the threshold of the year and the gateway of eternity. If we would only stop our toplike whirling, we would see the dry path through the waters of our days. But man rarely considers time, and if he does, he believes that it is the stuff of which he is made, and he despairs, whereas through the thread of time, through the woven fabric, the sun is shining. I have painted the seasons of life; I have painted Children's Games and the Woes of Old Age, the Pleasures of Youth and the Tasks of Maturity, paintings for the cardinal points. And that is how the friend for whom they were done placed them: at the center of his house, around a circular table ablaze with a tapestry sun. Slowly I spun the carousel of our four ages, with their tools, their toys, their emblems. I painted the ball and the hoop, the anvil, the hammer, the plowshare, the sail, the helmet and the sword, the pot and the bellows, the spindle and the distaff—everything from keel to crutch, from cradle to grave. The images were worn, but I touched them with new color. And I silently recited the end of the *Metamorphoses:* "The course of the year is like our lives, and what we have been, or now are, we shall not be tomorrow. Helen weeps when she sees herself in the glass, wrinkled with age, and asks herself why she was twice carried off. Time, the devourer, and the jealous years that pass destroy all things, nibbling them away, and consume them gradually in a lingering death."

I shall paint the Triumph of Death. Mine will be even more frightful than the one in Palermo, in the Palazzo Sclafani, and the one in Pisa. Bosch portrayed the world as a haywain, with mankind, priests in the lead, rushing to fill their sacks and coffers, and killing and slaughtering till they fall beneath the wheels, and all for a fistful of fools' gold; while the devil-drawn cart passes as through a farmyard gate into the all-consuming fire. I would like to have invented this great proverb, this parable. And I will equal it, God willing. I shall paint the universal reign of death. All those children I used to paint in their wagons I will now show taken as babes-in-arms, a fly on their taper-white brow. I will not paint the Danse Macabre. I will not show bishop, king, pope or plowman coaxed by a skeleton or their own shade to join the reel. I will not show the skeleton enfolding the pretty girl who admires her face in the glass, blind to the hollow-faced putrid reflection she is to become. Nor pompous death's cortege riding on its wagon, wheels crushing miters, scepters and objects of ordinary life. I will not retell the meeting of the Three Live Men and the Three Dead Men on their way to town. I shall paint death's monumental task, his cartage, his graves. My painting will be a vast landscape the color of clay. The whole earth will lie before our eyes like a killing field, the harvest of death. I shall paint the grand Battle between Life and Death. I shall paint the snares he lays for us from our first breath, his lair, the war he wages, to our face or at our backs. I shall paint the battle of the quick and the dead. I shall show the immense armies of Death. I shall paint the Agony.

7

He is dressed in black velvet and wears the Golden Fleece about his neck. He is standing in his darkened study. He is Philip II, king of Spain. He signs: *Yo, el Re,* "I, the King." Sometimes in the margin of reports sent by the police or his spies, he writes *oho,* "eye." He thinks he looks upon the world with an eagle's eye, but his is the eye of a vulture.

Plans for the Escorial are taking shape. The palace will be built of huge blocks of granite, on the outskirts of Madrid among the Castilian boulders where black bulls graze: the summer sun is broiling and the winter snow and ice make this an anxious spot, a desert for the devil's court. The Escorial is designed like an instrument of torture; it is laid out like Saint Lawrence's grill. It will be the dwelling and reflection of a king by whose hand enemies of the Catholic faith are roasted to a turn each day.

This will be an agreeable lair from which to keep an eye on the world. He sees the caravels sailing in with their casks of gold, returning from the New World that God has given Spain. He sees the gold changed into barracks and guns. May the gold that Thou givest me, O God, be used for Thy glory, and with Thine aid, Lord, may I crush Thine enemies. Praised be Thou, who givest us the fortune with which to defend Thy glory and Europe from the Turks! He sees the Indian gold turned to power, sails, and canon—the Armada, that invincible police of the seas and the globe.

He sees those other Turks, our brothers in Christ, alas, heretics and worse than Turks, for they renounce their baptism and the true faith they once held. He sees Germany. He sees Geneva and London. He sees Flanders, and Antwerp. He sees Brussels. It is true that these countries bring him as much as America. But if only he could burn that land and those people like so much straw!

The Escorial is dedicated to Saint Lawrence because Saint Quentin fell under the blows of Spain on the feast day of that martyr. The city was bigger than Madrid and its environs, and very wealthy because it was the warehouse for the various commodities that were shipped to the Low Countries. The guns pounded the city walls for hours. Then the signal was given to attack, and the sack began. They fell upon the dead, tore open belly and bowels in search of gold. They walked among naked cadavers whose entrails spilled onto the ground. Several soldiers picked up nearly two thousand ducats. All around them was in flames. They stole everything, even the copper plaque on the front of the town hall. The king had ordered that the women be respected. But he was not there when they were seized by the lansquenets: they undressed the women and searched them for concealed money and jewels; if they found nothing, they would slash their faces or cut off their arms to make them talk. On the evening of the third day, the king arrived; of the city only flames and embers remained. He advanced among clouds of feathers from mattresses eviscerated in search of gold and silver, he looked away from the naked corpses and the dogs, he wanted to thank God for this victory in the cathedral, but it was so full of filth and stench that he was unable to enter. He directed the living to a nearby town: three thousand five hundred women, naked, starving, ill and wounded. The Escorial would be the real Te Deum for this victory. They would beseech Saint Lawrence once more to bless the canons and arms of the Most Catholic King. The king's grandmother was Joanna the Mad. The crown prince Don Juan was a madman who had been shut away, and perhaps poisoned, for the good of Christendom. This was the secret pain, the wound that Philip II bore with patience. Treading between death and madness, the king of Spain fastened the Escorial over this hair shirt like a spiritual armor.

8

It begins with a vision of sorts—a place, a landscape, a man playing a bagpipe in front of an inn. Raising his eyes he sees the sign—a Blue Ship, swinging in the wind. In a darkened window a couple, a girl laughing and embarrassed, a man's hand, a haymaker's hand, touching her red bodice, and her throat flushed with pleasure. The black beams of the bedroom, or the attic, are barely visible. The painter sees details of no concern to the lovers: the mossy tile roof, the tits on the ridge, next to the chimney; more birds in the green sky, through the branches of an aged tree, half-harvested fields, a farmhand in shirtsleeves bringing two jugs of water through the wheat, the harvesters napping in the corner of the field in the shade of a towering oak, a boat in the distant light of the horizon. The piper plays on. One of his cronies listens: is he offering advice or a tankard to quench the player's thirst? The square has now filled with couples lurching into the dance like skaters on ice. The men and women form a garland, weaving in and out in a fabric of red and white sleeves.

Or it may begin with a color, with the desire or an inkling of a certain color: a countryside russet like the throat of a fox, a clay-brown rock, the green tunic of a horseman against the gray of the horse, the candid blue of an apron, the red or white of a sleeve next to the yellow of an earthenware jug or the golden brown of a loaf of bread. It begins with an obscure craving to paint a certain piece of panel—like that straw-yellow facade that sets off the Easter fool, which at once demands a reply and a suggestion from other colors, those next to the first, then all the rest: the ones summoning the others, the others responding, changing tones with their surroundings, like the composition of a bouquet that evolves as it stands and fades; as instruments tune up before they play in perfect pitch. Colors have natural likes and dislikes; one must learn to be happy when they get along and to understand that it is not a matter of placing two pretty colors side by side, but one darkish color alongside a vivid one; bit by bit the one will serve the other.

You are not truly a painter unless you feel the pleasure of laying on a color, a satisfying matter, of losing yourself in it, as before a winter fire, in the evening, beneath a snowy roof or before the sky hung with leaves, or in the gold of a buttercup, or among the grasses. You would not often pick up a brush if you did not feel, in the presence of the white or *grisaille*—but *grisaille* is already a color, it is already painting—the timid, hesitant yearning for a color which will take shape, soul, and life and sing in chorus with its neighbors. When you paint in this way time goes imperceptibly by: evening falls, night; your mind is filled with the soothing painting in store, with no room for thoughts of eating or resting your feet. It is a pleasure that springs from somewhere in childhood, when you modelled figurines out of clay and smoothed or raked patches of mud, dreamy eyed; a pleasure from that time when the mouth waters at the sight of a thick slice of bread smeared with butter by a liberal hand; pure gourmandise.

It happens that the painting comes as a dream, and sometimes even in a dream.

It may happen that it begins with an idea. Then the work closely resembles the trade Bruegel learned at Cock's shop. The subject was The Virtues and the Vices, The Fall of Hermogenes the Magician, The Ass at School, The Land of Milk and Honey, The Fat and the Lean. Sometimes the theme was a proverb: Every man for himself; Big fish eat little fish. Sometimes it was a pun: Alchemist, al ghemist (loosely translated: Alchemist, all amiss). Bruegel was not content simply to illustrate the alchemist's ruin by drawing the half-starved artist in front of his cold ovens and broken beakers; he delighted in imagining the whole laboratory in detail and showing, through the window, his wife and children going out to beg. At a stroke, the neighboring houses appeared, the town, the whole surroundings in which these poor creatures spent their lives. The experience acquired by the draftsman in the Chambers of Rhetoric, his acquaintance with their recitals, now found its use; the task of the illustrator is to choose, in any given action, the most meaningful moments, the most striking and memorable gesture, and, in the tight paper space, surround the main scene with its compactly illustrated consequences. But if the stage and the engraving are to be analogous, it was also necesary to squeeze the whole length and variety of a story into a single image, and in such a way that a child could understand. He must therefore be economical. It is not merely a question of intelligence, but of draftsmanship. How must a group of beggars be drawn so they strike the viewer with the force of a proverb? The composition of the whole picture implies that of each detail.

It was no doubt from this exercise that Bruegel came to understand those composite landscapes that combine a mountain range with a plowed field from Kempen; those vistas that exist nowhere but which ring truer than any that one encounters because they proceed not only from what our eyes have seen, but from the picture our mind has created, which is truer—because it is of the mind—than Nature, which is of a merely sensible order. It is at this price that a drawing (when only ink and paper lie before the eyes, nothing else) makes us feel it is real. This was the art by which Breugel won van Mander's praise in the following terms: "On his journeys, Bruegel drew many views from nature, so that it was said of him, when he traveled through the Alps that he had swallowed all the mountains and rocks and spat them out again, after his return, onto his canvases and panels, so faithfully did he follow, here as everywhere, the appearance of Nature."

No one was better able to imitate Bosch than he. Not only had he swallowed up the mountains of Italy, he had fed on the works of the previous century. "Peter Bruegel of Breda, gifted imitator of the craft and imaginings of Hieronymus Bosch, which earned him the nickname the Second Hieronymus Bosch," writes Guicciardini in Bruegel's lifetime. Lampsonius, in his anthology *Pictorum aliquot celebrium Germaniae inferioris effigies,* inscribed at the bottom of a portrait of Bruegel the following epitaph: "Who is this new Hieronymus Bosch? He breathes new life into the master's dreams, even surpassing him

The Tower of Babel, 1563, Kunsthistorisches Museum, Vienna

The Fall of the Rebel Angels, 1562, Musées Royaux des Beaux-Arts de Belgique, Brussels

The Triumph of Death, 1562–63, Museo del Prado, Madrid. SCALA/ART Resource, N.Y.

Dulle Griet, 1562–63, Museum Mayer van den Bergh, Antwerp

The Fall of Icarus, 1562–63, Musées Royaux des Beaux-Arts de Belgique, Brussels

The Wedding Banquet, 1568(?), Kunsthistorisches Museum, Vienna

The Carrying of the Cross, 1564, Kunsthistorisches Museum, Vienna

Hunters in the Snow, 1565, Kunsthistorisches Museum, Vienna

The Gloomy Day, 1565, Kunsthistorisches Museum, Vienna

Winter Landscape with Skaters and Bird Trap, 1565, Musées Royaux des Beaux-Arts de Belgique, Brussels

The Census at Bethlehem, 1566, Musées Royaux des Beaux-Arts de Belgique, Brussels

The Adoration of the Magi, 1556(?), Musées Royaux des Beaux-Arts de Belgique, Brussels

The Tempest, 1568(?), Kunsthistorisches Museum, Vienna

in his use of color and his draftsmanship. Glory to you Peter, glorious in your art; for your humorous pictures in the old master's style you deserve the highest praise that can be conferred on an artist."

Bruegel was certainly conscious of his own talent. But this praise would not have vexed him. Like his contemporaries, no doubt, he considered imitation of the masters one of the conditions for achieving mastery, not only of their methods, but of their vision, and its underlying principles; this was so true that, when imitating Bosch, for example, and reproducing, at the behest of Cock and his clients, similar scenes of devils and death, desert hermits, the young artist had the sentiment that he was not copying a closed work, but drawing on a source invented by the master. He felt his mind to be inspired by another; he felt that, for a time, he had been given the task of accomplishing on earth and in his flesh the desires and visions that another mind, in passing from one world to the next, had left behind.

Bruegel had also used Bosch's *Excision of the Stone of Madness*—which was probably not his own invention—for his engraving of *The Witch of Malleghem* (Malleghem means the village of the mad): madness is but the other side of wisdom, and, as they say, since alchemists find the philosopher's stone in their own noggins, the fanciful stone must surely grow in the madman's head: all you have to do is take it apart. Bosch had painted a credulous fool tied to a chair and surrounded by three figures, a nun leaning on the round table and wearing a closed red missal on her head; a cleric who resembles someone offering good advice to a condemned man at the stake; and, dressed in a long pink robe with a pitcher hanging from his belt and a funnel on his head, the surgeon with scalpel in hand. He had set the scene on a grassy tapestry against a deep yellow-green rural background of orchards, roads, thickets, a white horse standing in the shade of a clump of trees, the steeples and the towers of distant towns, the blue strip of hills or low mountains beneath the blue and white of the sky, a few minute windmills, a wheel, a gallows. But Bruegel has changed the location and multiplied the figures. He has set the operation and the cruel farce in the village of Proverbs (the same ship is putting out to sea at the top of the picture). A crowd of madmen is pushing and shoving about the medicine stall. They are pressing in from every side, hands outstretched and mouths gawping. You can hear their cries: "Me next, me next, it's my turn." A curious couple lifts their shutter to have a look at the carnival (perhaps they are interested in the profits to be gained from such a pilgrimage?)—all of this in a tangle of crutches, jugs, and knives. They elbow in to be cured of their madness as though it were a toothache. A mill wheel turns—what grain is it grinding? And several monsters from Boschland stroll among the legs of the writhing figures and perch on the roofs. What are those pious members of the mad brotherhood, the Good Friar and the Good Sister, discussing as they lean on the bricked-up corner? A bird with a ladel through its beak sits on a demijohn. A soldier— more likely a highwayman—waits, his helmet over his eyes, to be cured. Are the physicians not just as mad as the madmen? In the lower right-hand corner, like a beached boat, lies a huge egg, a string of seeds of madness, hare-brained notions, spills from one end, and a gaping hole reveals a doctor probing the head of a lunatic. This egg is not found in Bosch's meadow, but Bruegel took the idea from *The Concert in an Egg*, in which the chorus of human folly in an eggshell boat sings an air for several voices—the Egg of Fools or the Concert in a Ship.

But an idea, a proverb, a witticism did not always do the trick. Often it was a book that fueled the imagination. And the Bible has pride of place. Becoming a painter meant learning not only to read and to understand the word of God, but to see it in order to make it visible. How is it possible to represent with dignity the divine story, show the faces of the prophets and saints, the Virgin Mary and Our Lord Jesus Christ. How does one go about finding the most memorable and clearest composition, the one most faithful to the Holy Scriptures? A concern almost as old as the wish of the crippled king of Odessa, who sent a painter to look for Christ in order to paint his portrait, almost as old, too, as Veronica's gesture. That is why the painter's guild took as their patron Saint Luke, who drew a portrait of the Virgin Mary.

But how is one to paint that which cannot be looked upon. What preparation is there for portraying the triumph of death? He read Petrarch. He saw the broad land so full of the dead that no words could tell, nor prose nor verse. He read the last canto of Lucretius and watched the plague smite Athens. Then he set aside his books and looked at people. Under the hats and the hoods, beneath the helmets he saw livid cheeks that would soon be hollow, in the sleeves he saw armbones and fingerbones, for each passerby he imagined his own individual death. At the kermis he watched the dancers and the piper by the table, the procession following its banner, the crew hoisting the sail: corpses and skeletons every one. He saw the wedding guests: so many bodies in a grave. The haymakers in the summer gold: so many blasted trees. He did not close his eyes when he saw Mary's face dissolve with the others and her vertebrae scatter like a broken string of beads. He did not put aside his thoughts when, in the sudden night, they nailed down his coffin lid. He regarded his bones as a bundle of firewood where slugs and snails crawl.

As he composed *The Triumph of Death*, Bruegel was painting for himself. Perhaps he had set before him, as a reminder of salvation in the midst of this disaster, a small pen-and-brush *grisaille* on gray paper. In the center, against a partially revealed opening in the rock, is a round stone taller than a man, a sort of millstone that has rolled to one side of the hole. Behind the stone is the mouth of the tomb, gaping like the gullet of Jonah's big fish. It comprises shadow and clay and verges on a flawless black. A radiant-winged angel dressed in a long robe is seated on the wheel of stone: the viewer must raise his eyes to see the face and the light that streams from it. In the fore-ground, at the foot of a blasted hollow tree, some soldiers are waking, like the shepherds of Bethlehem long ago, and are dazzled by the angel: one of them raises a hand to shield his eyes. But others are still sleeping, like the child in his mother's womb; their head rests on their arms, and their arms on their knees. One soldier, a knee still to the ground, is attempting to stand; he catches sight of the angel and seizes a weapon; his neighbor, still half asleep at the foot of the stone, has not seen the angel; he approaches the grave, holding his lance as though it were a pole. A group of more alert soldiers—no doubt the relief patrol—armored like beetles, are peering into the depths of the tomb, pointing to the darkness of the cave where they remember having laid the body, but the tomb is empty. The waking soldiers fight off a stupor deeper than any produced by drink. Will such be our sluggish efforts at last to raise our eyes to Christ and his light? Will it be this hard to wake from our long, fast sleep of death? The Holy Women are coming down the path bearing spices. They see the stone rolled away and the empty tomb. But they do not understand. They had been wondering: "Who will roll away the heavy stone, for we are mere women? And what will the soldiers do to us?" They see the soldiers on the ground, as though drunk. Have they, perhaps, been knocked unconscious? The frightening thought crossed their minds—but why?—that robbers had come to steal the body of Jesus. Then they notice, calmly seated on the stone, a young man dressed in white. They hear the angel's voice. No one has yet seen Christ rising into the clouds, triumphant over death.

5

THE THEATER OF DEATH

Not a lantern, nor a candle. Black as night. The breathing of those waiting for the lights to come up is barely audible. In the distance, far in the distance, in the distant wings of the world, behind the black mountains beneath their snow and the unseen stars (if the moon is shining, it gives off an icy light, a frozen pond in the sky, lip of the well of the dead), and somewhere behind us a trumpet is playing the *Dies irae*. A double drum plays against the beat. The noise echoes like a barrel, a cave, like a tun, like thunder, reverberating to the very marrow of your bones. A footsore music for a catafalque. Then the cracked voice of a hurdy-gurdy.

And the wind that suddenly rises. Stage right, a bright pool of light, which will grow, illuminates a young man who puts his hand to the grip of his long sword. He starts. He takes fright. The walls, where are the walls? The walls have gone as one sweeps away a tablecloth. The walls are gone, and the ceiling! The whole house has been plucked up like a cover from a cheese plate. The soft light from the candles and chandeliers was dancing in the mirrors and glancing off the delicate Cordoba leather, off the crystal on the table; the banquet was drawing to a close amid music and laughter; and the woman at my right was making eyes at me. And suddenly the walls evaporate. It is not that the house has become transparent, like glass: we are out of doors. We are in the garden, the countryside. I stretch out my hands and touch nothing but air. Nothing. The wind is rising. I feel it on my face and hands. An odor of manure insinuates itself into my nostrils. I take a deep breath of a horrifying smell of charnel house. The smell of death penetrates my lungs. Where is the person for whom I was about to pour a drink? It is pitch dark and one sees as though it were day. I can still hear nearby the harmonies of a love song. But what a racket and creaking of wheels from the roads! And that abominable smell of rotting meat on the wind. Against my hipbone I feel the round table, with its white cloth, its cloth too white in the flashes of light and the storm. Icy fear grips me despite my courage. The diamond-clad fool, about to show us some sleight-of-hand beneath his habit of black and red check, how I understand his slipping terrified under the table and the white cloth, hiding like a poodle. Myself, I am of noble birth, young, in good health and I am drawing my long sword.

Behind the young man, on the round, white table, white like a November moon or the tapers round a deathbed, in the middle of the table sits a pewter plate, and in the plate, an earthenware dish, and in the dish, an eye—no, not an eye! But a socket, trying to see, peering over the edge. There in the plate lies a death's head, like some dessert just set out. There lies a death's head watching us, looking as though it were laughing at the joke played on the guests. There is the dirt-caked cover of the skull.

You can hear the sound of the wind, and in the wind, confused shouting, groaning, the laughter of rattles. An Italian love duo (next to the skull's table) glides and slips by, like a leisurely boat in a tempest. A voice seems to come from a skeleton, saying, your neighbor, your gentle fair, gallant neighbor, who melted at your words with flushing brow, she has already gone from your mind. I have seized her by the waist, by the breast, as you dreamed of doing. She is as plump as I am thin and dry. Crying out, she shakes her long furred sleeves. She opens her raspberry mouth in an animal cry. Still she flees me, slipping from my bony fingers. It is true that my breath does not smell of ambrosia. It is true that my face has grown somewhat hollow, that my skull is bald, that the moldy casing of my ribs is more visible now that I go about naked as a dog. Her girlfriend, whom you used to make jealous, in vain hides her eyes: she has seen the green monk bearing a stew of bone and skull. She sees the green monk and his cowl from which dangle the ears of a fool's cap.

A few feet from the banquet, a lansquenet draws himself up in his ruffles, ribbons, and slashed sleeves. He is doing battle with a shrouded skeleton; but this insect, bracing his heel against a deadman's helmet, blocks the other's raised sword and, with the aid of a rope, snares the adversary's leg. The two look like they are dancing, steps for a wedding dance! One soldier has fallen, mowed down by the skeleton finishing him off. A peasant hurls a bench at an oncoming hoard. An armored knight sprawls in the dust, as still as a stump. But what is there to do? Our attackers are already dead. Their armor is a shroud, their rampart an ossuary. Games and counters, cards and goblets, tric-trac and backgammon have fallen to the grass: there are no winners. A steady-handed corpse lights me with his lantern. Another has plundered our wardrobes, he has garbed himself in golden yellow and donned a carnival mask. Like a cupbearer, he empties the wine from our silver ewers into the stream.

On a hillock stands a tree from which hangs an enormous bell rung by two indefatigable bony figures. The love duo continues amid the clicking of bones. The lover plays the lute while his lady holds the book. Behind their backs a deadman accompanies them on what looks like a famished cello. A crowd is making good speed. These are the people of the town. They press together and hurry along as though it were rush hour. They are prodded with lances, struck with axes, mowed down, butchered, strangled. Like a heap of rags, they pile up in limp bundles. Those untouched by the bony militia imagine they can flee by a sort of porch, a high, wide trapdoor. The reinforcements are waiting behind upright coffins. There they stand, at rest, refreshed, youthful troops, blocking all escape. They are encamped in the garden. Since when do we quarter regiments of death? I see the torches smoking above the skeletal horde. They bide their time, marking time. At the signal, they will charge. Meanwhile, with a clacking of mandibles, they chat. They whistle at the pretty girls; they would like to wink. I hear their barracks jokes. Death does not improve a man. And the crowd enters pell-mell, thrown upon one another like fish into a basket. The couples embracing are not those who embraced in life. A scraggy flayed nag, ridden by a skeleton weilding a scythe, tramples the pile under foot. And children with familiar faces are shoveled into the belly of death. They will return, empty skulled, thin-limbed mercenaries in this chalky army of the night. They pass like a tide swelling the rivers of dead, and back they come again. The earth vomits squadrons of shoulder and thigh bones. The land disgorges legions of dead; no other century ever brought so many under arms.

Lift up your eyes! You saw the villagers walk into the Tartar's trap like a herd streaming to the slaughterhouse. You see the whole world in the throes of death. You see the seat of death, and death riding out. You see, on the horizon, shipwrecks and fires. You see ships burning at sea and sailors caught between the grill and the deep. You see the full measure of death's ruses and ploys. You see the Black Death and the Blue vying for the checkerboard of country and town. The bony brotherhood traps us in its snares and tips us into its nets. It drives us to the water's edge and drowns us there. A bloated body floats in the green river; a convent of shrouds waves as it goes by; a naked man with a millstone around his neck is about to join the corpses. Cohorts of bones stream from a seaside cemetery and from a tower built upon a reef. The first born among the dead help the newborn from their coffins. Two monks pull a decomposing woman along in her box; her head rests on a bundle of straw and her broken child dangles over the edge. Look and see: gibbets, wheels, instruments of torture. See the tattered corpses rotting in forked trees. See the gallows and the skeletal ladders upon a thousand golgothas. See the executioner at the base of the wheel, mere backbone and ribs, raise his sword above the neck of a man already half dead with fright. We are always glad to lend death a helping hand. Look! They fight us, they track us into every corner, these manikins, these machines without heart of flesh, and they seem to be laughing. They seem to invite us to the biggest feast ever! They look like they miss us. Look! Look at the thousands of ways to die, the thousands of macabre postures, the frightful buffoonery, the great combat, the battle of battles, our lives harvested like grapes, our breath reaped like stands of grain, our blood trod under bony heels, the thousands of ways of trampling out our flesh, our eyes given up to the crows, our entrails to the worm, the hooves of pale horses striking temples and skulls, the crimson spots of fever, our members thrown onto the refuse heap. And up there, above the disemboweled corpses, the tortures, the wheels, the murders, the bloodstained judges' garden! Stage left, the king staggers about. Which king? Nimrod, who no longer thinks of the Tower of Babel, nor of his palaces and ships. Is that you, poor Charles, in your crown and ermine and purple! No. It is myself. That prelate helped along by a skeleton—that is me, a humble modest parishioner. The pilgrim they are assassinating has my face, cries out with my voice. I am the guest and the lover, defending his table and dice. I am he who hears not, who hears nothing, subjugated as I am by the charm of the lute and the delicate breast, who does not hear the cart creaking in the arpeggios, nor the glanderous laughter of the desiccated dobbin, a crow perched on its rump. Lift up your eyes and see the convoys of skulls, the harvest of white crocks with their gaping orbs, and astride his scrawny nag, scythe in hand, loathsome Death. Lift up your eyes, look, listen! Everyone is exiting—and I am exiting! Into the gaping hole in the clay. They are disappearing into the wings. Where is Christ! Where is the hell he promised, or his Heaven? Hell, I see, its stronghold, its furnaces in the center of the picture, with old-fashioned devils, dragonflies, web-footed moles. The hell of nightmares and crackling flames. Go on, keep moving. Already there is a hint of Last Judgment in the air. Return to the clay and wait for the Last Judgment, if it comes. Lights out. The end.

6

RUE HAUTE

1

In fact the house was not that small. Over the years, the oldest part had gained one room that had originally belonged to the house next door, a storeroom made over into a dining room, a cellar, a staircase with wardrobes. The house had grown after the fashion of a tree, which had given it a wealth of nooks and crannies; and the attic was made up of several attics that were not all strictly on the same level or of the same height. It formed a sort of widow's walk from which you could look out over the plain, the fields and woods, the harvests and deep-lying snow, the roofs of the town, and finally, from the narrowest gable, the harsh rise of the mange-colored Galgenberg. You could see both country and town. You could see clouds, the long caravan, the slow fleet of passing clouds, the flocks of clouds in their blue pasture, their islands of wool, raveled and dispersed by the wind, dyed by many suns to resemble fabrics of India and China, or Flanders cloth. You stood on the shore of the sky as on the shore of the sea. The winds coiled in the air or filed by like some endless troop. Gently the days and the seasons changed the color of the air and the house timbers. Bruegel had built windows in the top story to let in light. There he had set up his workshop, or rather workshops, since his drawing table stood at some distance from where he painted. Sometimes he would spend long moments motionless before his canvas, not lifting his brush, just looking, as one observes a valley, the brilliance of the river, and the activity of men in the fields. He seemed to be listening to his painting. But he also liked to stride through this attic, to take walks, and on these walks meet the finished painting and the one barely begun. But he did not always look at his works; on these walks, he would also think, and dream. It had always seemed to him that his thoughts became more vibrant and free when he could pace the floor. On his attic walks, he rediscovered the fervent reveries he had relished on the roads of Holland, the roads of his childhood, the roads of Italy. Scattered rugs muffled his footsteps;

94

between the carpets, the wood floors shone like a ship's deck; terra-cotta tiles gleamed red. Here and there were low tables, lamps, books: the Latin poets, Homer, the Bible. There was a high-backed armchair in which Bruegel sat to read, dream, or lean back and look at the paintings that astonished him, but were his all the same. Under the eaves, in the silence of the attic where the winds and the rain could be heard skittering across the roof tiles and slates, and the sounds of birds' feet, little by little, like so many hamlets and constellations, like the seasons of a lifetime, his paintings had arranged themselves into a number of localities. A few steps took the artist from a group of dances and wedding scenes to snow-covered Bethlehem. Among these large pictures, he was like a man standing amid the dreams of his nights, surrounded, like a child who delights in slipping between the sheets that women pull and stretch before folding. This was his oratory, and his laboratory.

Next to his own, there was another, smaller workshop, normally occupied by his two apprentices, where the necessary preparations were made. You could leave the attic by several doors. The largest opened on to a study and, from there, to the rest of the house. Another led only to the bedroom and was draped with a length of gold-worked cloth. The whole attic, in fact the whole house, was like a spiral shell. A few narrower passages, invented by time and the handi-work of builders, made it possible to come and go by a shorter way. It was one of those houses children loved because it provided them with niches and nooks where reverie delights to wander and dwell.

Sometimes Bruegel would catch himself thinking of the time when this house did not exist. He could see a densely wooded landscape with trees, swiftly trotting wild boar, deer's antlers. Where today's soup was steaming, mistletoe once garlanded the oaks. A curving, almost circular wall in the center of the house made him think that, on this spot, on this windy hill, all had begun with a windmill. But had the windmill perhaps come about only because a tower had been erected? Perhaps the tower of a chapel, or a cloister. Or of a strong-hold, or a camp. Yes, the windmill must have been installed in the tower. Wheat had replaced the weapons, or the prayers. The miller's songs had succeeded the guardhouse chorus, the sounding of military trumpets, the hymns, and the bells. Inside his house, Bruegel trained his ear to the sounds of the past. As we, looking into a mirror, would like to recapture the faces and the gaze of those who, passing, have gazed at themselves. They say that when a witch is given a dish, she can hear words. One day a witch had paled in front of her client; the soup tureen she was handed had witnessed a murder. Bruegel listened to the murmuring of the past hidden within the house. As you imagine you hear the sea, and even its vessels, in a shell, whoever has ears can hear the walls whispering, telling even the black secrets of the cellars beneath your feet.

Perhaps it was the tower of an ancient fortification, a watchtower from Roman times. A windmill took up its quarters, centuries later, in the deserted, useless tower—or some long-bearded son of Saint Anthony, the hermit, in the thicket, setting out the Book and the cross before his eyes, to pray, but, amid the drops of mistletoe, in the moonlight, assailed by burlesque yet terrifying duck-billed devils with cauldrons for rumps, by the brothel and the cortege of false queens. Nothing remained of that tower but the shape, the design, the mold. Then the guard had changed and the oaths of ancient Italy had rung out. He saw the soldiers asleep in the straw; some had barely loosened their armor to be ready for their coming watch: in the foggy night they lay like Pilate's men, fallen asleep beside the tomb and whom the snow-white brilliance of the angel does not awaken, weighed down as they are by an unhappy sleep. They were dreaming of their family in Campania, of a little garden for their re-tirement. When would they once more see the fruit-laden, twining vineyards of their childhood? Was it possible in those days to see, from this hill, in the far-off silver of the fog against the silver of the sea, the fleets in from Rome? They got up. The sound of their march-ing feet, the iron of their mail and arms could be heard, as today the sound of Spanish troops, in the streets. A helmet glittered, and a cap-tain's purple at the shoulder. Then brambles overgrew the barracks. And the time of milling began, while the heavens rang out the Chris-tian hours and feasts.

He had arranged his books in the mold of the tower. They rose like a wall of words and thoughts. Like the grain, the finest wheat of minds. At the base stood tall volumes of maps, and compendia of drawings of birds and fish. He felt a bit like Noah in his ark, with the pictures and the memory of the world about him. He liked to read in his torsaded armchair, while, at the window, the rain washed or beat the leaded panes and their colors. He sat at the heart of this round library, like Jason in his clearing listening to the sound of the Oaks of Dodona counsel him the voyage.

There were also the coins that he had brought back from Rome: a Minerva leaning on her spear, half-effaced emperors, horses and chariots, triremes. There were a few small bronze statues found in the sands of the Scheldt—poor gods rolled about in the silt and fished out head down by a some dragnet. There was also the Mercury, or rather the rough-hewn milestone, equipped with purse and staff, a

winged cap and a face that looked a little like that of his host: it had
been discovered there in the foundations of the house. Other bronze
Mercurys in various postures had been found in Velseke, in Flanders,
near Oudenaarde, in a location thought to have been the town of
Belgis.

In the center of the room, Bruegel had placed a globe that he had
constructed and painted in Antwerp, in the geographer's workshop,
for his own pleasure (the pleasure of patience and colors) and to learn
about and understand the world, even though he was still hardly more
than a child, and Pieter van Aalst gave him whole days that he did not
have to account for. It was by making the sphere that the geographer
had taught him the shape and the configuration of the earth, the old
routes and the new. He would enter the red-brick house near the
wharf. He would be coming from the waterfront or the countryside.
He could still feel the wind from the fields and the sea on his face. And
suddenly silence. Past the heavy coffered door, his feet would sink into
a deep carpet, a Persian garden of wool. This was the place of study.
Green light. The still heart of the world. The geographer wore an old-
fashioned long robe of green velvet with ermine or fawn-colored cuffs
and collar. The room was a sort of well, surrounded by tall bookshelves against which leaned copper and wooden ladders, like those
on ships. A stairway led to the turret. Up there was the spyglass. All
you had to do was to swing it around, raise or lower it, and the story
of the world unfolded anew. You could see the harbor, and, in the distance, the sea and its ships fairly engulfed in light. You could see men
in the rigging, who thought themselves far away; little did they suspect the eyes trained on them. And yet you almost held them in the
hollow of your hand. You could see people conversing on the piers,
the trading, the barrels, an egret feather in a toque, the great crane as
thoughtful as a grasshopper. On the fortifications, at the other end of
town, you could see the woman watering the red flowers on her balcony. She too thought she was alone. You could see her as though
reading her story in a book. Then they would turn the spyglass on
the moon, suddenly as close as a field. They observed the sky. They
observed those other countries, the stars. They wrote down the
phases and signs in the tables. And so they would grow dizzy dreaming in the well-like observatory, open to the bottomless heights.
Downstairs, in the geographer's workshop, wide green-leather tables
with copper tacks held maps and books. The world was reflected in
this workshop like the garden in the ball on the staircase.

Midway up the library stairs, a narrow door led to the bedroom.
Beyond lay the private house, almost a house within a house. When

Mary would appear on the landing, dressed in gold, golden yellow, or blue, as Bruegel stood dreaming by the globe or choosing a book, he thought he was seeing the young Sibyl of the house in Antwerp.

The room contained a wealth of deep chests, fabrics, quilts, heavy, full draperies; and the wood of the mantle and beams was gorged with wax. Other bedrooms, next to the master bedroom, would be for the children. From the window you could see the garden, a patch of country in the distance. You could see a door at the far end of the garden, in the brown-brick wall, and a brook flowing beneath the willows.

2

The Triumph of Death hangs in Madrid, *The Fall of the Rebel Angels* in Brussels, *Dulle Griet* (Mad Meg) in Antwerp. There was one moment, the year Bruegel moved to the rue Haute when it was possible to see these three intense paintings side by side in his workshop. In fact, few were admitted: only his closest friends, or an occasional colleague who had come a long way. And sometimes Bruegel would draw a curtain in front of the work in progress. He was not given to commenting on the meaning of what he had done. "Isn't it clear?" he would say. "And if the meaning of these figures isn't obvious, isn't that a sign that some uncertainty is necessary? Things often have more than one meaning." To those who insisted that he divulge the key to his compositions, the detail that changes everything and that no one sees unless they are in on the secret, Bruegel liked to give Bacbuc's reply: "Interpret what you do yourself." Was this simply elementary caution in those times of religious burnings and slaughters? Or was this his taste for teasing that van Mander writes about, or his sense of the secret that must be kept, the sense of things that are clear to those who know, but remain obscure, or invisible, for those who do not. In the last line of his life of Bruegel, van Mander writes: "He did one more painting, entitled *The Triumph of Truth*. It was, he said, his best work." Of this unknown masterpiece, which may have existed only in his mind, all we know is that we cannot see it. And so is invisible Truth portrayed, since it triumphs by staying ever out of reach and never ceases to draw, as a magnet, our desire, even along our darkest paths of error and lies.

In Bruegel's workshop attic there were the three paintings, then. I can feel them radiating in the dark house. With such paintings, nothing can ever compare with the moment when the painter is the only one who knows them. The time when he thinks of them at night, in bed; as though he saw them glowing in the dark, through the walls, the partitions, the floor. At daybreak, in the pink and gray dawn, he will see them once again. The painter's visit to yesterday's work is his morning prayer. Sometimes, even, while his young wife slept, he would get up in the dark and soundlessly climb the few steps to the workshop to take one more look at his work, in the night. I feel as though I have been, in the dark of the moon, to this workshop where Bruegel comes, candle in hand, to question those dreams on their wooden panels. And so, for a few nights the three paintings stood not far apart. Today they light separate museums. But how they did radiate together, those nights in Brussels, in the rue Haute!

To think of them together increases their force and their mystery, their self-evidence. This could be the entire work of some master known only by these three large scenes. And *scene* is the right word. The three paintings, all the same size, are three scenes from a play, the three acts of a tragedy. They are three battle scenes. The first takes place in heaven, as it says in Revelations: it is the battle between the archangel Michael and his angels, and the Dragon and his armies. The second would be more aptly named the Universal Agony: it shows the living caught up in the arms of death; this battle takes place on earth. The third is fought below: it is a burlesque scene set in Hell. The *Children's Games* and *The Proverbs,* and even the *Battle between Carnival and Lent* are far away indeed! A door has opened in Bruegel's soul, and windows, and a wind blows through bearing dreams and truth, a wind from the other world. He has climbed to the attic of his own accord, he has descended the slippery stairs into his cellars and caves; he has thrown open the window of his house onto the battleground of death, the swamps of felled bodies, and the snow of ossuaries. He used to imagine; now he has *seen*. Something more than simply painting has occurred. Now the three large panels are separated and so well known they barely draw a glance, but to those who saw them together in the workshop, they were not so much paintings as *apparitions*. As Bruegel raised the candle slightly, the dumbfounded visitor found himself standing before the three scenes, like Virgil and Dante at the meeting of the three worlds.

All the while he had been conceiving and composing them, Bruegel had felt something akin to the warm, strong, fatherly hand of Hieronymus Bosch on his shoulder, felt him at his back, looking on, affectionately. He heard Bosch, he heard the way he had of being still and watching; in this silence, he received his advice, his energy and inspiration, and sometimes this exchange of the heart would blossom into a few well-chosen words. The young painter spoke to the old master, the father, as a man sometimes speaks to his guardian angel. Bosch was often present, beside him in the workshop, and Bruegel could almost see him, like a living man, an earthly companion. Sometimes the old master stayed away—for hours, days, weeks. Where was he? What heavenly path did he take, through what dewy emerald meadows did that pilgrim go, praying? On what still fragile shoulder did he lay the warmth and strength of his hand. At those times, Bruegel matured alone. He grew used to the idea of deciding what he thought, what he would do, alone. He progressed. And then, suddenly, once again the warm weight on his shoulder, and the fatherly, brotherly gaze fixed on the large picture that was taking shape, coming to life.

No one sets out to become a painter, or a poet, unless some master or father precedes and guides him to that point from which he must go on alone. In the early years he does not always know who they are. No doubt, Pieter Coeck van Aalst and Hieronymus Cock were Bruegel's living masters. But Bosch was his inner master. He became aware of this only upon his return from Italy, when, rid of the temptation (but had he really been tempted?) to pursue a career in Venice or Rome, like Jean de Boulogne, he traveled in his own country, with Franckert of Nuremberg, and found in Flanders both a foreign country and his native land. He would have been proud to have been born Italian and, crossing the Alps, he realized that he could have been as much a man of the mountains as he was of the plain and the sea. But he felt himself a son of that other country. He belonged to the family of those who dwelled, all who had ever dwelled, between the Meuse and the Rhine. He traveled through Flanders and Holland with the same curiosity that, in Umbria, Tuscany, Apulia, Venice, and Palermo, had driven him to learn from everything he saw: habits of speech and dress, ways of eating, building, scratching a living from the land, and that turn of mind that shapes a people beyond all that can be said or seen; but there he felt at home. He discovered his lost childhood and its distant headwaters. He felt a deep bond with Jan van Ruysbroek, our Saint John of the Forêt de Soignes. And one day he set out, unhurriedly but not unimpatiently, for 's Hertogenbosch, and the first man to pour him a drink, the keeper of the hotel on the great square was named van Aken. From the open window, Bruegel saw the same sky in which Hieronymus had watched Saint Anthony fly imperturbably by on a toothy fish.

In the foreground a throng of gaping monsters rushes past. They plummet from the sky like frightful fish spewed up from the sea: slack gullets, pointed teeth, and flabby, livid bellies. With lightning speed they have traded their luminous face and heavenly form for unsightly eellike snouts, they have changed into toads, serpents, crabs, hideous masks of the depths. How could they? One, in his fall, his downfall, drags with him a superb theorbe, which he used to play before the Eternal One, which he will now scrape in the stagnant ponds of hot coals and disgust. They fall belly up like so many dead sharks. They are cast into the sinister mud, a mass of entrails, and their bellies crack and split like a pomegranate, their guts are full of wormy eggs and teem with more devils yet. They list. They founder! They sink! Irresistibly they are cast down by the might and radiance of the faithful angels! Like tons of refuse they fall, like a rotted vintage into the winepress of nothingness. They are fat and very close, obese, obscene, and they fall. Like an enormous outpouring of grotesque sewage, they come tumbling down. They have only each other to stay their fall, but all are falling. What can they have done to be driven out in this way? A shaft of light beams from above: a sun and a home of glory. Will they remember, in their exile, and burn with remorse? Croaking, they slide. They are already far, far from the divine light. They pitch into the abode of shadows and frost. They squirm in the ice that blazes and burns. Their pursuers are youth and grace embodied, nearly children, choir boys on a short leave of absence from their heavenly home, called to active duty, knightly duty, clean-up duty. They are dressed in long white robes, and their swords are not so much weapons as rods, no heavier than light. Neither strength, nor muscle, nor the jointing of armor, nor the metal of arms are needed to vanquish these beasts, but light, obedience, and the Spirit. They hover like purest springtime above the corruption below. They are the snows and the snowmelts. They soar above this vile melee as in an aerial dance; theirs is the elegance and the perfume of swinging censers. We have seen them before: the angels of Paradise, of course, but also van Eyck's angels, the angels of Bruges, of ancient, holy Flanders; these are the spiritual brothers of limpid Flanders, the Flanders of mirrors and swans, of white lace bonnets, of clear eyes, and radiant tenderness. Some blow lustily into delicate curved horns. Their breath becomes a battle cry, a cry of joy; as the walls of Jericho came tumbling down to the sound of trumpets, so the unclean armies fall and Jerusalem shines forth. In their midst, as though amid his armor-bearers, the knightly archangel, Saint Michael, in his golden mail, with his round shield bearing the red cross turned to the abyss, does battle with the crux of evil, the Serpent, the Dragon with seven heads.

A black dragonfly can be seen, and a few dubious-looking animals circling the tower of hell that glows red in the center of *The Triumph of Death*. The same dragonfly was fleeing before the archangel's blows. But in the midst of our life, our laughter, our business, we are caught up, not in the clutches of some devil, but under the mechanical arm of a laughing, desiccated skeleton. An army of deadmen snatches us up, tracks us down. They have invaded us like a foreign host. Our ramparts are scaled by their clattering cohort, and they cannot be killed. They sail our rivers, camp by our roads, they sit in our homes and sleep in our sheets. I open a wardrobe and find a battalion. If I kneel in the paupers' pew, my poor body all atremble, they shift and then press closer, drown me in the baptismal font, bring on the catafalque. And that bell, who tolls it with such fury? A skeletal sacristan announcing the town's fall. The horse in my stable has turned to bones, he carries me through a dead man's land! Helmets peer from behind the haystacks, or the rim of helmets, but beneath the helmet, the empty cranial jug, and the senile laughter of the dead.

And who is this tall, stark woman striding through hell with her soldierly gait? On her head she wears an iron pot shaped like a skimming ladle, she carries her sword like a prod or a skewer, her white apron bulges with kitchen utensils, a pewter-colored breastplate covers her flat chest; over one arm hangs a basket of odds and ends and a frying pan that sticks out the back, under her arm she clutches a heavy chest full of coins or pearls, and her left hand is gloved in a man's gauntlet. Behind her a pack of village women is pillaging hell or something very like it; they go at it the way they wield their baskets at market. They are garbed in small-town colors, in the colors of proverbs, bursting with health and high spirits in the reddish glow of the hellish shores, flanked by ponds of splashing monsters. Their excited band surges onto a little bridge, arms upraised to fall upon the devils; they crowd into a house that they will strip of its contents, like a gang of soldiers kicking down doors in a hostile, or a friendly, village. They wage their war with the zeal of women at spring cleaning. Astride the roof of the looted house, a curious robed figure dips out the contents of a broken egg that serves as his bottom; gold and excrement fall onto the heads of the shrews below. The roof is on fire and someone is brandishing a cauldron through a hole in the thatch. Not only is the ladling figure scraping out his eggshell, but on his shoulder he balances a rowboat containing a glass ball inside which curious figures busy themselves around a table bearing a large roast chicken. A purse dangles from the straddling figure; a bold woman rummages through it. But the small band of rural harpies is unworried about these no less worrisome things. These Stygian washerwomen cannot see past the end of their scrubboard. It is no surprise to them that hell holds houses like their own, the everyday landscape, the ordinary square. Could it be that this is hell? The conflagration in the sky, these blazing haystacks, these revels spawned by bad wine, these creatures born of too much drink, do they reside in the depths of Tartarus, or somewhere in our countryside? Banners fly over the ruins and the crumbling walls, from the pinions of Beelzebub's courts. What do they say? Nothing clear, nothing good. This is a bad land; the barracks and the fleets belong to one whose name is Legion. A bell growls and barks from the crotch of a tree. There is a tower rigged with wheels and gears. There are eggs, cages in which mice are dancing a round, white eggs inside black eggs, eggs like a basket, eggs like a house, and pots and jugs. Armored patrols drill beneath archways. Absurd creatures flap in the glowing coals of the nether sky. A skinny leg protrudes from the mouth of a fish: I hear the cries of the swallowed victim, smothering in the entrails of this modest Leviathan; he shouts that it stinks of fish, he has bitten the gall, he was a sinful fisherman and was caught by a fish, and perhaps he already sees, in the dark gut of his fish, a hell with an idiotic landscape like the one in which we see him waving his leg like an arm, one of life's castaways. More cries, or rather the sound of soldiers singing, come from a round basin in the lurid village where a thicket of gendarmes lurks in bundles, in sheaves, helmeted and spiney speared. So it goes in hell. In the middle of the red marsh, naked, small, and chilled, a minute couple contemplates the scope of the calamity. He is Adam. She is Eve.

He who knows the Fall begins the Return and the Ascent. While, in Antwerp or Brussels, Bruegel was painting this now dismembered triptych, he descended into hell. He descended a nightmare into the seething and the folly of his own heart. His mind dwelled below the ground, in those places trod by the shrew, derision of ourselves, in that Babylon of caverns and depths that we all are. He saw this queen of Babylon stride with bestial gait; this appetite for earthly hardware, this yearning for the laying up of things, of thoughts and knowledge, even; this yearning to possess, everything, even the angels who come to our door; this yearning to dominate all things, all life. He saw the heart of man, vast and bare as a desert. He painted, he worked; his face was like the faces of other men, but, as in a dream, he descended into the secret depths and chambers, the roots, of our heart. A hell of a wind was blowing up. Painfully he dragged himself free of the slough. A dark sun shone on the fires. He descended as in a dream, but he kept his mind alert, as one holds a lantern aloft, to see and to understand. He was able to laugh at this fierce burlesque ego. He saw the architecture of nightmares and he measured the contours of fevers. His eye pierced the belly of the earth and saw the horses of death. He found the strength to lift his gaze above the macabre mountains, and he saw the angelic battle in the air. He saw the everlasting light resplendent with a memory and a promise. And he strove upward toward that light.

To paint this triptych, to descend into himself, into the hells, the subterranean passages, the abysses, and the ocean troughs of the Leviathan that blows and stinks in the depths of our heart; to descend, to capsize like Jonah, and to surface and cross the mournful plains of life, the festering wounds and the skeletons, the feeling that all is vain since, in the end, everything is swept away, this was Bruegel's temptation, like that of all hermits, beginning with Saint Anthony of Egypt. While he was with Cock, he had taken pleasure in composing a carnival of vices, a bedeviled world with corteges of dancing jugs, fish eddying in the wind, huge fish the size of hogsheads, their gaping scaly bellies revealing dens in which souse fell upon souse, snout to snout, eggs the size of a small boat discharging banner-waving armies, seductive frogs, toads puffing beneath their tiaras, cellar shindys, oriental palaces moldering beneath their moss, sacrilegious acrobats, bone-headed cows playing the harp, the crowd, the tohubohu of sabbaths, taverns in hollow trees, roast chickens, dragonflies from his conflagrations, the twisted brigands of the lord of the flies, his small winged army, the din of drums and off-key pipes, the screech of untuned strings, and even the smells that must go with the billowing smoke rising from towns and bivouacs, all the arms that hell turns on the unswerving ascetic. And then he became a hermit himself, and gravely he represented the old man on his knees, facing the Book and reading aloud, to ward off the mad bells and the plague-ridden words of evil, or reading to himself, by heart, but with such an inward voice that the bubbles of that grim world burst with each new verse, with every syllable uttered. He was this old man, watched over and sheltered by a tree, and fervently he inscribed a halo about the wise head soon to be free of the din of the world. He had taken the measure of the temptations told in books, portrayed in pictures. The hardest had been to look squarely at death and the whole vanity of life. And he had transformed the skull on the stump that Anthony contemplates like a looking-glass into that immense army of skulls and the whole revolting gala of *The Triumph of Death.*

A hermit, was he? This man who had just taken a young, gracious wife and who painted in the comfort of a workshop in the sky, in the falling November snow.

The heart is ever a desert where wild beasts seduce and strike us with terror. And the soldierly mitered beasts are no less troubling than those seen in the visions of Egypt's tombs and caves. Could I keep my nerve in those storms, neither falter, nor weaken, nor betray, nor curse? Bruegel drew Patience, holy Patience. She is seated on a dressed stone, her eyes raised to heaven, praying amid the churning shadows and the monstrous agitation around her. A hollow, wooden cardinal rides a hollow egg from which a head protrudes, smoking and burning. Where are they going thus, emptiness and death? Darkness covers the world. Darkness fills the heart. A screech owl sits on a dry, twisted tree in which brothels have found a perch. Can the Church visible be anything but this rotted cardinal mounted on his whitewashed egg-tomb? But the True Church is within. May Patience keep us faithful, she who is the strength to suffer and endure; she who is hope and faith in the Light. She sits in the darkness that burgeons and teems with monsters; but already an infant sun is rising on the far shores of the sea. A new dawn awaits us on the other side of the world, and already its light sustains us.

3

He works long hours. Since he moved to Brussels he has worked harder than ever. He rises earlier. Sometimes he even leaves his bed at night, to read, think, dream in front of a panel barely begun. To draw or sketch in the broad lines with charcoal, chalk, silver point, brush, or to indicate the large masses of the picture. The yellow brushstrokes are almost invisible, and the chalk or charcoal lines so light that the slightest breath disperses them: once the painting begins, the process erases or covers the sketch. In fact, he continues to draw as he paints. He moves imperceptibly from the drawing to the finished painting. He hardly needs a working drawing. The panel itself is his sketch pad. He takes pleasure in this sort of giant print spread over the space of his future painting. He likes its vistas and the black-and-white picture. He waits for the colors to rise, like dawn in

the forest to the still sleepy calls of birds, or on the hill to which the
harvesters will soon be returning, sickles hanging from their belts. In
the gray-and-black lines he already sees a painting. He enjoys these
potential pictures that only a painter can see, which will bow to other
pictures, efface themselves. The Tower of Babel or the mountainous
road to Damascus were once as fragile and inconsistent as a cloud, as
a butterfly's wings. But then, was Babel ever more than a large cloud
in men's minds, a shadow on the earth, like its own faint shadow on
the ground?

All his time was devoted to his work. Does he finally, does he already sense that life is short, and that, if he wants to see with his eyes
what he feels stirring in his heart, he must make haste? He rises in
the night hours like a monk, but he is not a monk, he does not want
a cloistered or retiring life. All he must do is not lose sight, even in
the midst of idle chatter, of the work in progress. He does not close
his heart or his mind to things around him. He avoids invitations, but
does not want to drift away from his friends, as always, Franckert
and Ortelius. A man cannot live without friendship and a few brothers looking on. He does not flee new friendships if the occasion arises.
He loves his wife as a young boy loves. They have long conversations,
for the pleasure, for the love of it: and this wedded friendship, which
he is discovering, is the most precious of all. He, already an old man,
confides in this woman, a mere girl, and he marvels at so much wisdom. Sometimes he tells her his stormy sorrows; he tells her what he
sees, and what he almost sees. We would have a truly beautiful book
if only we had Mary's recollections.

They had redone the dining room and built more rooms in the old
storage space. There were tall, deep fireplaces, long wide tables with
carved lion's-paw feet and emerald-green stained glass in the windows representing the lives of Saint Roch and Saint Martin, and no
unfortunate soul had ever been disappointed who knocked at this
sign, begging a bowl of hot soup and a loaf of bread, or sometimes,
when the first snows fell, a warmer wrap than the rags he wore. The
walls were covered in gilt-stamped tawny leather from the workshops
of Mechelen. Here and there hung a tapestry by Pieter van Aalst:
Ulysses recognized by his nurse, the goose that guarded Philemon
and Baucis taking refuge on the laps of Jupiter and Mercury, An-
chises consoling one of Ulysses' comrades left behind in Sicily. Seen
through the glazing, as through magically arrested rain, the street and
the passersby, framed by the leading, looked like figures in a stained-
glass window. Bruegel liked the soft light created by the small tinted

squares; everything was near, and yet seemed more distant, almost
dreamlike, and more restful; even voices were muted; life had the
velvet texture of an old picture. The rumble of handcarts could be
heard; horseshoes sparking on the pavement; sometimes a mounted
patrol, the harsh voices of the men and the jangle of weapons and
tack. Sometimes the patrol would halt, for what reason? A mass of
rumps and the snorting of animals next to a milestone. You could
feel their eyes slew round beneath the visors. They would set off
again. They would ride down toward Hal Gate, then out into the
country. They would surround a farm, roughly interrogate the inhabitants, children and all. Night was falling. Lanterns and a few
passersby. Laughter and voices were stifled. Curtains were carefully
drawn so that nothing could be guessed from the street, so that the
house would seem asleep, or deserted. At night the house set sail.
They bathed in its light. This was the house of reveries, of grave
thoughts, of friendship. A thought for wind-battered, war-battered
Flanders. The countryside, the troops out there. And the danger that
could threaten, even here. Antwerp wrapped in fog, and the hamlets
glowing like embers in the plain.

When they were alone, Peter and Mary took their meals in the
spacious kitchen. They enjoyed eating by the fire and the cooking pot.
They liked to see the blue-and-white wall tiles and the polished brick
floor gleaming in the firelight. The hearth and andirons were already
black as though from a hundred years of fires. The kitchen gave onto
the dining room. The door was left open. The pots and plates suited
the more solemn room. On the other side, the low branches of the
garden sometimes grazed the windows and the top of the door when
the wind blew and bent them. It was a tiny garden with low walls
along which trees had been trained, the door of a beguinage in the
back wall, a stream flowing through the tall grass, a bridge of old
planks and bricks. This green kitchen garden was walled by more
houses, slopes, an orchard, trees whose delicacy and height, standing
out against the green of the orchards and the red of the roofs, was
startling. From lark to owl to meadowlark, the birds lived a very different story from that of men, a story still beaded with Eden's dew,
despite the fierce pecking order of life.

Some evenings friends would call, and then Bruegel would neither
write, nor draw, nor read. They would celebrate friendship. It was a
joy to be of one heart around the white table, in the light of candles
and the fire with its logs that would sometimes whistle and hiss. History has not recorded the names of those who, of an evening, shared

Peter and Mary's life in Brussels. Perhaps they were neighbors. No doubt there were painters, colleagues, his old Antwerp friends Hieronymus Cock and Ortelius, travelers from Italy. Sometimes Bruegel would take them up to his workshop, sometimes not. Occasionally they would make music. They would play airs by Roland de Lassus. They would sing "Dessus des marchés d'Arras," or old tunes as peasants do. "I would like to paint with the frankness and simplicity of our Christmas carols and May songs. As a child, I loved to sing and twirl the rattle as we went, from door to door, begging eggs on Easter morning. Now I take an even greater pleasure in the songs. It is not only because hearing them reminds me of the child I was, in the hoary grass, the sugar-coated meadow, where the steaming breath of the oxen and fog slips among the willows and hovers above the stream, the river. I also see everything they are singing about, I hear them in color. It is as though these songs, so soft sounding in Flemish, were invented that same night by the shepherds of Bethlehem going home to their huts, their eyes still dazzled by the sight of that ordinary child swaddled in a light that was not of this world. Did I say invented? Rather learned from the lips of angels, through the snow, and directly taken up on their pipes never to be forgotten. Surely at that time there were Flemish shepherds watching over the sheep of Palestine." And according to the season, Bruegel would sing with his guests those songs that he would soon be singing with Mary for their first child, who would surely be a boy and who, as custom would have it, would be called Peter. They would sing "Ons genaket die avont-star, / die ons verlichtet also claer . . . ," and "Het is een dach der vrolichkeit . . . ," and "Kinder swycht, soo moochdi horen; / Ecce mundi gaudia! / hoe heer Jesus is gheboren . . . ," and "Daer kwamen drij Koningen met een sterr'; / Uyt vremde landed: het was soo verr'. . . ." He planned to copy the songs into a notebook and illuminate them with animals and people so that his children would learn to read as they sang, or to draw, for he would leave some pages for them to draw figures in the snow or on the roads.

When Philip Marnix, from Saint Aldegonde, came to the house with a friend, he joined in the singing. One day he would compose the *Wilhelmuslied,* the song of the comrades of William the Silent and the hymn of the free fatherland. One day he would be one of the leading figures of the Lowland insurrection against Catholic and Spanish tyranny. He would be a great Northern writer. But, when Bruegel met him, he was a mere young man of around twenty-five. He was born near the castle of Nassau, in Brussels. He had been back

in Brussels for four or five years, having finished his theological studies in Geneva under Calvin. But Calvin was not the author he most
often quoted—this was Rabelais. He was one of the gentlemen who
would fight for freedom with a copy of *Pantagruel* in his pocket; he
would be accused of having gone over to Rabelaisianism. But it was
not Rabelais's farces or puns that fascinated him. He saw the light
of Erasmus in those pages. He fed on his philosophy. The question
that preoccupied him for the moment was the education of children.
And tyranny. How to put Picrochole out of the game? How to build
Theleme? What education to give the prince? If the prince were properly educated, he would repress his tyrannical tendencies, he would
be a bastion against all tyrants. Rabelais answered in fables. Beneath
the laughter and games must lie reason and wisdom. This doctrine
must be put into practice. Bruegel looked at the young man in his
jacket of green suede, his hair falling onto his shoulders, his sweet
face, his eyes superb with enthusiasm. He seemed frail, almost weak,
but something about him said that, come the day, he would be among
those who died heroes, or martyrs. Was he there to talk about Rabelais and Pantagruel? Did he have in his pocket the *Fifth Book*, which
had just been published?

But they did not talk about Rabelais. They spoke of the love one
should have for one's enemies. Each was thinking of Spain, squeezing
the flesh and heart of Flanders in its unfeeling fist. And each foresaw
even greater savagery, greater misery. How can you not hate the brute
who shatters your door, judges you in the name of the Gospel that
condemns him, and burns you?

"For the love of Christ," said Marnix, "let us not hate our enemies.
But let us pray that the persecutor change, that he be touched by
grace, and repent."

"Yes," said Bruegel, "but when he is a savage beast, how can I
believe . . ."

"Who was more savage than Paul? In the beginning he was too
young to do his own biting. He minded the cloaks while the others
hefted the stones and the skull-sized rocks. He watched over the
cloaks and satchels while the little band of marksmen stoned the dea-
con Stephen."

And Bruegel could see Paul wearing a pale green cloak, standing
by a pile of red cloaks. In a depression, in the pale white aura of a
reddening linen robe, Stephen. It caused no more stir than when
children chase a dog along a wall and pepper it with stones to see
who is the best aim. There are people walking behind their donkeys,

one hand resting on the straw-colored sack. Others are talking under
a tree, an olive tree. Are they discussing the price of oil and wheat?
Are they trying to agree on digging a well? Are they debating two
passages of Talmud or speaking of the sages of Greece? Perhaps they
are talking about the weather. All around them stretches the countryside. No angels pour forth from a rent in the sky as in an Italian
painting. A man is being stoned, that is all. Because he does not worship God the right way. Stephen prays. He prays as Christ prayed for
his killers: "Forgive them!" Did he pray for the young man he sees
standing over there, by the cloaks? The light from the sky is ordinary
light. He alone saw the heavens open, just then, while he was addressing the wall of judges before him, and the glory of Christ rain on
that band of sacristans, now casting their last stones, catching their
breath. Up the hill in an April mist stands Golgotha. Bruegel sees the
wheels and gallows, like those here. A bell tells the hours in the Brussels night.

For me, Josse of Oudenaarde, in the *Book of Arras,* has Bosch's face,
so does the tramp in *The Haywain* or *The Prodigal Son,* in Amsterdam.
He is dressed in gray, in beige linen and blue gaiters. He wears a big
hat to keep off the sun and rain. By trade he is a peddler. What he
peddles depends on the year, the season; it can be shrimps as well as
needles, but it has to be light: the satchel does not bother him, but a
handcart would; it would keep him from taking the shortcuts he so
likes through brush and woods. He is also a peddler of words. He is
always surrounded by children who have dropped their hoops, left
their marbles and tops to listen to tales of giants, the life of Gayant,
Aymon's Four Sons, Genevieve of Brabant. Sometimes he tells other
tales, for grown men and women. Funny, lively stories. Does he make
them up? Are they, as he says, things he has seen, or stories he has
heard from a reliable source, his grandfather in the first place, who
was a bigger trader, a better walker, who went from Bruges to Constantinople and from Constantinople to Kiev, speaking all languages,
selling ivories and jewelry, whereas Josse keeps mainly to the Provinces? It is true, though, that he knows his Flanders, every street and
glen, like no one else. He is Flanders in person, its lore, its memory.
To hear him talk, you would think he had seen with his own eyes
everything he evokes. You would think that he had seen Cæsar's first
soldiers, muddy and shivering, pushing their boats and carts through
the snow, driving in the square of stakes around their tents. You
would think he had seen the miracles performed by Saint Martin and
Saint Eloi. He raises his eyes and gazes into the distance: you would
think he was seeing it all again. Has the weather changed so very

much since then? The fog banks rolling in over the fields are like the
memories and thoughts of people who lived like us, in this place.
You would think that, in times gone by, Josse was already finding
the words for familiar things, for the way of the world, the village
chronicles. And when he falls silent, they still listen, they join his
silence and accompany him. He is a word-bearing tree, and it feels
good to sit in his shade. He is always at ease, always at home. If he
enters the tavern, voices call out and everyone moves over to make
him a place. Or at the farm, in the house in the evening. Sometimes
he says nothing. He stares into the fire. His eyes change color, but
most often they are blue, like fields of flax in bloom, blue as the flax
flower, and sometimes as gray as the sea beneath a gull's wing. Tall.
Fairly tall. Lean, pretty lean. He is people and prince. Old with the
old, a child among children. Bruegel knew him at home; he was
already a peddler. He was no different from what he is now. They had
often met on the roads of Flanders, as he and Franckert were going
from village to village. He had met him at the Antwerp market, down
by the waterfront. Jokingly he called him Blue-gaitered Hermes. Occasionally he would ask his advice: his advice was gospel, inspired
words. A wanderer's word, a word of the people, that came forth only
when asked, so short and sweet that you wondered if you had heard,
but over the years it would take root and grow—to the point, enlight-
ening. An unwritten word and, if ever repeated, it will ring with the
round modesty of a proverb. Josse. Josse of Oudenaarde. Everyone
knows him. As fleeting as a cloud. Seasons go by and no one sees
him. Then one day, he is there.

From time to time he would call on Peter and Mary. He often came
by way of the stream and the garden, following the track of the hare
and the bird. He would sit down and make himself at home. Bruegel
listened as he would have to the sound of his childhood and the
prophecy of the road that still lay ahead. He listened to the voice of
Flanders and the spirit of the Bible. Josse carried not only stories, or
plain advice for a better life, or tales of the ordinary, but also tales of
pain and misery as well. He recounted what he had seen. He would
say: "There was this woman, a good woman; I knew her, a good
Catholic, good Christian; and they came and they burned her. Another woman who spoke up for her was buried alive."

4

One day Hugo van der Goes knocked at the door of the Rouge-
Cloître. He had come through the noise of Brussels, come through
part of the Forêt de Soignes, and now he stood before the monastery

wall of crushed tile and cement. He had dropped his reins, and his horse snatched a mouthful of linden bark (had he come on foot, like a poor man; or had he saddled his horse for which he now had no use?), he knocked at the studded door blessed by a tall wrought-iron cross that also blesses the traveler, the wanderer, the brothers; he had come seeking help. The man standing there so wretchedly was a famous painter, a proud man. Two years earlier he had been dean of the Ghent painters' guild: severe, scrupulous, judging his colleagues' work, punishing fraud and weakness. Today—why didn't the door open—he was begging to be received as a lay brother by the Regular Canons of the Priory of Saint Augustine de Rouge-Cloître; he hoped that his half-brother, Nicolas, an oblate, would put in a word in his favor. But it seemed that Hugo had taken leave of his senses. Was it last year's insurrection and the corpse-strewn streets of Artevelde, and all the cruelty his eyes had seen that had left him horror-stricken? Was it because he had been unable to marry Elisabeth Weytens? He had painted *David and Abigail* for her father; it had hung above the mantelpiece; her father set it on fire as he was asking for Elisabeth's hand. The door opened, he was drawn in, warmed, he wept by the high fireplace, he repented of his pride and shook like a child. He bawled that devils spat on his paintings and broke his cups and brushes. A novice from Tournai, who had entered the order in 1475, was to accompany him during his probation. He was entrusted with the priory chronicle. Hugo's unhappy life had just been entered.

At first his life in the convent was easy. He wore a gray tunic that came to his knees. He painted. He attended offices. Everyone watched over him with affection. He painted in the large cell he had been assigned. The brothers were struck with admiration when they passed his open window. But they were startled whenever their gaze crossed his, whenever they saw his face while he was at work. He would remain immobile for long periods, and sometimes tears rolled down his cheeks, his harsh beard. They could hear him sighing, and weeping at night; sighing that he could not paint what he saw, that his hand was too heavy and cramped with bitter cold. And yet he painted. He painted the Adoration of the Magi. He painted the Virgin and Child. He painted the Descent from the Cross. He painted a Death of the Virgin whose colors were so like storms and lightning-lit wheat, so like a cry and a wound that the brothers could not see it without being troubled. Sometimes the painter shut himself up in the darkness of his workshop. Sometimes he would walk among the flowers that bloomed in the cloister, the meadow, along the narcissus-

banked stream. He would be amused by the antics of a bird. He received visitors. Leuven's alderman invited him, with the utmost
courtesy, in order to consult him about several paintings that Thierry
Bouts had left unfinished. He quit the Forêt de Soignes, and the city
of Leuven gave a great banquet in his honor, at the Inn of the Angels.
Did he think he was cured and free to travel a bit? His half-brother,
Nicolas, and Petrus Rombouts, canon at the Trône-de-la-Vierge convent in Grobbendonck, accompanied him to Cologne. The chronicle
does not say whether he went to paint or simply to look at pictures
and forests. But it does state that, when he returned, Hugo's mind
was deranged. Perched precariously atop his horse; at inns where a
sudden burst of flame from the fire would alarm him; along the roads
to the squall of the winds, the cawing of the crows, the creaking of
the carts; relentlessly he cried that he was damned, condemned to
everlasting hell, whatever he did! He would have done himself bodily
harm, and most cruel, had those present not forcibly stopped him. In
vain they reminded him of the recent pleasures, and those he had
promised himself, in his workshop, surrounded by his friends. This
sudden infirmity cast a deep pall over the end of the voyage. Notwithstanding, they came to Brussels, but Hugo did not recognize the
town. The very convent walls set him shouting as though he had seen
the glowing gates of hell open before him. The prior was called to the
painter's bedside, the latter having been given a draft of linden and
pavot. It was his opinion that Hugo had been stricken with King
Saul's torment, and, recalling how David's harp would calm the king,
the prior allowed them to play music for Brother Hugo and to include
games of a nature to tame his troubled, wandering mind. With
mournful hearts, and sometimes in terror, the monks sang hymns
and drinking songs, played the flute and played the viol, with angelic
gestures, at the foot of the bed where the painter lay sweating in
agony.

In spite of all they did, the chronicle reports, Brother Hugo's health
did not improve. He said he was a child of perdition. Tirelessly he
repeated it. He wept and he suffered. The help and succor that the
choir brothers gave him, the love and compassion they showed him
day and night, trying to anticipate his every wish, will never be forgotten. But no one could agree on the cause of the illness. Some held
it was a fit of madness. Others thought he was possessed. And to tell
the truth, Brother Hugo showed signs of both; and yet throughout
his misfortune, he was bent on harming no one but himself. This is
not what is said of the mad or the possessed. Only God knows the
truth of this ailment. The doctors know only that such a sickness may

be caused by certain foods that incite to melancholy, or by heady wines that consume the humors, or by the actions of a vitiated humor on the body of a man already inclined toward such infirmities, and finally, by one's passions. And Hugo was devoured with passions. He worried about how he would complete the works he still had to paint, even nine years would not suffice. He often poured over a book in Flemish. And as for wine, he drank with his guests, and this may have aggravated his state.

The malady may have been a stroke of divine grace. Honors and fame had troubled Hugo; the misery that he could not hide dissipated the giddy pleasure he took in appearances, the concern he had for worldly renown. He became more modest. He no longer took his meals with the prior but with his lay brothers. "Sepultus est in nostro atrio sub divo," is the chronicle's last entry: he is buried in our grave-yard. The Burgundian court painter and Maximilian's friend did not receive the honors of a chapel tomb, a stone near the choir like so many of his colleagues. Was it his desire to lie with the poorest of the poor and those whose name would soon vanish with the dust? Does this grave mean that van der Goes took his own life?

It was in his delirium that Hugo saw *The Meeting of David and Abigail* burn. He saw the picture in flames and ashes because he could not marry Elisabeth Weytens. In Bruegel's time this painting still hung in Ghent, in a house surrounded by water, near the little bridge over the Muyd, owned by one Jacques Weytens. It represented Abigail coming to meet the king. David on his mount shown like the sun. As he was painting this wonder, van der Goes knew that he equalled van Eyck and his tender Apocalyptic hues. And Abigail had Elisabeth's features. When Elisabeth looked at the painting, it was as though she were looking in the glass. Did Bruegel see this procession of women as, in Florence, he was able to see the shepherds and peasants of his *Nativity,* and in Bruges, *The Death of the Virgin?*

Perhaps, as he painted, his thoughts sometimes wandered to the art of the painter who died at Rouge-Cloître. But he also thought about his madness, his suffering. Entering into madness is like falling asleep and trudging through the copses and forests of a dream. Is being mad not living in a world of daydreaming sleep, but with the eyes wide open, taking the shadows and colors of the imagination for bodies more real than those we can touch? And who keeps us from madness? Who stays our slide into this sad realm? Saint Anthony in his cave, his desert, among the dry bones, before the onslaught of monsters, encircled by their scales, their claws, their hideous jaws and teeth, could have given way, and spilled into the depths of hell. Madness is hell. Who is to say that hell is not the bulging pocket of madness, its realm, its petrified kingdom? You descend into the caves as down the stairway of damnation. And within these visceral depths loom more peaks to scale, and vertigo. In the distance stretch jeering plains, fields of bones, parading horses, folds and furrows, the pale gray-faced reaches of desert. This is not the folly that sent Erasmus to his philosopher's pulpit; it is the madness that tricks and torments the mind, the horrifying companion of Death, the frightful ghost of our reason. It was true folly, true pain that afflicted Hugo van der Goes. He believed he was damned. He saw himself damned. He clung to his painting like a drowning man to his boat, on the sea, in the storm and the sarcastic winds. His nightmares took on bodily forms. They growled and barked inside his cell. He held to his painting as his head was buffeted by the sound of bells and crows' wings. The very colors of his paintings groaned out loud. The venom seeped into paradise. Sometimes there was neither painting nor madness: only a glimpse of snow and countryside from his narrow window, nothing, nothing but the frost-laden sky, the black-and-white fields with their pitchfork trees, a scattering of winking stars, the world; that was the purest terror, the angels slaughtered in a ruined sky and the devils beneath the stones biding their time until the onslaught, the attack. A theater was going up in the glade. He could not tear his eyes away. A procession of monkeys came bearing his paintings and covered the sacred scenes, the Holy Scriptures, with their spittle; before a hastily assembled tribunal of rats, they accused him, they accused Hugo of having authored these vile deeds. A trap door opened: new hells and live coals. They let down the sacrilegious painter like a barrel.

The children of Saturn are a melancholy lot. Why are some who seek the paths of the golden age held fast in the lead of horrors? Bruegel, whom everyone took for a serious man, a steady mind, was acquainted with our common frailness. He knew within himself the breach through which terrors of the night surge and take hold, the carnival of vices, the folly of perdition. He knew that Hugo van der Goes's misfortune could have been his own. He knew the grip of melancholy. He knew his own fascination with black thoughts. He knew the path of darkness. But one day he had sworn to be happy. He had sworn himself an oath of happiness. He had promised himself never to work at his own undoing. He had resolved it. He had decided to forswear complicity with the enemy within. And the flock of insanities had kept away.

He had never spoken of it. He had never disclosed that period of his life. Had it lasted days, weeks, a season? He had been neither mad nor dreaming. And yet it was not ordinary life. He had been with Hans, his friend from Nuremberg. It had happened during the Hoboken kermis. They had joined one table, then another, in the midst of the laughter and belching, the boasting and the effusive greetings of the drinkers. They retired under trees. They made their way through jostling crowds. To tell the truth, it was a heavy drunken night. At one point, he lost sight of his friend. For a while he searched among the tables, in the street, the inns, by the stream, on the bridge; then he gave up. He was overcome with fatigue and sank down under an elm. When he woke, the festivities had died away, the square was nearly empty, and a man was standing before him. Dawn was breaking, there was a morning mist, and he was cold. Or better, his first impression was one of chill and dawn, but as soon as he had risen to follow the beckoning figure, he found himself in the dark of night, on the edge of a forest. The man had uttered only a few words. Had he even spoken at all? It was clear that he was to follow the man and tear himself from the heavy, futile celebration. He had said: "Your fur-lined cloak is too fine for the road that lies ahead. Leave it at the foot of the elm, there on the moss. It's the feast of Saint Martin. Think of the joy such a windfall will bring. Now come!" He drops his mantle and is surprised to see himself clad as a beggar. Are they both going begging? He knows the man and yet does not recognize him. He can never really see his face. He hears his voice, more than his words, but that is enough for him to understand all he needs to understand. His step is light upon the grass. Do they go from village to village, through hamlets, crossroads, and forks? The hike could last years, centuries. Begging at church doors, the smell of hot soup in cottages. They walk. They see a picture-book Flanders shining like a windowpane. Shining like a window reflecting the glowing evening sun or a pane behind which the fireplace and the family candle make a nighttime sun. The breath of plants and grazing herds. The distance grows; they walk on. He feels that he is walking in some other time. All he has to do is leave the wide road, turn onto a path, veiled at first glance by a wisp of fog, and he is in a land living a century ago, or more distant yet. One step to the side brings him to a land as discrete as the ripples left by the tide on the sand. The Flanders of old is like those towns and their bells that surface alongside boats. Where are they going? Is this to be a time of pilgrimages and poverty? He has removed his warm wrap and left his purse at the foot of the tree. Has he perhaps lost his name? Dogs bark in the distance.

And sometimes bulldogs snuffle at his legs. A red sun on the horizon in the grayness of the journey. Is this a time of wandering and penitence? Or perhaps the way of the dead? And is this plank bridge they are crossing coffin wood leading to the other side. Is it already time to die? He has done nothing on earth that was worthwhile, he has wasted his life, he was waiting for tomorrow. His poverty, his miserable garment show his true worthlessness. He has thrown the time he was given to the winds. He has walked through the fog and the cold like a scarecrow of straw and rags. He has slept away his life. He has not lived. Flanders weeps at his passing, and the sweet sound of the bells accompanies him and would console him. What he is begging, in the mud and the cold, is not a handout of bread and a coin, but God's mercy and everlasting life. They have come to the edge of the forest. They make their way through the brush. Birds peep from beneath the leaves. Soon his companion says: "I'll leave you here. Go. Don't be afraid. We'll meet again. Go on." The night grows blacker. He walks with his hands outstretched, touching tree trunks, catching his elbow here and there on a thorn. How is it that snow is falling so beneath these tall trees? No longer is there slippery mud under foot, but the crunch of hoarfrost. The stream he is following glistens like a crystal thread. Snow falls on the branches as slow as a flame. In the clearing, through the snowflakes, is a monastery behind a stockade of birches. A few brothers are wandering about with lanterns. They are searching for their prior who should have returned long ago. They call the prior's name and their voices echo through the ancient stand. I saw their pink faces. One of them was quite young. They seemed not to see me. They did not ask if I had seen the missing man. I stepped into the monastery courtyard. A dog was asleep in his straw house. The snow was already sticking to the logs along the wall. I do not know why I did not go into the kitchen where I saw pots boiling. I ventured into the chapel where a few candles burned. When I came out, the wind was whipping up the snow in front of the porch. And the noise of the storm was racing through the treetops. I set out once more on the forest path. I knew I was deep in the Forêt de Soignes. The storm ceased. The snow fell more slowly. At my back I could hear the hermitage bell. I saw a glimmer of light, glowing above the trees. I turned in that direction. At the foot of a linden, illuminated by a light that came from neither the moon, nor the snow, nor any earthly flame, an old man, wrapped in a cape, was praying, radiant. He raised his eyes and looked at me. Then it was back to the trail.

7

THE VOYAGE OF ICARUS

At last he let his apprentices see the nearly finished painting.

"I don't know what to call it," he said.

"Isn't it a *Landscape with Plowman*?" asked the youngest.

"No," said Bruegel, "It's *The Fall of Icarus*."

And he told them the story, and they were moved. They saw the father and son, fitted out with their wings, escape from the island, flee Minos, swim in the blue air, to the astonishment of the peasants who saw them flying in the bright April breeze. The apprentices felt the wax holding Icarus's feathers melt over his shoulders and down his spine. They saw him stumble in the wind like a skater unbalanced. Was Bruegel trying to warn them against daring too much in their work? Was he telling them to follow a middle course? They would think about that another day. They were less aware of the moral of the fable than of the light the painting shed on the world. They looked at the sun shining on the sea like a buttercup under a girl's chin, the green sea; the proud ship maneuvering, her sails billowing, her sailors on the ladders; the islands and the coast in the summer haze; small boats and ships making for the horizon; the pinkness of the glistening, distant towns; the fisherman on the shore, his basket beside him; the shepherd standing amid his sheep, his dog; the horse, the plow, the plowman in a red shirt under an old-fashioned tunic; the earth sliced open and the furrows folded like stacks of linen or kneaded dough; the big tree separating the two fields; the brush, the birds. They were looking at the glory of the world, the simple glory of the world.

Everything is slightly rounded as in a convex mirror. Everything is clear and yet somehow hazy, the way certain days glow with a particular joy. Could it be that the everyday world is so lovely; could it be so glorious and noble to go, one foot on the green land and the other on the plowed furrow, behind a steady horse with neatly groomed mane? The shadow falling on the brown earth is a delight.

The branches and leaves of the big tree are a celebration reaching to the bare sky. The marble of the far-off mountains, their snow cover, is the dwelling place of angels, gods, travelers we met last year in our villages. The sea curves down from the horizon to join the bend of our little plot. The sea is radiant with morning light, and the afternoon shadow is already creeping over the bushes, the edge of the field, the clump of trees. The plowman with his wide, red sleeves, dressed as though in sunlight, the plowman with but his profile visible under his cap looks like a peasant lord. Glory of the world and peace on earth where the sap rises, where the wind bears the birds from one season to the next.

"But," said an apprentice, "what about Icarus? I don't see him. Dædalus is already way ahead, he's left the patch of sky you've painted, the shepherd with his eyes raised surely still sees him and is watching him vanish like a lark; Dædalus thinks his son is behind him, hidden in the glare of the sun; but I don't see Icarus."

"He's already beneath the water," said Bruegel. And he thought back to the painter from Mechelen in Rome, who, needing money, painted *The Flood,* showing the earth and the sky, and the tightly closed ark in the rain, like a simple chest on the horizon.

"Where are the people?" they would ask.

"Drowned. If the water goes down, you'll see them in the meadows, on the peaks, like wineskins. The survivors are snug in the ark with the animals."

The jest became known, and soon everyone wanted such a *Flood.* But was it merely a jest and a way to make quick work of the job? Bruegel wondered if the artist had not hidden a lot of philosophy in his joke, like his people beneath the opaque sea. He told his apprentices that he sometimes painted on the back of his panels the other side of what was on the side he signed; and as they watched, in amongst the waves near the shore, he painted a leg protruding above the foam, and a few feathers drifting down to the surface of the water. They fell gently on the wind, the very wind which drives the ships and turns the stones in mills—in windmills with linen sails.

What he had painted surprised him and moved him to long reveries. Was he less naive than his apprentices, he, the master of this painting? He had known what he was doing. But had he? Or had this picture come to him as in a dream? He had followed his vision as the plowman follows his horse. The plowman is indeed the master. But it is the horse that does the pulling. The man who plows will sow tomorrow, and then harvest. But what force causes the grain to sprout and ripen. What force enables him to do his work? The force which will perhaps fail him shortly and oblige him to leave the field before it is all turned? He is not the master of the force. And the painter is not the master of his visions. He does his best. He does his best not to fail in his duty. He does his best not to weaken. He follows. He strives to be faithful. Perhaps it is within his power to be faithful and to rise at dawn like a good servant. He waits for the image to appear. He is like a man looking into newly troubled water, who waits for the blue of the sky to clear, for the clouds to settle. And when he deemed that the last brushstroke had been laid, the last feather painted on the waves, the last touch of white foam on the sea, the last shadow on the furrow, the last russet leaf on the trees, he stood before his own painting more astonished than before any other. His vision had taken shape. Every line, every stroke had passed through his hand. Yes. But where did they come from?

Did he even know when this *Fall of Icarus* had first come to him? Was it even the fall that he had wanted to paint, or the father flying with his son above the plowed field, the great ship, the daffodil and narcissus shore, and the marble pollen-colored sky beneath which the flock of sheep blossomed like a small bouquet. Did he know what thoughts and reflections had started it all? This was as hard to discern as the fine line that separates the last thoughts from the first dreams. Memory has no memory of the passage. It irons out the wrinkles as it goes. We fall sleeping into sleep. There is no memory of passing from waking to sleep, nor of what there was before our birth. Will we feel the passage of death? The beginning of a poem or a painting blots from the mind all trace of its inception, if it was not commissioned. And even then, the first tremor is forgotten. He should really keep a record of his projects, he thought, like a trade register; but he never had (would he ever? Did he keep a diary, one which would burn in this fireplace—before which he daydreamed—with the papers he would have destroyed after his death, for Mary's peace of mind?). But this record would not tell the humble beginnings. Beginnings are humble only when looking back, when the race is run. Youth seems a shining time only when looking back, when the race is run, only when autumn draws suddenly near. The young man is surprised that others envy him, that they praise his days of glory: he does not understand. When things begin, when they began, the pieces were inextricable, insignificant, invisible. What people take for a beginning often contains its end as well. Man cannot live without a plan. But the wind decides the outcome. He seeks to guide his thoughts, his work, but he does not determine their birth. He tends them like a flock to which he has fallen heir. He is only a steward, faithful, unfaithful, obedient, disobedient, clever, or shy. He works his mind like a field that was there before him. Were he to soar to the source of his thoughts, he would surely be blinded and fall. We seek and find the truth only in dimmer light. Our bodily sheath, our spirit's earthly dwelling is a thick foliage which filters the sun, too harsh for this life. God willing, one day we shall know as we are known. We shall see the sun face to face as, on an April day, we gaze at a meadow buttercup and the golden fleece of a flock.

Perhaps it all began with his reading Ovid. Bruegel sat in his armchair, the cat asleep on his feet. Dusk mingled with the flickering flames of the fire. The wind could be heard scuttling along the rooftops. Almost without looking, he picked up a small, tawny, leatherbound copy of Ovid lying next to the other books on the shelf. He had bought this one in Italy, near the Coliseum, his first day there. The feel of it in his hand always brought back the radiance of that day, the humorous prints flapping in front of the shop in the shade of the columns, and the autumn of his return, when under a tree looking out over the vast slopes and meadows, he reread a book of the *Metamorphoses*. He cherished Ovid. The poet had left Rome for Athens; just as he had left the Scheldt to loiter on the bridges of the Tiber. The emperor had exiled Ovid to a land where the sound of reeds had tormented him even in his sleep. There he dreamed of the changes in the universe and the turning of time—the matter of his poems, that and love and sadness. He would have liked his memory to be associated with celebrations and Rome; death took him before the year was out. Our calendar was born in the catacombs. The ink used for the Psalms served to copy the Golden Fleece and the allegories as well. Ovid, and Æsop, were the grist of our fables.

Bruegel thought of Ovid, of the fate of books and pictures. The Latin poet imagined these tales read in the villas and vineyards of Sicily; Irish monks read in them the journey of the soul. And he had said to Mary—she had drawn closer to the fire and was doing her tapestry accounts in a large ledger—he had said to her: "I shall draw you something from the *Metamorphoses*." Four cartoons, or even six. Why this desire? Perhaps because of Philemon and Baucis, the picture of that couple who sent the roots of their love ever deeper and whom the visiting gods blessed. (This was one of his favorite passages.) Or did he want to illustrate the many disguises Vertumnus donned in his attempt to approach Pomona, the garden nymph, laughing, unlaughing, secluded in her orchard, straw-hatted behind the garden-wall, indifferent to his courting, caring only about fresh water for her lettuces, her apple trees, her cabbages and her radishes? Vertumnus, dressed for the harvest, brings her a basket of wheat. He sticks a wisp of hay in his hair and looks as though he has just been harvesting. A prod in his hand, he becomes a cowherd; a knife, he has been pruning trees and grapevines. With a ladder on his shoulder, he looks about to pick apples; with a rod, to fish for rudd. The tapestries would praise the ruses and patience of love and the carousel of the seasons. A small bucolic god speaks all the country roles. Here he assumes the accent of Kempen, a little farther, the slow Brabant speech.

But the book fell open to Minos and Dædalus. Ovid shows the fisherman plying his quivering rod, a shepherd leaning on his staff, a peasant bearing down on the handle of his plow. The shepherd who saw Icarus and Dædalus passing in the clouds watched open-mouthed and thought these travelers walking on the wind were gods out for a stroll. But they have already passed Samos on their left, Delos, and Paros; on the right Lebinthus and Calymne, whose bee-hives are the richest. The wave that is Attica combs, rippling like an oriental fabric over the bazaar floor. They see paths and lakes, peaks, mountains, coasts, and the ships on the sea, like a painted map. The breeze whispers in their ears. No man has known the pleasures birds know, this princely view of the world! They swim and glide in the blue of the air as in the clearest, freshest water.

"I warn you," Dædalus had said, "not to fly so low that the mist or fog weighs down your wings, nor so high that the sun scorches you: fly between the two! Avoid too much heat and too much damp, too much dryness and too much cold. Keep to the center of their wheel. Don't look at Bootes or Helice, or at Orion's drawn sword. Take me as your guide and follow!"

But Icarus grows excited. He forgets the advice. Soon he masters the beating of his wings and swoops in wide, playful circles above the sea. Does Minos see him laughing and dancing on the invisible crest of the world? Like a swimmer, turning his back on the cries from shore, he is already far at sea. He has tired of following his father's shoulders, his snowy wings and shock of hair. He enters into glory as into a garden, a garden of flames that surrounds him; and he breathes in. "O Sun! Father!" he cries to the encircling fire. Once more he kicks on the wind! Again he beats his wings on the torrid wave of the wind! Once more he thrusts up into the light! The wax is melting now, and his plumage scatters like snow and forsakes him.

He would not paint Dædalus arranging the eagle and dove feathers in a panpipe pattern to make the wings, nor the flight of father and son above the ships, as he had done for an engraving not so long ago, nor rash Icarus spinning like a child's pinwheel in a cloud. He chose those verses which Ovid had made only to show the extent of Dædalus's feat. He would show the plowman, the fisherman, the shepherd; even the partridge that sings at the end of the poem would be singing in a bush. He would follow faithfully the poet's order and invention. But he would find a way to celebrate what Ovid had neglected: the Virgilian earth and the tilled fields, the woods, the water, and the wind visible from the window. He would find a way to give pride of place, in the foreground, and as he liked to see him in his childhood, bent to his plow, his black hair falling along his cheek, to a peasant dressed in the style of Kempen a century ago, the folds of his Greek tunic matching the plowed folds of the ground. Had he seen that he would not paint Dædalus and only show Icarus in the trough of a swell? Had he seen the opposition between the large ordinary figure of the peasant and this small heroic figure who appears as a mere fugitive heel behind the door? Had he seen them back to back, each unaware of the other, one engulfed by the sea, the other planted on sturdy legs, one gigantic, the other minute, one who would have drunk dew from the chalice of the sun, the other sweating and slaving in the groove of the plow? Was this farce or philosophy? No one would ever know. He would put his heart into painting the fairest of landscapes. His rhymes and meters would be the harmony of curves—shore, hill, and tongue of land, the bosom of the fields and borders—and ideal lines, like the fine, noble triangle of peasant, fisherman, and shepherd, his constellation. He would build on golden numbers. Suddenly a great ship with billowing sheets is sailing in the glory of the day and of his painting. A large vessel glides before us, while the last feather from Icarus's wings settles on the refreshing foam and sinks, a snowflake of a feather.

All that can now be seen of Icarus is a toenail; but he is discovering to his terror the depths of the watery sky. Pallor of pearl and colors of the moon! Again on the edges of the sea slopes and ravines, he reels, stricken with vertigo. He trembles. He reaches to enfold the sea-green sun of the depths, but his arms embrace the fugitive scales of the waves. He slips through the petrified roots of the Flood. He who once soared higher than the eagle and phoenix now glides over the ruins and moats of Babel, its wells, mines, dungeons, dens, the broken spiral of its parapet, the stone blocks of its stairways and quarries, the gaping domes with their hovering, roaming armada of crabs, the hollow circles of amphitheaters, the side streets, uprooted graves, the rot of temples and prisons, arsenals, wharves, and ports. He weaves in and out beneath dismembered arches. He touches the moss-covered porches where mussels cling in garlands, shields, bucrania! Icarus, Icarus, where will your journey end? Little Ulysses of the deep, winged sailor laughing in the blue, light as the snow, where will you find your Ithaca, and rest from your labors? But he drifts on. He has entered Babel and the inverted ocean peak. He is lost in the clouds of the sea, its storm clouds, its whirlwinds. Deeper and deeper! He is a weight from a fisherman's net, left to sink. He sails on, flying over heaps of Babels and God-made abysses; he sees, looming at him, their creeks, their circuses, their rents, their shadowy estuaries, the immense coliseum where whale and wreck of Babylon play out the end of the world. Down and down! That was only the threshold and the first few steps. You are growing heavy, Icarus, you are growing numb. Let yourself go, foolish Icarus, flighty Icarus! Fall like an arrow to the heart of the mark! He falls. He rises irresistibly toward the snout, toward the black maw of the Leviathan, as he fell into the fiery furnace of the sun. All around is slime and rot, enveloped in the slow, indolent movements of the seaweed. Never did Dædalus build fortress or maze as secure as these avalanches of mauve walls traversed by fleets of octopus or these green crystal palaces, whose halls ring like bells. Icarus wanders lost among the ramparts, strays, is sucked into the mud. At his approach, the sea-bottom horizons recede and slip away. No cry can rise to the gentle wind and green leaves of yesterday. Ah, the wild strawberries, the dew, pearl-like drops of rain drunk from the cheek, cool of the evening, and the gaze of a girl, blue-eyed, chewing at a blade of grass! No voice in these dull caves comes to him, to guide and console. He descends like a falling leaf the inclines of the current, and hovers on Neptune's cold, deep trade winds. The Minotaur that sucks him to the bottom of the world, endlessly swallowing him, is a hole the color of night. He has passed the flaccid gates of hell, crossed the sevenfold river. He loses his soul in this vulvar grave.

Did he see, as he sank, now rolling, now tumbling, the black crescent on the sea dome, that island, shadow, the hull of the ship, shrink and vanish? No sailor heard his cry as he fell three cables from the poop. Can one really die amid such indifference? The fine ship quivers contentedly in the April wind. The heavy structure of canvas and wood turns and moves as easily as a toy wagon. The voyage is over, and the sailors have waved to the fisherman bending over the water, a red scarf around his neck, but the fisherman thinks only of his line and his creel. The wind carries the broken litany of the sheep behind him, the curt intermittent response of the dog, and the smell of grass mingled with the odor of turned earth. Down below, fish dance at low tide. The plowman in the picture is as large as Icarus was small. One makes but a brief swirl in the sea, the other turns the dark land fold by fold, offering it up to the wind and the rain, to the sky, to the meteors, for his winter's bread. Here the furrow's swell, there the vain spit and spray of the talkative sea. Here bread, a house, life; while there the sea-grave closes over Icarus, and the marble of the sea entombs him. Does the plowman know that the way to the sun lies through this sweat, this tilled land, this harvest hard-won like a battle? Soon the flock will again descend the slope and the bank to the village, snatching as it goes a spinning leaf from the bush. The great ship is not visible from here: it is entering the harbor, simple and stately. The field is now plowed to the edge, as pleasing to the eye as linen and sheets on a closet shelf. The plowman unharnesses his horse, which looks at him with friendly eyes. He buckles his belt and sees the smoke from the hamlet rising above the treetops. Ulysses came home and the next day had taken up the handle of his plow. The sun is sinking and already touches the horizon. Soon the night, its gentle winds, stars, love, and sleep between rough sheets. The plow is collecting dew, and the nearby thicket sends out the gleaming song of a nightingale.

As he read Ovid, he saw his painting. He saw that unearthly light. Everything was there, in Ovid. The dumbfounded shepherd, the fisherman, the partridge beating its wings. He saw the coast and the shore, the pale, glorious background, the curve of the sea at land's end. He had only to follow the order of the words and, too, find an order for the eyes, for the picture, intertwining the two subtly as the flute mingles with the voice, the branches and boughs with the light blue of the sky. He saw the light of the sky where young Icarus vaults exulting. And as soon as he had done with drawing and begun to paint, everything changed again, as when suddenly the sun breaks through the clouds casting the acre of wheat into supernatural relief. He was close to the earth, the horse. Once more he saw the light of Sicily, as though the two slopes of his life had merged. He was the boy flying in the air, the wind, the sun. He had been the young Icarus watching his father build a kitelike affair, the boy whose hair will tickle his face as he flies and dives through the clouds. He felt himself become the wise Dædalus. Soon he would have to lead his own son in the paths of moderation. This story was for him, the story of a father and a son, of a father who must bury his son: "He saw the feathers on the water, cursed his invention, and sealed the body in a tomb."

But must not every man so mourn his youth? And so Icarus must be buried. And he must settle down to work. Like Ulysses after his far-flung travels, he must again put his hand to the plow and savor the pleasure of watching the seasons of his youth wash over the hills of home. He saw himself after his wanderings in Italy, among the goats and temples, in Sicily, at the straits of Messina, the end of Europe. Beyond lay the world. Africa. Like Pieter van Aalst, he could have gone on to Constantinople and become a merchant; or he could have taken up the pilgrim's staff, gone to Jerusalem, and lost his way. Perhaps return and perhaps not. He was tempted off the coast of Sicily. And he decided not to go another step. It was time to turn back. The end of the road. Who knows what would have become of him had he gone on? And why did he come back? To live here, to take Mary for his wife, and to paint Icarus today. To live here. And he chose to paint a Kempen peasant—a peasant, yet dressed like Ulysses, dressed like the king of his realm, the king of his patch of ground, the king of his acre. He stood before the picture of his life as sometimes we do in our dreams: the different sides of our life converge, the friends we have known in far-off lands converse as though acquainted. Youth and manhood are two walls of the same house. In the background, there is the long journey and the Italian earth with its peculiar light; in the foreground, the land of his birth and his life. And the pleasure he takes in painting those ships bathed in light! And that island, Dædalus's island.

   If the Brussels aldermen ever came to inquire about their commission, he would show them this painting. The aldermen would voice surprise: why Icarus, when he was supposed to celebrate the construction of the Willebroeck Canal? He would explain that it was not about Icarus, who was already out of the picture, but Dædalus, patron of all arts, a model for architects and engineers. He would tell them that he had painted the allegory of the invention of tools and instruments, the eulogy of all labors, the figure of the transformation of the world by our hands and our minds. In this landscape, which you will recognize as Flanders, a Flanders which looks out onto the globe of the world, he would tell them, I have painted the glory and the wisdom of Construction. I have painted the conquering of the world by Dædalus-like men. I have painted Industry: farming and animal husbandry, fishing; and Commerce, figured by the ships and the distant ports. He would not be lying. This painting was both Ovid's poem, the flight of Icarus and Dædalus, and the theater of human labor. I have painted the condition of Adam's children, the bread won by the sweat of their brow, and how men learned to change their sentence and punishment to happiness, to turn the thorn-ridden land into a habitable place in which to dwell. In this dwelling place, however, no one stops for long. Our eyes will see this light, where the ship's golden sail bows and billows, for but a little while. Will anyone wonder about the face barely visible at the far end of the field, under a bush, of an old man no doubt, who is dead or sleeping, his face the color of earth? Nothing obliged me to paint this face of a man stretched out in the shadows—not Ovid's poem, where Icarus stumbles alone and loses his life, nor my praises of man's industry. But had I not painted this face of a man sleeping or having died so recently that no one yet knew, had I conceived my picture without the sun of this gaze gone out, it seems to me that my painting would have been lacking in truth. I wanted this natural truth. Dædalus and his wings had no place in this ordinary landscape. I did not show him. Such mythology would have robbed the earth of its weight, would have turned the trees to vapor. Was that why, from a chance spot beneath the bush, there came the idea to do the face of a dead man? A nameless man, a nearly faceless man, like the poor men in ditches, when winter comes, lying there; you do not know if they are drunk or sick or if they have died that night, alone. A few steps away, the nurturing plow continues its furrow, and the horse snorts; the plowman is looking down, not thinking of his own death; the lips of the earth he sees promise him only harvest and enough to eat. He does not see, beneath the bush in the next field, the man lying dead. It is true that cart and plow do not stop for a dying man. The tolling bell does not stop the wind working in the mill. I painted this man in the corner of the picture; was I thinking of my father, who may have died like him, far from home, unknown to those who noticed him the next morning? Did I, the painter, imagine myself the plowman of this painting, laying on my brushstrokes as he plows his furrow, standing amid my thoughts like a shepherd whose sheep and dog bump about his legs, casting my line toward the shimmering of my daydreams? Did I place the face of an ordinary man, whose hand death arrests one day, in the corner, like a date and signature? Peter, Peter, in the midst of your work and the pleasure of your labors, remember that you are dust and to dust and mud, perhaps tomorrow, you shall return.

Bruegel suggested to some of his friends that the painting might be an allegory of Hermes, the god of commerce and herding, of roads and crossroads, but also the god of messages and those who interpret them. He pointed out that the image he had composed was the true labyrinth and that Hermes, in the guise of a shepherd, the end of his staff marking the center of the picture, was guarding the entrance. As the mind proceeds from that which is most visible to that which is least, and as it can proceed by analogy with that which is least visible to that which is invisible, and from that which is invisible to the eye to that which is invisible in itself, until it comes to the idea, which in the end makes all visible and intelligible; so the skillful eye of the beholder will, without becoming absorbed by Icarus's foot, move from the large plowman to the small drowning figure, then, following the shepherd's gaze, will search the air for Dædalus, and turn, in thought, to the artist's masterpiece, the labyrinth, only to escape by means of one last invention. How very Platonic this all is. At first the eye takes what it sees for all there is to see, but by degrees it passes out of the initial shadows and ascends to the intelligible meaning. Platonic, too, the philosopher's descent to the folly of Icarus, who, because of faulty method and philosophy, falls back to the darkest chambers of the cave of the world, whereas moderation would have brought him to the courts of heaven. It was at this point that, somewhat nonplussed, Bruegel's friends began saying what was later often to be repeated: "There is even more thinking than painting in our Bruegel's painting." They wondered how this man with his slightly heavy, almost peasantlike appearance—admittedly a great reader and of lively curiosity—how this man, who, in the street, could be taken for a merchant, could have acquired a taste for these subtle games? And Bruegel, as though he had heard their surprise, but making no reply, looked warmly out at them from beneath a bushy eyebrow.

Dear Icarus! he thought to himself. They think I have left your heel on the foam and that I have painted you so minute in mockery. Mine was false mockery and false indifference to your misfortune, which remains your glory. Everything must be reversed to be understood. Everything must be turned around, beginning with the usual moral, for your reversal to be understood. What did you want, new soul? To pass through the fire? To dwell within the fire? Were you not satisfied with dominion over land, water, and wind? Were you not satisfied with dominion over Nature? You wanted to return to the heavenly dwelling. Is that forbidden? The sun was your Ithaca. Who is to blame you? I listen to Dædalus's lesson, a lesson in moderation; but I also listen to your folly, your exaltation, your loss at sea. If the plowman listens to his own heart, and the fisherman and the shepherd, they know that they, too, are Icarus. They know that they possess this passion for life, everlasting life. They do not want to be but blowing dust, a furrow soon covered by next year's plow, a wave washing instantly back on itself. They do not want to fade as the grass of the field. The dark sun of earth is not enough, it is not their homeland. They are children of the true sun. I painted the shepherd, the fisherman, the plowman and the sailors in the rigging to paint man, the family of man; but I painted the plowman large and Icarus nearly imperceptible to show the inner man, Adam. Adam plows and strains: that is the peasant; Adam falls from paradise, and the archangel's fiery sword bars the gate to the heavenly orchard: that is Icarus. Does Adam plowing his plot of land know he once dwelt in the garden of light? He walks, he labors, his eyes on the ground, having cleared the briars and stones. But the child sinking in the watery night, whom he does not know, whom he has forgotten, is his innermost soul, his memory. He was the one tempted by the forbidden tree, in the center of the garden, and who, beneath the shadows of the sea, still hopes to return, having crossed the barrier of fire. He has fallen, but he will rise again. One day the sun will come and burst the gates and hinges of death. The sun will open once more the closed book of the depths, illuminating the world, dethroning death. He will dive and save the lost child like a pearl, as Elijah came and stretched out his hand to Jonah in his abyss. It is not true that the strapping plowman and the foolish Icarus do not know each other. They are the obverse and reverse of the coin. The plowman and the castaway child, the sun-lover, are one and the same. I am that peasant with downcast eyes, whose heart in the depths of the sea remembers and knows that the incorruptible sun is his true home. Do not take it amiss, Ovid, my friend, if I read you in my own fashion.

8

MARY

Had he fallen in the forest, in the brambles, harried by fever, wild beasts, brigands, spirits from the other world? Who had carried him to the side of the road where he lay, shivering, in the dawn light? He had never spoken of that night to anyone, nor of the freezing morning, nor of anything that had followed. Every man, in the course of his life, has experienced some things that are inexplicable and which time encourages him to believe he has dreamed, but he knows that they happened in the density and the reality of this world and that they altered the meaning and the color of his days. A cart emerged from the fog and stopped. A man stepped to the ground and bent down; his face and voice were those of Josse. Then sleep. Sometimes, product of his dreams or the world outside, a few trees, the road ahead, a bridge, the blue of the warming sky. And sleep. He woke between soft hospital sheets, the ringing of a carillon, the milky walls, a glint of green grass outside, birds chatting by the window. They would tell him he was in Bruges. He drank the hot soup and bit into the springy, floured bread. The women in blue dresses and stiff winged caps moved and spoke like his mother, in her village, among her neighbors. Their faces were those of the Holy Women on the road to Calvary, as seen by Mestys and Memling. Tomorrow he could get up, he should be patient. He would get up tomorrow: the purple evening fell and then the arc of the night. He got up, he walked, he mused and strolled along the Minnewater, near the lockhouse, and watched the swans gliding through reflected willows and clouds. Every step he took on that shore, among the mossy trees, gave him the feeling that he was advancing through Flanders of last century, and more distant yet, so far away that the country seemed celestial, like the sky looking out from the depths of remembering waters. The air in which he walked and breathed had the nobility of snow. He picked a primrose growing in the grass of Saint John's Hospital. He could stay as long as he liked. He was well. He was strong. He helped with the work. He painted the doors and shutters of the Begijnhof. He basked in the light of the day, the hour, the falling evening. He took long walks in Bruges, a city as soft as a pigeon's wing. Sometimes he would go as far as the sea, to Damme, with its sand and oblivion, its wind and gray-and-white birds on the ruined ramparts. What should I do with my life? Then he would return to the city, delicate and pink in the distance. Once the harbor had been as thick with ships as Antwerp, and Bruges had had more bankers and money-changers than Beguines. Dawn-white rays of sun glanced off the roofs and the turrets of the silent, still silent town. He knew all the churches. Bruges was a maze. He walked and he prayed. For him, the heart of Bruges was the Jerusalem church. He liked to see its oriental dome jutting among the roofs. Bruges was the mirror of Jerusalem, and Jerusalem, the promise of the world to come. Inside, a folded cloth lying on the Holy Sepulchre told him that the grip of death was broken. And it was in Bruges that, one morning, the image of a young sibyl in a green velvet dress, rose within him and filled him with confusion and joy, with certainty. In this street, with its pink and white housefronts, in this street of lacemakers and their glistening threads, he was no longer alone.

People happily traveled thirty leagues to attend a wedding. And Guicciardini marveled at the sumptuous trappings. "Every wedding, each according to its station, is celebrated with abundant and sumptuous ceremony and feasting, numerous invitations being sent to relations and friends, and lasts ordinarily the space of three days. The bridegroom dresses well, and the bride even better, changing on each of the days for new garments richly and gaily adorned."

The match was often found in the neighboring town, or even in foreign parts, so that marriages helped build peace. In short, sailor and peasant, burgher and craftsman, all in the the Low Countries married like princes. And the splendid presents as well as the banquets bespoke the love felt for young people, the regard for their affection, the good wishes for their life, their home, the children they hoped for. Although weddings in Flanders might well be enlivened with spicy language, they still glowed with the light of Cana. They were reminiscent of a harvest meal in the barn. The smell of straw hung in the air. The smell of wheat stalks. Harvest was over, and now it was time for weddings. Harvest of bodies in love, harvest of babies, and with this rush of life the family was prepared to live till the end of the world, until the last drop of time on earth, for an everlasting glory, the time that would encompass all times, the eternity of everlasting life. If I can smell the odor of straw and wheat, if I hear that laughter in the barn and the sound of wooden spoons, the sound of jugs being filled and poured around a sturdy table, it is because I am thinking of Bruegel's *Wedding Banquet*, which hangs in Vienna. It is because I see the solemn, pink-faced bride, crowned with a wreath of leaves, sitting regally before a green wall hanging and straw ramparts. I still see this young woman as an image of the earth: the great triumph of life. My eye falls on the flushed child in its red cap adorned with a peacock feather, greedily gobbling marmalade. I can hear the stocky servers bearing plates of mush or pancakes, carrying the litter or the door that has been pressed into service for the occasion. I eavesdrop on the guests seated on the oak bench, the milking stool, the upended milk tank. And, entering by the wide-open door, I see a flock of neighbors who will not be left standing outside. Bruegel is among the guests, wearing plumb-colored velvet and a round cap cocked at an angle. He pretends to listen to his neighbor, but he cannot hear above the howl of the bagpipes. If he was fond of attending weddings, as van Mander reports, in the company of his friend Franckert, bringing presents for the bride as though he were part of the family, it was no doubt not as a city-dweller come to observe the lumpish preening and rustic games, but because he loved these outpourings of life. He sensed something biblical in them. He could hear Sara's laughter when the three lordly travelers, rising from their meal, promised her a son, in spite of her age. He thought of Rachel and Leah: when Jacob worked for Laban so long in order to marry first one, then the other. He thought of Ruth amid the sheaves of wheat. He was moved by these faces, rarely handsome, always slightly ruddy, faces of those who work in the wind and the sun. Real faces of men and women. And those two loved each other. Flanders is a biblical land.

The day of their wedding, Peter was grave, and Mary more radiant than ever. The dinner was held at a country house that Pieter Coeck had acquired and Mayken Bessemers would inherit. In and around Brussels there were many wooded spots for the flocks to graze. A stream ran through the bottom of the meadow. There the newlyweds stood for a moment, silent, almost too moved to speak, their hands, on which the new gold of the rings glittered, intertwined, and watched the bleaks and sticklebacks swimming against the current, beneath the drifting leaves. Clouds and clumps of trees cast fluffy shadows on the water. How long will we live together, shoulder to shoulder, Mary? How long will we be this happy, Peter? Birds were singing. The wind rustled the leaves and the grass. In the distance, the bells of Brussels were ringing. They started back up the meadow. Long tables stood under the hangars. Looking at the faces of his friends, Peter could retrace his life. There was Martin van Vos, with whom he had traveled part of the way to Italy. There was Niclaes Jonghelinck and his brother James, the sculptor. There was Hans Franckert and Herman Pilgrim, who had come from Amsterdam. There was Ortelius. There were many of the poets of La Giroflée waiting for the moment to read their epithalamium; many brothers from Saint Luke's; merchants from Brussels, Antwerp, Mechelen; a few of their future neighbors. The elderly woman in peasant dress was Peter's mother. Mary chatted engagingly with her. One sensed her vaguely out of her element in this gathering, but she did not seem ill at ease. Peter kept an eye on her. He knew she did not really like to leave her village. Her son and daughter-in-law had invited her to come to Brussels, and to live with them. She had declined. Visibly she was someone who had chosen to live in silence, alone, like a recluse on the island of old age. Mayken Bessemers watched Peter and thought of the time when he was an apprentice: so far, so near. Imperceptibly, the day passed, then Mary and Peter had left the table, and the meadow.

9

FOR JONGHELINCK

Soon he was able to earn a living with his skills. Even before entering Saint Luke's guild, he had worked with older colleagues. In Mechelen, he had worked for Pieter Balten, painting the *grisaille* for a triptych dedicated by the glovemakers of the town to their patron Saint Gommary and to Saint Rombalt. Cock paid well. And as soon as he began painting, he had customers. Van Mander alludes to Hans Pilgrim, of Amsterdam, who "owned a very beautiful *Peasant Wedding* painted in oils, in which the faces and all the exposed portions of the body appeared yellow and brown, their unbeautiful skin being very different from that of the townspeople." He mentions Hans Franckert, a merchant, but also a member of the Chamber of Rhetoric, La Giroflée, "for whom Bruegel often worked." Perhaps Franckert taught his friend about business. I can well imagine Bruegel owning a stake in a ship. The income would free him to paint without regard for fashion. Surely a painter who observed the cranes working on the upper levels of Babel knew how money increased when well invested.

Niclaes Jonghelinck could have been a sculptor, like his brother James, or a painter: he loved beautiful things; and perhaps it was only to acquire such objects that he became the merchant banker that he was. The Medicis were his model. He once owned as many as sixteen Bruegels. *The Carrying of the Cross* hung at one end of a long hall (opposite *The Tower of Babel*; the other walls were bare). From a distance, all the eye sees at first is a landscape with a crowd strung out between a wood, on the left, and a pale, barren hill, on the right. A crowd out for a holiday, no doubt. Perched atop a tormented pinnacle is a windmill. On closer inspection, one sees in the foreground four figures larger than the others, Mary and the Holy Women with Saint John. Bruegel has drawn them in the old style. The Holy Women are weeping, as the painters of Bruges portray them at the foot of the Cross, but they are not at the foot of the Cross; they are kneeling with Mary and Saint John on a red-clay knoll near a torture wheel and upon the knoll, slightly above a human skull, the broken skull of a horse lies bleaching. A little lower and facing the passing throng, stand the daughters of Jerusalem, lamenting on the way to Golgotha. In the background, on the hill, two tiny crosses have already been erected; and around these, on the mangy, trampled ground, a circle of the most impatient has already formed. Near the center of the picture, in a hollow, two condemned men standing in a cart about to ford a stream are being comforted by monks; a figure is slipping a crucifix into the hands of one of the men. Other days the cart, a big box mounted on four wheels, probably carries cattle or produce; the carter riding on the shaft daydreams. A large crowd throngs at the city gates. Some have come to watch the execution, and others are going about their business. The road rises in a sweeping curve toward the spot, and the rows of gallows, and wheels, and crosses. Horsemen in red tunics, like those worn by the Walloon guards, keep an eye on the proceedings. Everything is going smoothly, except for one incident: a woman with a rosary dangling from her belt is resisting with might and main the efforts of the police to enlist her husband's help in carrying the cross of the third man—the one who did not get to ride in the cart. You must look even more closely to see Christ, fallen under the weight of his cross. And yet Bruegel has placed him at the center of the painting, but so small in the midst of all the human commotion, in the broad landscape, that we pay him no more attention than did the people there that day. Instead we see a big white horse looking at us and showing its teeth.

Bruegel liked to paint as a philosopher, as Erasmus or More had written their books: following their own movement. He also liked to work on commission. The commission aroused in him that which was merely waiting to surface. He had acquired the habit while working for Cock. He only accepted a subject if he had, in fact, already *responded*. And no commission had ever hampered his freedom to invent. He was not the first to have represented the Procession to Calvary making its way across a broad landscape. Amstel, Artsen, Herri met de Bles had already done so. They had set the city of Jerusalem on the left, in the background haze, Christ toiling up the hill and the soldiers, the peddler resting on the roadbank, and up there, in the far distance, Golgotha. Bruegel had adopted this model as any of his fellow workers would have done. But he had had the idea of painting Mary and the Holy Women in the foreground, posed as they would be at the foot of the cross. He had had the idea of painting them in the old style—as a kind of image—and of painting Christ's torture as *chose vue*, something seen, an everyday execution. Was this to say that, if Christ were to return, we would crucify him as before? The Temple of Jerusalem rises in the haze. It is a spring day. People step over puddles, slip going up the muddy slope. Already a cloud darkens the hollow that will soon be covered by the shadows of agony and death. Near Veronica's companions, on the far right-hand side of the picture beneath a wheel from which a scrap of clothing still flutters, Bruegel has placed a few contemporary figures watching Christ and wringing their hands. Lost in this callous, cruel, curious crowd, they are His witnesses. And the man wringing his hands is no doubt the painter himself.

Jonghelinck asked Bruegel to do a series of paintings for his house in Antwerp. They would hang around a rotunda from which one could look out and see the far-flung fields and the sea, the river, and the ships passing. Bruegel replies: "I shall paint the world and the seasons." He is surrounded by what he sees from first one window, then the next. He is at the center of a vast world. Anyone catching sight of him at that moment as, already at work, he meditates on the world and on his painting would see that the Drawing of the Artist in his felt cap, with bushy eyebrow and stern gaze, that this portrait of a painter past middle age, brush raised to his canvas—a black-and-white drawing of the artist about to paint, but whose canvas is still untouched—is the image of his true spirit. Yes, that is how he stands in the round room, as in the tower of his soul, thoughtful, attentive to what he sees welling up from within; the age we see on his face is the age of the world, the image of time breaking on the shores of eternity. That is how he will paint, standing in the dream of his life, like a tree that suckles on the earthly night and unfurls its leaves to the invisible breeze. He is surrounded by the painting that has risen in his mind. He will paint the circular horizon, the circle of our life. The passage from one month to the next will be imperceptible, like the undetectable borders between one country and the next; they are like cloud-shadows passing over plowed field and woods. The earth is seamless, like mankind. He will show the day slipping by, and the days, and the year. So impatient is he to begin that he brings the conversation to a close and returns from Antwerp to Brussels as though in a dream, engrossed in his vision of the year. There will be no story this time, only his account of the visible world. He will show the seasons and the land. And the tasks of men, their life beneath the heavens. There it stands, the silent bible of our common life.

He feels that he has been put on earth to paint this picture *The Seasons* and that everything he has done to date was in preparation for this work. His last? Perhaps. He will paint as though, when finished, he must lay down his brush forever, and close his eyes on the world. When Hesiod undertook his *Works and Days,* he must have had the same look in his eye, on his face, the stamp of a solitary; he must have worn the same felt cap on an unruly head of hair. The fire is kindled in a man. The fire of fullness and vision, the fire coursing through his veins and quickening him is that of fathomless autumns.

He nurtures his work with long walks in the Brussels countryside. He goes out at dawn and returns at nightfall. Often he takes his son, perching him on his shoulders. The eyes of the child are higher than his father's. He looks at the snow, the approaching evening, the distant fires, the woods, stands of wheat, the wisps of smoke floating above the rooftops. The wonder of being there, of being in the world. Will you remember that moment when, from my shoulders, you watched a crow fly, glide, and then land in the branches of the big tree? Will you remember the sun's cauldron? The questions are unvoiced. He walks on. He walks through the wet grass. He feels the opacity of the world. How can he believe there is a world other than the one we see? No passageway. Our realm is sealed. We inhabit the world and its time. The child on his shoulders is as carefree as a bird. The man thinks to himself that each step bears him not so much from one place to the next as toward the end of his life. And, at that moment, standing there surrounded by visible things, he feels he is no more than a living mortal passing through a world that seems everlasting and yet consumes itself like a fire. What he paints is not what he sees. Evening comes. But the whole day has been dark and cloudy. The chimney was not drawing well. Some men are cutting the damp willow branches. In the distance, on the frothing green-and-white river, on their way to sea, some boats have been caught in the storm. By the sea looms a chain of icy snow-covered mountains, then the castle amid the crags, the town, a red-and-brown village roofed in thatch, the courtyard and the wall of the inn. Here is life, compressed beneath the roofs and among the trees. Eat your waffles, little man, and dance. And you, my paper-crowned child, shine your dark lantern over the broad landscape. How pleasant it is when evening comes and the fleeting lights on the fields and the banks cheer our hearts. The white speck of a solitary gull in the dark sky. And that whitewashed gable in the blessed melancholy of thicket and felled trees. One man is binding a bundle of firewood. A dance tune can be heard played by an indefatigable violin at the inn. Even the sap rising in the heart of the willows is audible.

As he lay dying, Bruegel asked that many of his drawings be burned. It has been said that he regretted their asperity or that he wanted to spare Mary the reproaches they might bring. But the drawings that blazed in the fireplace of the rue Haute, as he felt himself leaving this world, did not depict executioners, judges, or informers. They were the preliminary drawings for *The Seasons,* which he had kept. Sketches of grape pickers bending between the rows, and the gallows on the riverbank bathed in soft September light. A sketch of a peasant drinking from an upended jug, of a girl carrying a large basket of cherries on her head and who seems to dance along, of a skinny dog in the snow with its tail curled over its back. A sketch of the big tree and the ship shattered by the sea storm. A sketch of the cow looking out at us while the others make for the barn, and the village in shadow at the bottom of the hill. A sketch of a roof undergoing repairs. A sketch of people lighting a fire. A sketch of the well-muffled man, his arms raised above his head pruning an unkempt willow. Among the sketches could be seen calculations, harmonic divisions. One could see the interplay of circles and angles: the diagonals of paths and slopes, the broad swaths of landscape, the circle of ripe fields and hills, the generous lap of the earth, the nonvisible crystal of paintings, of the world. Here were the beginnings of a handbook for his own use. Painting had to be the *coincidence of opposites.* As he had combined the curve of a tree and that of the ship's sail in *Icarus,* so he combined distances, the bank in the foreground and the far tangle of forest, the depth of the world and the wall-like solidity of the finish, the precise draftsmanship and the effusive coloration, the boldness of the colors and their pollenlike texture. Sometimes he would move an empty frame about in front of the picture: everything that appeared within the frame had to justify stopping to gaze or reflect; every detail had to be a perfect picture, and their composition as fluid and natural as a river flowing. It was then that the painting brought together the manifest world and that other world, the manifest dream. Each picture was an adventure, the invention of a new song.

He painted the cycle of the year, of the months and seasons as they go round. He painted the cycle of the world. Here comes the red-and-white herd down the sloping path back to the village—and the eyes of the animals, earth red, milky white, looking at us as, in the sweeping background, the river and the clouds go their own ways. Has the world ever been more beautiful than on that late-fall afternoon? The day is drawing to a close, and the cowherds are coming home to a meal, a lamp, and a bed. And here in the deep, still snow, the hunters are returning. The mountains and the hard, glinting, stingy day are behind them. They are muffled in thick wraps, and over their shoulder they carry long steel-tipped pikes. We look down at what they see: more snow and the pure, blissful snowbound village. Ithaca made the heart of her exile beat no faster than this village with its snowy roofs nestled in a rapturous landscape. The fields have turned to ice ponds, where children are skating. One figure holds his umbrella sail-like to the wind, and it pushes him across the ice like a ship. A cart is being pulled along a white-edged road. Little bridges straddle the frozen river. A woman is carrying a bundle of firewood. Birds walk on the ice or perch warily in the bare branches. Chimneys smoke in the clear air. In the cold and the harshness of the world we have found matter for life and dreams. The family of man is here, huddled between the rimed garden and the reassuring kitchen kettle. If, at times, I thought I had lost my way amid the cruel ways of the world, here I see, glowing in this peaceful snowbound setting, the childlike candor of the days, of the place of my birth and my life. And so we emerge from the forest and turn our steps homeward. This evening we will hold our hands to the fire and we will know we are alive for yet a while. A large bird hovers above the valley.

10

FRAGMENT OF A LETTER
TO ORTELIUS

I don't write you often enough. But then I write very little. I had promised myself to keep a dairy of what I saw on my trip to Italy, a promise quickly broken. The best was in my drawings. For the rest, I relied on my memory; and I have forgotten what deserved to be. When I happen to read a few of the pages I did write, I see that I gave movements of humor or minute things an embarrassing importance. And yet I have no doubt that the man I was ten years ago and the child standing, one stormy day, by the frog pond, under the willow, that I can still see, so far from the life I lead today, yesterday's man, the child in the pasture and myself, writing in our house in rue Haute, with the rain pouring down on Brussels as it has been for the last three days and the sky the color of black slate and the drops running down the windows, are indubitably one and the same! But I am astonished at the portrait that emerges from those pages or the letters I never sent. I once put everything into my drawing, and now into painting. At times, for no particular reason, I am transfixed by a moment of my youth or childhood: I see a certain day, a gesture, as though in the background of a landscape, distant, yet close and clear. *I experienced that.* It was so long ago. Like the high note of the great bell, I have at the same time the sentiment of life's fleetingness and its immensity, endlessly unfolding. How will we see it when we reach the other side? I have finished Niclaes Jonghelinck's commission: a painting of the year. After such a work a man feels he can die because he is sure he was not born in vain. It is a major piece of painting that sums up my life, and God has given me the strength to carry it through. I told myself that I had reached the pinnacle of my career and can now sit down with those I admire.

Now I would like something entirely different. I have just finished a small picture, the bend of a frozen river, the Scheldt, no doubt. The

sky is yellow, the river is yellow, a very soft, as though distant, yellow.
A golden glow backs the sky, like a lamp behind a windowpane. A
sky still heavy with snow. Figures are skating on the frozen river, or
walking. Children spin tops or slide pucks. It is a freezing Sunday (or
perhaps a weekday). The clouds are high; no one is looking at them.
They are looking at the ice, which is paler in the middle. To the right
is a blackish tangle of branches, firewood, more like twigs; just looking at them makes you cold. And tall dark brown trees, the top
branches dusted with white. Two birds fly off in the direction of the
gray town on the horizon, toward the estuary and the sea. Some
crows are perched in the tall trees and in the brush. The ones in the
foreground are the same size as the figures on the ice. The rushes of
a willow fan out in front of a yellow house. A small-town church.
And then houses lining the riverbank, and the distant white hills and
the expanse of fields and the clumps of bare trees. The houses stand
pink (but also gray or brown) beneath roofs covered in snow like a
table under its cloth for special days. A solitary black crow on a thin,
high branch, looking at none of this, but pointing its beak to the sky
that we do not see. At the base of the tree, under a trap, some crumbs
for a handful of birds that come to inspect or sit ruffling their feathers
in the underbrush. The birds are no more thinking of the old door
that a trip-cord will bring down on them than the skaters of the ice
that might crack. The cruelty of men, and of winter, danger behind
an innocuous facade, but above all I wanted to paint those houses,
the village, the boats trapped in the river ice next to the poles, the
water transformed into a road and paths, and the snow, the snow . . .

I liked Italy, I learned many lessons there, but never, unlike so
many others whom the journey has estranged from themselves, have
I felt the desire to paint in Italian. Today, as I turn to winter and the
snow, my season (together with autumn), I look even more carefully
at the work of our old painters, my homeland. We were lucky enough
to have, at the house for a few weeks, a painting of the Holy Family
arriving in Bethlehem, between the red houses along with all the
carts. That, I said to myself, is how you should paint.

Try to imagine a small Adoration of the Magi. The travelers have
come to one of the narrow village streets. They have difficulty seeing
ahead because of the heavy snowfall. And we can barely make out
the scene through the dense flakes. On the right, a palace with no
windows or roof; a thick beam braces the wall: it is snowing inside
as well as out. The donkey carrying the king's pack waits patiently. A
snow-covered shed overhangs the frozen river. A child poles his sled
between some white branches, alongside a half-buried willow. A man

carrying a bucket climbs the three wide steps in the wall: he has just broken the ice in order to draw water. His wife is waiting on the bank with a second bucket. A worried mother calls to her child: what if he got too close to the hole in the ice? You can see snug houses, trees, red chimneys standing straight and tall, a little red-brick bridge, and arches through which you catch a glimpse of other streets of the little town. One of the kings kneels before Mary and the child; he is hard to distinguish, despite his ample yellow cloak. The scene takes place at the far left of the panel. Even more difficult to see, in the shadow of what looks like a hut, a tumble-down barn with the snow falling even faster, are the child and his mother. In the street, people walk with their heads down and their hands in their sleeves. It is as cold as it was here last year. No one notices the travelers. Too cold, too much snow! And nothing indicates that they are kings and have come from a far-off land. Jesus' birthplace is barely a house; it is a shelter with two walls, there are holes in the roof and the wind and snow blow through. Can you picture all this, my dear Abraham?

11

IN THOSE DAYS . . .

It has been brought to the attention of our lord that in recent times, in wooded and secret places in the vicinity of our town, nonconformist and heretical meetings have been held, and in particular in what is known as the "Heegde" Wood, on the third day following Christmas, contrary to the orders and placards published a number of times by our gracious lord, The King. The aforementioned meetings are held in the name and guise of a new religion, by which nonconformists and atheists attempt to seduce the common people, children, and the simple, without parental consent, which religion tends in reality to encourage riot and revolt in town and country, the common possession of all goods, to the great deprivation and desolation and perversion of widows, orphans, and all God-fearing people, who would be left in great danger of death, conflagration . . .

The 17th day of January, 1565
Jean van Locquenghien
Amman of the city of Brussels

The number of sermons preached in the vicinity of Brussels by the Church of the Fields and the Woods was growing daily. When a preacher, an apostle, arrived from Germany or France, from England or somewhere in the interior of this country, word would go out a short time in advance. It was never certain. That evening, on last-minute notice—and blessed be the fog!—people would remain outside the city gates under cover of night or scale the ramparts to keep a rendezvous made by someone who would take them to someone else. Those wishing to take part in the meeting were examined carefully, and if the day was not safe, if there was fear of being surprised by soldiers or the danger of a trap, it was still possible to disperse in time. The real danger began when they all reached the woods, the clearing, the isolated barn, and formed a crowd. A watch would be set on the road: their part in the praying was to help the common cause. Certain members of the meeting were assigned to keep an eye out.

Some men carried pistols under their cloaks; others, sickles to hamstring the horses, should they come. They had already given their lives to protect the greater number and to save the few women who were there among the peasants, craftsmen, roofers, woolcarders, and all those who depended on charity for their living. Sometimes there would be a few lords and ladies. It was not wise to look at faces: if you were taken, it was easier not to give out names, under torture.

This praying, psalm-singing, fraternal throng was Israel in the desert; they were the Church of the Apostles on whom the flames of the Spirit descended· they were the crowd in some unlit house in the East, listening to Paul or reading his letters. The Apostles who came to them had no home or bed. They would be arrested and burned alive at God's pleasure. Others would rise up from among those gathered there, from among those who still spoke as children, and would repeat the fervent message. As long as they were free, they walked, spoke, read aloud the Holy Scriptures, called down the Spirit, sang a psalm. The wind shook the forest. The wind shook the willows, and the river running through their plains was the river of a land in which they must hide in order to pray together. They sang the Book. They listened to the Book. The walls and columns of their temple were the tall oaks and the wind, the gray and brown plowed fields just visible through the woods. Their temple was the open Bible. The crow soaring above the plowed strips was Elijah's raven. The tiny plowman in the distance was Elisha plowing behind his oxen. The land of Brabant is holy, like the land of Judaea. Christ invisible walks our roads. He walks beside us, in the coming night, and our hearts are burning, as they burned, long ago, when through the branches the travelers saw the still distant roof of the inn at Emmaus.

Never have Bruegel's trees been so forceful. They do not grow straight up. They are twisted by their effort, especially the one on the left. They writhe like the river in the background, on a much lower plane than the clearing where John the Baptist is preaching and prophesying. What is he saying? He is telling the listening crowd: "Change your ways. Turn from your path, go back! Repent! The kingdom of heaven is at hand!" In the crowd Bruegel has placed several worried faces, looking at us, who could well have been appointed to attend each of the preachments of John, whom they call the Baptist. A listener looking too indifferent to be true. Two hooded monks— their candor frightening—are deep in consultation: these are the bishop's eyes and ears. John is not looking their way. He is looking at those big trees, columns of the clearing, and the red-breeched boys who ride the crotch and, with one ear to the orator, survey the ladies' mushroom hats or search the branches for a nest with eggs to suck or unfledged chicks. He is looking at the mighty trees that rise slowly out of the darkness of the earth, like man toward God. "Even now the ax is laid to the roots of the tree. And any tree which fails to give good fruit will be cut down and thrown on the fire." And then he says, "I baptize you in water for repentance, but the one who comes after me is more powerful and greater than I. He is coming and he is close at hand and I am not worthy to put on his sandals." Of whom is he speaking in this enigmatic style?

Those who are watching John and have to report back question him. Is he Elijah? Is he the Messiah? No, he is not Elijah. He is not the Messiah. He says, "I am the voice crying in the wilderness: 'Prepare a way for the Lord,' as the prophet Isaiah says. 'Every valley will be filled in, every mountain or hill made low; crooked ways will be made straight, and rough roads made smooth. And all flesh shall see the salvation of God.'" The crowd listening to the prophet pronounce with Isaiah those bewildering words could just as well be a crowd at market. There are children, godly women, ladies, a pilgrim in a scallop-shell hat, a lansquenet with dangling sword and many-colored breeches. There are old men who look asleep. Boys proud of their tall red caps. There are bonnets and headgear of all colors and shapes. The faces of many humble people who do not understand much of what they hear, but they hope, no doubt, in a vague way, for something like a miracle, a breath of goodness on their hard lives. A couple of gypsies are standing at the back. At first we see only the superb stripes of the blanket that serves as a cloak. A man, inattentive, has turned around and is holding out his hand; the gypsy tells his fortune. The image of all those who would rather rely on soothsayers than on the Good News. And since the secret service has no further questions, a few people, their faces drawn, ask,

"Rabbi, what must we do?"

"If you have two cloaks, share one! If you have something to eat, don't eat alone."

Even some tax collectors come forward, despite the threatening stares: "Exact no more than the rate."

A group of soldiers ventures up and faces become even harder. Is the prophet going to tell them to throw down their arms?

"Abstain from all mistreatment. Be content with your pay."

As he painted, and took immense pleasure in the gypsy's many-colored blanket, his wife's Chinese hat (all we see of her is this huge

straw hat and her red-and-white woollen garment, while her baby
munches on a piece of bread and watches from the safety of her arms
those coming along the road), as he took such pleasure in the tightly
packed bouquet of faces, as diverse as humankind, Bruegel listened
to those words, to John the Baptist's replies. The prophet asked little:
that soldiers be content with waging war. That they abstain from
plundering, and all brutality to villagers. And then, barely visible in
the painting, a spot of gold, he painted the face of Christ and the
family likeness he shared with John, his cousin, who has not yet seen
him, even as he announces his coming. Christ is dressed in a gown
like those going to the river to be baptized, like those going to the
stake. Down the hill on the riverbank, with a few flicks of his brush,
Bruegel paints in the baptism. What is that scene on the horizon,
those churches and mountains? Is it Judaea? Is that the Scheldt flowing down to Antwerp; the Meuse, the plain of Flanders? The river is
the river of time. I can hear the murmur of Jordan's waters from here.

Now Jesus is alone. He has gone into the wilderness. Wherever he
looks, nothing but sand, bare glinting tan rock, red sand, the color of
jackals, or pale, white sky, the sun an open wound, at night wild
animals stalking. No water springs from the rock; no bread in the
sack. Only a tunic on the body that will soon be shaking with hunger
and fatigue. Sometimes a slight hollow in the rock cradles his back,
sometimes. Watch, pray, and fast. Forty days and forty nights. One
day for each year in the desert when the Hebrews won their freedom
from pharaoh and the deadly labor in Egypt. This time it is all mankind that will be freed from bondage. Jesus descends into the arid pit
of solitude. God became man, he came down to earth, he must learn
just how forsaken man can be when he no longer feels his fragile tie
with God. And the fortieth day, when he can no longer stand for
hunger, the devil comes. This is no artist's devil, not even a ghost; it
is a thought. He comes in the form of a thought. And it says to this
man who is now skin-and-bone, this wasted man kneeling among
the stones: "If you are the Son of God, you can change these piles of
stone to warm bread."

He is so weak from fasting, his head aches so, he could easily
doubt that he is the Son of God. Would God be mad enough to
plunge himself into such wretchedness, which starves his very being?
Would he be so cruel as to leave his own son in dire need beneath
the midday sun? But Jesus replies: "It is written that man does not
live by bread alone, but by every word that comes from the mouth
of God."

Then the devil takes him to the parapet of the Temple of Jerusalem: "If you are the Son of God, if you are certain, jump! I too can read, and I have read: 'The Lord will command his angels to carry you so gently in their hands, on the feathers of their wings, that you will not stub your foot on the smallest stone.'"

But Jesus says: "Read again! It is written: Thou shalt not tempt the Lord thy God."

Then the devil, the spirit of darkness, the father of lies, the killer of killers, takes Christ up on a high mountain. He shows him the whole world, down to the last scroll of horizon. He spreads before him the rich tapestry of earthly realms. Is this the scene that the painter is moved to represent? Here stands Christ, with the dark shadow throwing its arm across the wall. This mountain is the Babel of old. It is higher than the other mountains of Palestine or the world. It is a mountain of wit and guile. It is the world and overshadows the world. Jesus sees the plows in the fields, the boat on the stream, the fleets from Tyre and Sidon as they pass at sea, the cluster of villages and towns glowing gold in the sun. A wide river cuts through the countryside. A cow nuzzles the water. There lies the whole earth of those days, and the earth of all days to come, as in a book, the pages lie waiting to be turned. But such is the world, until the end of time; and the centuries groan and froth like ocean waves. And the shadow says: "Worship me. Kiss my feet and cloak! And all this will be yours."

Jesus says: "Get thee behind me Satan! It is written: thou shalt worship the Lord thy God and serve him alone!"

Then, says the Gospel of Saint Matthew, "The devil left him and angels appeared and served him." Has any painter represented Christ's banquet in the desert, served by angels in the cool shade of their wings? Once again the Bethlehem snow is falling about him and the angels' song sparkles in the starry night. He is left with the angels and the wild beasts.

The scene shifts to a village both Flemish and Judaean. The roofs creak with the weight of the snow. The fields are blinding. It seems that winter will never end. We are sentenced forever to dwell in frost and ice. We must find a way to live with it. Herod has ordered a census. Everyone must go to his father's village or town. Unfortunate for those who must cross the mountain. And no question of waiting for spring. It is in the thick of winter that you must go and enroll. And pay your taxes while you are there. And if robbers waylay you? Those waiting comfortably at the inn, their feet on a warmer, do not worry themselves about such details.

The inn where the tithe is collected takes up most of the left side

of the panel. We look down on it, as on the whole scene, the people
and the carts in the snow, the little town and its gate, and the derelict
tower next to the roof in which the owner has neglected to repair the
hole. The sign of the inn is The Green Wreath: a snowy wreath of
greenery hangs over the door. A small band of people waits patiently.
Pressing around the window keeps them warm. The red-capped hal-
berdier is leaning against a tall tree whose black, naked dead-looking
branches bear a bright sun sinking on the horizon. Under a cart
loaded with two snow-covered casks near a basin, a rooster and some
hens peck at the snow. Some men are counting out coins on a stool.
Servants from the inn are killing a pig: the frying pan is at hand to
catch the blood, and the bundles of firewood lie under an ax ready
for the singeing. The inn is built beside the river, now covered with
green ice. On the other bank, another village and its pink brick
church. Next to the inn, a large flat boat, white with snow, is trapped
in the ice. Some peasants, their knees bent under the weight of their
packs, cross the river clutching walking sticks; others are pulling and
pushing a barrel on runners. Come spring, the flatboat will ferry us.
At the corner of the roof dripping with icicles, on a red background
can be seen the arms of Cæsar: a two-headed black eagle. And the
green wreath hangs just above a sturdy wooden cross that defines the
windows in the wall.

*And as everyone was going to his own town to be registered, so Joseph
set out from the town of Nazareth in Galilee, and traveled up to Judaea, to
the town of David called Bethlehem, since he was of David's house and
lineage, to be enrolled with Mary, his wife, who was with child.* Yes, it
was the dead of winter, December, a time of wolves and hoarfrost, of
biting winds. They passed other wretched travelers on the frozen
roads, as though they had packed up their essentials and were fleeing
before an oncoming enemy, but they were only obeying Cæsar's
order and making their way to the family seat. The groups hardly
spoke in passing. Each kept his hands under his cloak. The inns were
turning people away. Night had fallen and they had to go on, to some
farm, an isolated shepherd's hut in a field, the meager shelter of a
wall and a few boards to make a fire that would not see out the night.
At the inn, the price of lodging sometimes discouraged even the most
wealthy. Oats for the horse, a crust of dry bread, the least item cost
days of work. Joseph, who was a carpenter, had brought along his
tools: he had tried to find small jobs along the way. All he had found
were a few logs to split for a gamekeeper who had sprained his
shoulder. Would they find lodging in Bethlehem? At last they saw

the ruined tower of the little town. They followed the willows. The streets were freezing, and an icy wind swept the town square.

Across this snowy square in Bethlehem come Joseph and Mary. No one looks up. They are a couple like all the others, heading toward the official inn. The man, wearing a brown coat, a basket on one arm and over his shoulder a saw that touches the broad brim of his hat, is no doubt the carpenter from a neighboring village or one of the men working, despite the cold, on the barn or shed that we see over there. The young woman holds herself straight on her donkey, she is wrapped in a great mantle. They have just crossed a stream on which children are sledding and spinning tops. An elder sister is pulling one of her brothers along on a stool tied to a rope, while the youngest brother waits his turn. A big bird is standing on a barrel trapped between ice and snow. All this takes place in the lower right-hand corner. On the bank a child is fastening his skates. He is in a hurry to go running and sliding over these pastures that are never so pretty as at Christmas, covered in snow. Another couple is crossing the stream: the man, a yellow hat on his head, is carrying a child bundled up in a length of red wool; his wife finds it hard to keep pace, on the ice. Scenes from daily life.

Joseph approaches the inn, passing between two snow-covered carts; one carries a load of wheat, the other, wine, no doubt, which a man is drawing off (if it has not frozen). In the middle of the square stands the poorest house in town; more like a shabby hut, with a sagging roof; a bottomless beehive serves as a chimney pot; a scrubby tree keeps the walls company; a small cross sticks out from the peak of the roof.

The ox walks close to the ass that bears Mary. He turns one worried eye in our direction. Does he see the mounted troops arriving in close ranks, beneath their spinney of lances and pikes? A band of hunters is returning from the hunt, behind a hound. A woman is sweeping snow near some children who are building a slide. Slowly the wheel of the world turns. Caught in the snow, and a rut, a cart has broken up. One wheel has come to rest nicely in the center of the picture.

Noiselessly, Mary carried little Peter upstairs to show him once more the snowbound village of Bethlehem. It was snowing in Brussels as well, and from the small windows on the staircase, they could see the muffled garden and the white roofs of neighboring houses. The door of the workshop is open. Next to the picture of the tithe-paying and the numbering stands another, of which Peter has said nothing. It is the same village in winter. With the same snowy roofs, the same deep snow on the square, the same snow-covered barrels and branches trapped in an iced-over pond. The yellow-and-red, low-roofed or step-gabled houses, the tall bare trees with their black branches against the green sky are the same. Against this pure, dazzling background, a closely packed mounted troop in armor, somber, helmeted, their raised lances bristling, has ridden up and now blocks the exit on the far side of the square. Others, in red tunics, guard the roads. Already soldiers are kicking in doors and wattle walls, battering them down with posts and battle axes. They take their axes to the shutters, climb onto a barrel and jump through the window into the house. *Herod was furious when he saw that he had been outwitted by the wisemen, and in Bethlehem and its surrounding district, he had all the male children killed who were two years old or under, reckoning by the date he had been careful to ask the wisemen.* He personally led the hunt in Bethlehem. He sits in the midst of his horsemen bunched beneath the purple banner and the black eagle, on the other side of the square, and his gray beard hangs down to his breastplate. The soldiers are calm. The village is surrounded. And if some mother managed to scale the brick wall in the back yard and get away, she would be fleeing over a field of snow: a quick canter would catch her. One woman, entangled in her skirts, blinded by her little boy's hands over her eyes, is rooted to the spot with terror and anguish: a lance brings her down, with her child. That is why the soldiers are in no hurry. Kill the children, yes, that we will do. But why pass up the chance to grab something that could be of use. The worst is those wailing women. Two years, maybe a little over two? When in doubt, kill. The snow is trampled smooth by the horses, the soldiers, and the women. One by one the children are struck down. *It was then that the words spoken through the prophet Jeremiah were fulfilled: A voice was heard in Ramah, sobbing and lamenting: it was Rachel weeping for her children, refusing to be comforted because they were no more!* They wring their hands, they cling to an arm that shakes them off and prepares to strike. A group of men kneels around a young horseman who does not look vicious: he was a friend of the village. The fat soldier is carrying away a child, it is already dead and dangles like a killed rabbit. Another, who used to be a butcher before entering Cæsar's service, has found the old knack and wields his blade. What can we say to these mothers whose children are dismembered, and who are thrown to the snow by a kick in the face, we who believe in Christ. To these women crying in the wilderness of their village, beneath an icy green sky, confronted with these black arms, ground under the hooves of horses, and whose only knowledge of sacred history is the story of their children's slaughter.

The silent painting cries out. Mary is standing in front of Peter holding the child in her arms, who reaches out to grab his father's beard and his shoulder. The white and red painting overwhelms the dim light of the workshop. Is it Bethlehem, is it the world, is it our own country? Mary feels as if she is in Bethlehem at this hour of slaughter, among the women whom nothing will comfort. But Peter not only feels that he saw what happened under Herod. He has the foreboding that he has seen what will happen here as well. Cæsar's troops are not Romans, in the picture, but Spaniards. That pale thin rider at their head, sitting as still as a judge before the stake, his long gray beard falling onto his breastplate, he knows he will see that face in the snow of his own country.

A *grisaille,* painted in the same years, represents *Christ and the Adulteress.* Christ is dressed in an ample robe and is bending over, to write on the ground. The gown gives off a supernatural light which illuminates the sand where the words are being traced, the clothing and the face of the woman who was condemned to die and will now live; it even illuminates the old accuser who has dropped the stone he was holding and whose hands are still open. On the cloak and the ephod of the priest and scribes (one of whom carries at his belt a lamp also touched by the supernatural light), something is written in Hebrew. But in the pool of light on the dust, the finger of Christ writes DIE SONDER SONDE IS DIE . . ., "Let him who is without sin cast the first stone." Could Bruegel have painted this without thinking of all those who, in the name of Christ, commit murder? But this painting is a meditation. He painted it for himself. Does he not have to forgive those who themselves refuse to pardon?

The woman is like the sheep that the good shepherd carries on his shoulders, and saves. She is mankind, the lost sheep, bound for glory at the end of death and time. She lay bleeding at the ebb of night. Christ bears her up like a sun. The Samaritan receives the word of living water. And this woman, who was to die, now lives. Her face is that of Eve having eaten the fruit. She is the essence of mankind. Through her, the scribes had tried to trap Jesus. But he is the Forgiver. He says: "I am the light of the world; anyone who follows me will not be walking in the dark; he will have the light of life."

12

BEGGAR'S BAG AND BOWL

Count Egmont has gone to Spain to put the case for the homeland. He was sent by the council. He set out in January of last year. Brederode, Noircames, Culemberg, Hoogstraten, as well as many other lords, accompanied him as far as Cambrai. Banquets were held to see him off. Will he return? As soon as he had vanished beyond the line of trees, his friends signed an oath with their own blood, promising to exact vengeance if any harm befell him. For he is charged with complaining to the king about excessive taxes, crimes committed by inquisitors, the prolonged presence of Spanish troops. He is to convince the king that the Inquisition violates the laws of the land and that the Seventeen Provinces are exhausted from all the cruelty.

With the exception of William of Orange, who declined, what better ambassador was there? He was prince of Gavre, baron of Brabant, governor of Flanders and Artois, scion of the duke of Gueldre and descendant of the kings of Friesland. For the king of Spain, it was he who had wed Mary Tudor in Winchester Cathedral. First the emperor's page, then his chamberlain, at nineteen he was a captain in the cavalry and worked miracles at Tunis. He did wonders at Saint Quentin and Gravelines, as well. The latter was his most recent claim to glory. Under orders from the king of France, the marshall of Thermes, governor of Calais had taken Dunkerque and Bergues and was ravaging Flanders. Egmont was mandated by the king of Spain. He had had two horses killed under him. At the end of the day, two thousand of the marshall's soldiers lay dead among the dunes, and three thousand had been taken prisoner, including the marshall himself. Egmont was loudly acclaimed all the way back to Brussels! "He is a man who likes flattery," Cardinal Granvelle wrote the king.

The king personally invited Egmont to Madrid. He who was customarily so cold, so reserved upon meeting people, left his study and hastened to greet him in the reception hall, stopped him before he could kneel in homage and would not even let Egmont kiss his hand,

welcoming him with an accolade instead. He treated Egmont like a
Spanish grandee. And the greatness of Spain dazzled the count: her
court, her dominion over the New World, her poets, painters, her
power on land and sea, her incomparable art of fine manners, and
her proud nature. The king showed him the Escorial, which was under construction, born of the vow he had made at the victorious battle
of Saint Quentin. He received Egmont in his apartments in Segovia.
The entire court treated him in the most flattering manner. How, in
the midst of such pomp, so many honors, such a warm welcome,
could he speak of the suffering at home? And yet he did. He was
rewarded with personal favors. Philip forgave his debts and personally undertook to provide his daughters with magnificent dowries.
Each day compromised him further. And when, leaving the king at
Valladolid, he began his homeward journey, it was not without promises. He may have believed that all the generosity that had been
heaped upon him was addressed not to his person, but to the ambassador, and therefore to his country. He wrote that he was the happiest
of men. Brussels received him like a king and a benefactor to the
homeland. It soon became clear that the promises he had brought
back were empty. He, too, saw this. Staggered to find himself the
victim of a farce, insulted and bitterly reproached by William of Nassau, he thought he would die of grief and shame. He left the court
and secluded himself on one of his estates. Over and over he said that
by such guile, the king had wanted to discredit him in the minds of
his compatriots. "If that is how he has decided to keep the promises
he made me in Spain, let someone else be governor of Flanders; as
for me, by removing myself from these affairs, I will prove to the
people that I had no part in this treachery."

And yet had anyone really believed that such an embassy, coming
after so many appeals, complaints and warnings, could succeed?
Philip had never loved the Northerners or their country. He saw himself as the sword of the Church, the white knight of the Catholic faith;
and this entire country, lying so close to Germany, seemed to him
shot through with heresy: pick up a dry log and you find a slug. He
did not want to loosen his grip, nor could he. Were he to extract less
money from Flanders, how could he finance his army and his fleet,
and how could he maintain Spain's mastery over the New World so
recently won to God? Furthermore, this land was a bulwark against
the Germans, the French, and the English. It was the Low Countries
that enabled him to intervene in Germany, in France where he might
even one day reign, who knows; it was from Netherlandish shores
that he dispatched the Englishmen he paid to plot the downfall of

Elizabeth. He had sworn to his father that he would faithfully uphold the House of Austria, and so Spain must be strong and the Low Countries were vital to her strength. Self-interest, hatred, pride, piety all combined in one man to turn him to stone. It was impossible for him to deal humanely and justly with the Seventeen Provinces. From time to time his closest and most faithful advisers would discretely suggest that it was time he ease his grip, but in vain; he had ears only for reasons of state, and that was madness.

It was then that several young noblemen seemed to have hatched a plot. Sometimes two or three, sometimes more could be seen riding from castle to castle. They said they were off to take the waters at Spa, or going hawking. But it is rare to see such grim faces on men taking their pleasure. They were drafting a declaration that later came to be known as the Compromise of the Nobility, because it tried to satisfy both Catholics and Reformers. Some were jurists, and all urged caution. While reaffirming their loyalty to the king, by this writ they pledged to stop the Inquisition from gaining a foothold in the Low Countries, to call for the abolition of placards against heretics, and their replacement by measures adopted in consultation with the Estates General. They demanded what Egmont had been unable to obtain. Among the young nobles were Niclaes van Hames, dubbed Golden Fleece because he was king-at-arms of the order; William van Marck, who was to become admiral of the Sea Beggars; Escaubecque of Lille, a cheery Calvinist who wore a rosary around his neck and brandished a copy of *Pantagruel*; Giles le Clercq, William of Nassau's secretary; Louis of Nassau, William's brother; John and Philip Marnix of Saint Aldegonde; Henry Brederode, lord of Vianen and marquis of Utrecht. Having drafted the declaration, the little band filtered back to the provinces. Within the space of a few days, hundreds of nobles had signed the Compromise and sworn to stick together "hand in hand like brothers and faithful comrades." For the most part they were petty nobles and gentlemen drawn from vigilante groups. Louis of Nassau's signature gave the impression that William approved the league; it encouraged the lukewarm. None of the knights of the Golden Fleece had signed; but William of Nassau advised his friends formally to present their petition to the regent.

"The more peacefully you come," he wrote to his brother, "the better it will be. It will make it all the easier for you."

Count Brederode entered the picture as a giant carnival figure: less hero than herald and less actor than emblem. He was Silenus astride his cask of beer, but big-hearted, a heart of gold, a fast friend of freedom, loving justice as much as fun. He was a colorful figure of earthy

Flanders. All revolutions need a thespian mask: this one is laughing uproariously. Brederode galloped across the revolutionary stage and was gone. He touched off the spark, and it might have been taken for mere fireworks and the noise of celebration. At the same moment, William the Silent was speaking to the regent: "I have the feeling that a great tragedy is in the making." Brederode gave the traditional three knocks, announcing what, in this bright month of April, might still seem to be a light comedy. He came forward as the curtain rose, as for an Elizabethan prologue. His was the voice, the lungs that burst forth, as though in a tirade—an impassioned speech—in the Compromise, a declaration so grave that until now it had been read in hushed tones, almost secretively. A figure from Bruegel's *Peasant Wedding*? More like one of Frans Hals's drinkers, an orange sash across his breastplate and lace on his shirt, broad-brimmed felt hat and waving feather, or Jordaens's Bacchus. Eat, drink and be merry! And tomorrow we die from indigestion, or from a musket ball. "We celebrated a most merry Saint Martin's," William of Nassau wrote to one of his brothers, "because we were in good company. For a day I thought Mr. Brederode was going to die, but he is better." The people loved him. They saw him as one of them, who just happened to be a lord. He talked like a sailor, like a docker, a peasant, and he laughed like all of them. It was he who would speak for the young rebels.

On the third of April, toward six o'clock in the evening—do you remember that great swath of pink clouds, that soft glorious banner over the town and the countryside dotted with steeples clear down to the sea—superb, heading a procession of two hundred horsemen, all from noble families, pistols holstered or tucked into their belts, he entered Brussels and hobbled his horse at the Nassau Portico. You can hear him say: "They thought I would never dare come to Brussels, but here I am. Perhaps I will leave in an entirely different way." It was never known of whom Brederode was speaking nor of what exit he was thinking. They all dismounted and went in search of lodging. Some took up quarters in the Nassau Palace as though they had been invited; others in the Culemberg mansion. Their comings and goings had an air of a hunt or an outing on the river. They wandered back and forth between mansion and palace, to see each other one last time, even though they had just parted. Many words passed beneath the canopy of leaves. The April sky was light blue. Brussels was expecting an eruption. It came on the fifth of April.

What was Bruegel doing that April? No doubt he was in Brussels. Perhaps he was drawing the *Wedding of Mopsus and Nisa* for Cock or

the *Masquerade of Ourson and Valentin*. Both were commissions—
something Bruegel did not refuse—in which he used earlier subjects,
small scenes that he had already worked up for *Carnival and Lent*. He
probably did not give them any hidden meaning: nevertheless, the
soldier holding the symbol of the world and a crossbow . . . Or perhaps Bruegel was busy engraving the only etching we have by him,
a copperplate: *The Rabbit Hunters,* set in a sweeping landscape with
the usual river, boats, and vistas. There again is the crossbow, pointed
at the little rabbit whose hole we can see. Another man, carrying a
pike, peers from behind the tree: the two hunters, one of whom
wears a long curved knife in his belt, are not peasants; they are soldiers, men of arms. Are they not after bigger game than these rabbits
that sense no danger?

What was Bruegel doing? Perhaps he was starting on *The Attack*
(he was to finish and sign the picture the following year). In the background, a stretch of plowed or fallow field; in the foreground, a man
and a woman set upon by three fat soldiers, eyes hidden by their
helmets, grotesque, terrifying; the woman wrings her hands, while
the young man prays; they are standing at a crossroad, the furrows
and ruts recede as though taking flight into the wind; the plain is
stark and vertiginous; the pitiful, vicious scene is utterly forsaken. A
dead tree. The figures could be the Virgin Mary and Saint John on
Calvary harassed by the Roman watchdogs—soldiers or rather robbers, armed like regular soldiers, deserters who live by plunder.

Or was he painting *The Good Shepherd* who defends his flock when
the wolf comes and *The Unfaithful Shepherd* who flees and abandons
his sheep? The robbers' attack, the shepherd with the wolf at his
throat, and the other one, fat and sleek as a prelate, who runs away,
are all set against the same dreary autumn or winter landscape of
desolate clay. Where is that radiant morning when, not far from the
plowman in his handsome tunic, the shepherds watched Dædalus fly
by? It is as though the cold had chilled the heart of the world. Did
Bruegel's heart sink at the suffering he saw, and foresaw, in the countryside? Was he meditating on the reign of good and bad princes, of
plundering kings, that ends in the savagery of sergeants in some dark
wood? Or was he thinking of Christ, the true shepherd?

He lit his way with the lantern of proverbs; he lit his way with the
mysterious sun of parables. As he painted the large earth-colored pictures, where the landscape seems to vanish into the distance, numbed
with solitude, he kept before him the print for which he had made
the drawing last year and which Philip Galle had engraved. It resembles a common holy picture. And indeed it is now tacked on the

wall of hundreds of Flemish kitchens; and the villagers, when they sit down to say grace, can look up and see it. But for Bruegel, the engraving was not so much a commission as a statement of faith. Christ is standing in the doorway of a stable; the entrance is narrow; the sheep are huddled around his legs and he carries one slung across his shoulders. This is the stable of the Nativity, from which Bruegel has borrowed the manger and the straw; it is also the opening of the tomb from which Christ emerged victorious over death. It is all one place, then, the grotto to which first the shepherds, then the wisemen came, and the new tomb where Our Lord suffered death as we all shall. With his birth he entered the valley of death, as each of us does; with his death, he was born to the Resurrection. He stands in the narrow doorway. It is as though he were saying: "I stand at the door." On the lintel, for all to read: "Ego sum ostium ovium. Joha. 10.12." And anyone can open the Book if the words have slipped his mind: "Truly I tell you, anyone who does not come in through the door of the sheepfold, but climbs in by another way is a thief and a brigand. But the one who comes in through the door is the shepherd. For him, the doorman will open the gate and the sheep listen to his voice; he calls each sheep by its name and he turns them out. And when he has let out his own sheep, he leads them, and the sheep follow him because they know his voice. They will not follow a stranger; they run away because they do not know his voice. Jesus told them this parable but they failed to understand what he meant. Jesus said to them again: Truly, I say to you, I am the door of the sheep."

Fat thieves and robbers have hacked through the roof and torn their way in; others are breaking down the walls and carrying off the sheep; a fighting man, a monk, a man of the people, side by side, lay hold of fleece and hooves. A mountain rises above the roof. If this was the stable of the Nativity alone, we would see the shepherds in rapture, unmindful of their chilblains. And similarly the angels, playing flutes and pipes. In the upper left, we see the good shepherd giving his life for his flock, and on the right, the bad shepherd, running away. "I know my sheep," Christ said, "and they know me." And he added, "As my father knows me and I know my father."

What was Bruegel doing in April 1566? Was he too preoccupied with the gathering storm to have the heart to paint or draw? Or did he think that his duty was to resist, to keep up hope by working? He could not have been unaware of Egmont's mission and his return, of the confederation, of the Compromise. What did he say to Mary? What did she have to say? Did he think back on the evening spent with Coornhert, and to what they had thought at the time? I do not see him among those watching the confederation ride by. If he did see them, I imagine him filled more with anxiety than with hope. April was exceedingly mild that year. Many were saying that one day the Spanish winter would no longer weigh upon their lives; but I think that, as he stared at the grass in his garden at the foot of the yellow and pink wall, Bruegel's heart was heavy.

Applause and shouts of joy greeted the passing procession. The churches rang the noon chimes as though celebrating their deliverance. Two by two, Brederode in the lead (or bringing up the rear with Louis of Nassau, two hundred gentlemen (or perhaps twice that number) and a few burghers from Antwerp and other towns proceeded to the palace of the regent. She had known they would come. She was ready to receive them. She could hear the joyous clamor of the crowd coming from beyond the walls and the park, acclaiming their heroes as they rode by, so young and handsome, and the hope of the people. The daughter of Charles V and a servant girl from Oudenaarde would have liked to grant William all he asked, yet she could only obey her brother, the king. Her life had been so light in Parma, in Florence. And here she was obliged to play the regent and impose the impossible. She knew the people's suffering and she pitied them. She was so tired that she shook. And she wept. Was she going to cry in front of the conspirators?

"What, Madame," said one of her advisers—perhaps Count Berlaymont—"are you afraid of those beggars?"

Brederode entered the council chamber accompanied by only a handful of nobles. It was he who would read out the petition before presenting it to the regent. He read in a voice like thunder. The placards of Charles V shall be abolished: times have changed, and even were the placards to be enforced with moderation, they would only lead, shortly, to a popular uprising. The Inquisition shall be abandoned in all Seventeen Provinces, which cannot abide it. His majesty shall be so gracious as to enact a statute governing religious matters, with the advice and consent of the Estates General. Having read the petition and laid it before the regent, Brederode made a low bow. The others did likewise. These perfectly executed reverences seemed to taunt the regent and the king, and portend trouble. Thereupon they left the Coudenberg palace by way of the gallery where, ten years earlier, the Emperor Charles had abdicated, his hand resting on the shoulder of William of Orange, his page. Did the thought cross their minds? Did their minds hark back to the guarded, sick look on the face of Philip, king of Spain, as he sat listening to Granvelle, bishop of Arras, read the speech he himself was unable to pronounce in either French or Flemish? In it he promised to pay frequent visits to the Low Countries, to respect their customs, freedoms, franchises, and privileges; to uphold the Catholic faith. He listened in silence as the cardinal read. His Spanish silence was eloquent.

The nobles had spent months preparing for this meeting that had lasted only minutes. They were disconcerted. No reply could be expected for several days. Had Brederode foreseen the wavering that followed the presentation of the petition? They would not separate before celebrating one last time. Seven tables of thirty were laid at the Culemberg mansion. They spent the afternoon commenting and deriding the morning's meeting. Then evening came. The torches were lit. The musicians mounted the stage. The cellars and kitchens were bulging with victuals as one day they would be with powder and crossbows. Was it when the banquet was in full swing, or earlier that afternoon, that someone had the idea of seeking out the beggars of Brussels and collecting their bowls and bags? In any event, when a disheveled and uproarious Brederode stood up and bellowed:

"They called us beggars? Well then, long live the Beggars!" The gold and silver drinking vessels had vanished from the tables to be replaced by the paupers' wooden bowls.

"Long live the Beggars!" they repeated unflaggingly, each time they raised a cup.

"Friends," said Brederode, "since, for the likes of them, we are beggars, we have good reason, from now on to drink from a bowl and carry a bag." Which he did. The nobles had found themselves a name and a battle cry; they made it their emblem.

The joke might not have survived the harsh light of day had not Hoorn, Egmont, and William of Nassau come to take Hoogstraten away from the party to the side of the regent, who wanted them all for consultation. In the middle of the night? Such was her habit, and the events of the day had left her deeply troubled. They had not planned to go in, but when they heard the uproar, they thought it wise to persuade the heroes that it was now time to retire. Spain must be given no pretexts, and their rowdy mood boded no good. They saw the flushed faces. They saw a new kind of Golden Fleece, the wooden bowl, hanging around the necks of a few nobles, and from their shoulders, the beggar's bag. This carnival was distasteful to Hoorn and Egmont, and it worried William. But suddenly they found themselves holding wooden vessels and being urged to drink up and cry: "Long live the Beggars!"

If they drank at all, it was against their will. And they remained silent. But the others shouted for them:

"Long live William of Orange! Long live Hoorn! Long live Egmont!"

For a moment they were like three victorious generals surrounded by their troops. They renounced the idea of preaching moderation. Hoogstraten joined them, and they left the room. Later Hoorn was to say that they had stayed only the space of a miserere. But all of Brussels imagined William and his friends laughing and drinking at the Beggars' Banquet.

The regent soon made her answer known. A delegation would depart for Spain, and she personally promised to impose moderation on the courts. The nobles left Brussels. Did Bruegel see them pass through the Hal Gate, most dressed in gray or brown, like beggars? As they left the town, Brederode fired his pistols into the air and turned his galloping horse toward Antwerp. William was at his estate in Breda, and Louis took the liberty of opening the Nassau palace to those who were in the habit of gathering to pray in the fields and woods. The meetings were held, discreetly, at dawn: soon the whole town knew of them. The jewelers made tiny golden bowls for the ladies and for the hats of fashionable young men. People shouted, "Long live the Beggars," in the streets and as far as the Coudenberg mansion gates. As the people had defied Cardinal Granvelle by sewing red bells on their clothes or wearing foxtails, alluding to his duplicity—to his enemy Simon Renart—the beggar business was directed at Spain and the Church. And every day saw a new variation. Wax medallions were made, one side bearing a picture of hands joined in prayer and the motto "Loyal to the king," the other a beggar's bag with the words "if it beggars us." In the markets, musicians poked fun at the clergy in their songs, and the people took up the refrain: "Long live the Beggars! Long live the Beggars!" Daring broadsheets and engravings were printed: on one, a steeple about to be toppled by three figures, while a number of bishops and priests attempt to keep it up. On one side, the words: "German Lutherans, French Huguenots, Flemish Beggars, we will bring down the Church of Rome"; on the other side: "If they keep it up, goodbye Pope and Co." In Antwerp, edition after edition came off the press of a print of a caged *papegai*: a monkey named Martin (as in Luther) and a calf (for Calvin) sat atop the cage. If a peddlar was caught selling the print, they could do nothing but release him; the blow had been struck.

The viscount of Antwerp, William of Nassau, called by the people and delegated by the regent, maintained order in the town. Misery was rampant: there was no work at the docks. And the Reformationists—whether German, English, or local—had always enjoyed a degree of freedom made inevitable by the sheer size of the city and the teeming waterfront. William had persuaded the city to create construction jobs for the unemployed. He had persuaded the Calvinists no longer to meet in the countryside or, if they did, to go unarmed—with the assurance that this was not some trick on the part of the government. William was sent to Brussels. Once he was gone, the convergence of Calvinists and victims of starvation overwhelmed the city. He had delayed his departure to be present for the feast of the Assumption. It was the custom to parade through the streets with the small statue of the Black Virgin from the cathedral, decked in gold and diamonds, dressed in silver lace, wearing a crown and carrying a scepter. Not to attend the procession would have appeared to leave the field to the rebels and would have provided Philip II with yet another pretext. William of Nassau, his wife, and his brother Louis stood on the balcony of the town hall and crossed themselves as the Virgin went by. With the exception of a few children shouting: "Hey, Mary! This is your last time out for a walk," there were no incidents that day. Perhaps peace would gradually return.

On Tuesday, the twentieth of August, toward the end of the afternoon, a drunk took the pulpit at Notre Dame and made ready to preach—"Hail, holy carpenter queen, holy-picture Mary. You're one little lady riding for a fall." They ran him out. He came back. His pursuers were then beaten with the butts of muskets that had been concealed under capes. The mob rushed in and began to sack the cathedral—some out of piety and horror of idols, others to steal all they could in order to eat their fill and clothe themselves. Night fell. The mob grew. Inside the cathedral it was every man for himself, and the plundering continued by torchlight. Ladders were brought in to reach the stained-glass windows and the higher statues. The nave rang with the blows of hammers, pickaxes, sledges, and mallets. The priests had hidden the little statue of the Black Virgin in one of the side chapels behind an iron plaque; she was discovered and treated like a doll, her dress torn, the miraculous statue smashed to pieces. The vaults echoed with a single, enormous outcry. Soon all that remained of the treasures and wonders, of all that was precious and sacred lay in broken bits on the flagstones amid the vomit and filth. The frenzy spread so fast that by dawn not a single church, chapel, or monastery remained intact. The monastery cellars lay ankle deep in beer and wine.

Rapidly a band some three thousand strong formed, men from Flanders and Wallony who had the look of ditchdiggers or farmhands. They were escorted by two dozen riders of noble appearance. By groups of twenty, they broke into churches, smashed the statues, defacing and burning the pictures. They tore into long strips the dais covers and the banners, the tunics, stoles, chasubles, and the sacred ornaments, which were often made of brocade. They fashioned flags, turbans, and cloaks, laughing at their Turkish disguises. The reliquaries were profaned. The wildest elements broke them open, then pitched them through the leaded or stained-glass windows, scattering bones and relics to the winds, ironizing on the foul-smelling remains distinguished by nothing from ordinary skeletons.

The image-breaking (*Beeldenstorm*) spread through the country and lasted for weeks. Many griefs fueled the flames: theological iconoclasm, hatred of Spain, the wretched plight of the country, memories and the practice of torture, fascination with fire, grudges between neighbors, the love of evil and destruction. In Vianen, Brederode made the rounds of all the churches to the music of pipe and drum. He stripped the hangings and ornaments, took down the pictures, removed the statues, and left the sanctuaries as bare as a stone quarry. On his own estate, Culemberg had the altars hacked to pieces and then set up tables in the nave and invited one and all; and more people came to dine than ever to worship. In Delft, Utrecht, Amsterdam, Ypres, mobs broke into convents pillaging and raining insults—and sometimes blows—on the monks and nuns. In Brussels a broadsheet was nailed, like a placard, to the door of all Catholic churches: "Brabant, awake! It is not your custom to be governed by a bastard, and Margaret the bastard is betraying us. Out with the whore!" And yet Margaret had announced that "preachments held in their customary places would not be disrupted." She begged the rebels to give back the churches, at least, and promised that they could build temples. The temples were already under way, built out of wood, and often opposite the Catholic church; some were round with a dome, others octagonal. In rural areas, people met in barns.

Everyone was fighting everyone, or very nearly: Catholics, Lutherans, Calvinists, Anabaptists; peasants and soldiers. For years lansquenets, German Reiters, Walloon red-coats, and Spanish foot soldiers had been living off the local population. According to one chronicle,

they offered the excuse that, badly paid, they still had to eat. If and when they repaid their host, it was in *coin of the cavalry*, that is, by blows with the flat of the sword. A baker in Mechelen had his face split in a fight; that very

evening, three brothers who worked at the slaughterhouse laid hold of the
first soldier they saw and butchered him like a sheep. The gaping wounds
could accommodate both hands. In Ghent, even though it was the middle of
summer, poverty stalked the streets; the paupers' chamber could not keep
pace with the demand. The second-hand clothes dealers could confirm the
fact, as was evident at the weekly markets. There was barely one cast-off item
of clothing or copper or pewter utensil for sale there where there had once
been twenty of a kind. Was it because the needy did not want their pledges
sold? No, it was because they had already pawned all but the rags on their
backs, like people with nowhere to turn and no hope in sight. They wandered the streets, collecting filth and garbage. They sent little children to the
refuse heap where they filled hats, sacks, pots and other receptacles, using
their hands, most wretchedly.

Visiting Belgium's museums, we sometimes find ourselves dreaming of all that was lost, that year, to the ax and fire. How many paintings by van Eyck and Memling were trampled under foot like so
many old boards? And how many statues charged with the tenderness and the weight of the world, and the story of the Passion, were
smashed. Thirty years later, van Mander's heart still ached. Writing
of Hugo van der Goes's *Crucifixion*, which hung in the Church of Saint
James, in Bruges, he says:

The extraordinary beauty of this painting saved it from the savage assault on
the sanctuaries; but later the church was used for Protestant services, and
they took this work of art and inscribed the Ten Commandments in gold
letters on a black background. And it was a painter who advised and executed the deed. I will not divulge his name, so that no one may say that one
from our ranks lent his hand to the annihilation of a beautiful work, an
outrage that the Art of Painting cannot contemplate without weeping. For-
tunately the original finish was hard, and the gold letters on the layer of black
formed a thick layer of oil colors. This chipped in places and could be entirely
removed.

Bruegel thought back on the paintings he had studied so closely,
throughout Flanders, that had nurtured his own work. Many were
no more than a memory, which would soon fade. Why were some
Reformers so wild to smash the Image of God become man? They
feared and rejected idolatry. But did they not understand that someone praying to the Virgin or to Christ, or calling upon the company
of saints, goes beyond the painted wood or canvas to address the
heart of the invisible, present person? Had they never seen that the
poor women who pray with tightly clasped hands before the crucified
Christ have their eyes closed, or filled with a look and a light that are
not of this world? Have they never seen that someone who kneels

and touches the wood that represents Jesus touches it like the woman who timidly brushed the fringe of his cloak, and was healed?

God became man, he took our form and our features because our spirit, enfolded and weighed down by our flesh, can rise and reach out to the mystery only by means of that which touches us, by that which we can see. God put on a physical body so that, in the end, our spirit might put on a glorious body. We do not fly like angels. We need a ladder. Images are the ladder that leads to the heart's secret. Images are also the Gospel in its tangible form. They are the acts that accompany the word and support it. They are words for our eyes. The apostles related the life of Our Lord, and we must grasp it with the eyes of our mind. And so it is good to see it, as through a glass, darkly, with our earthly eyes. It is good to see Christ and his disciples hulling wheat in our field, a sign that he is more concerned with the fatigue and hunger of his companions on the road than the time and the day for liturgical celebrations, the calendar of priests. It is good to see his mortal eyes in the light of our storms, our summers and amongst the boats of Antwerp—or Dunkerque. Those who reject the figurative portrayal of the saints and Christ and who look down on their brother's faith soon find themselves slapping their neighbor's face, and it is the face of Christ. It is true that so many who venerate and cense the image of the crucified Christ can, when the day comes, the same day, also nail their neighbor to his door, burn him like a dirty sheet, or simply let him starve on their doorstep.

As he meditated on these thoughts, Bruegel tried to paint as though the last few days had been serene. To so many paintings destroyed, so many sculptures consumed, the only response was to work. He worked like those of old: stubbornly, praying that God might come to his aid, that he purify his imagination, that he open his heart to the meaning of the Gospels and the world, that he guide his clumsy hand. To so much obtuse savagery—but those miserable wretches who took up the ax against a treasure of patience were poor men that Catholic brutality had driven to despair—it was imperative not to respond with spite and resentment. Understanding was needed. Forgiveness was needed. How can I pity you, Church of Rome, for your broken images, for your plundered wealth, you who bless the executioners who torture the poor Christs of today? They only tortured wooden faces, and every day you put to death and drive mad with pain poor wretches for whom Christ gave his life, tortured by his executioners, your precursors.

He painted. He worked. He defied the ruin and the fury with his work as a painter and the wisdom of his chosen Art. On his board he gave birth to the image that took shape within him, welling up from the Scriptures. He listened to the word taken down since God first spoke to mankind. He set his steps in those of the apostles. He spoke for those men whose hands actually touched the body of Christ when he passed through the walls to strengthen their wavering faith, more frail than a candle in the wind.

Gray hair and white beards, grown old on the roads of the world, bodies already bent with age, stiff and lean, the loyal apostles are all there, like sons gathered around their mother, like the night of the Last Supper, and the day the Spirit came to rest on them, in Mary's house, with all the doors closed. They are there in the house where Mary is about to die, as one day we all shall die. And Paul, who did not see the Lord with the eyes of his body, but received the awesome sweet light of his Word, is with them: he had clasped Peter to him in the doorway, and John, the first to return to Jerusalem, the beloved disciple, the son. The apostles are gathered around Mary's bed as they used to gather around Jesus. Each heard the call where he was, far flung, preaching, laboring, not even knowing if the others were still among the living. Peter was in Rome, Thomas in the inmost Indies, James in Jerusalem. Mark was in Alexandria. They heard the call as the wisemen had. They saw the warning in a dream, even though it might have been high noon, and, as in a dream, they set out on dusty roads, rocky roads, dizzy ice-covered mountain trails, through snowbound, nightbound forests to come together one last time, on this earth. They are together. Andrew, Peter's brother, Luke, Simon, Philip, Thaddeus, who is no longer living, came to keep watch. Their hearts are burning with one sorrow and one light. They are the Church, and the Church is like a family, when it is united. There they are in the dimly lit house. When Mary has left the world, when they can no longer see or touch her, when they can no longer hear her voice, and her house stands empty, when she is gone forever, it will be as though Jesus has left them a second time, as though the bodily thread of his earthly coming has been cut. Of course he is with them until the end of time, in spirit, in love, and through the mysterious sacrament of his body and blood, but the apostles will always be dull-witted and slow to believe. They did not recognize God when he ate at their table, and the sun would strike a jug or pitcher with an unordinary light; now they want to hold her hand in theirs, to touch God.

A fire is blazing on the hearth. A cat sleeps hunched in front of the flames. The light glints on the copper warming pan on the wall. A candle burns on a table amid some pewter plates and ewers. Two tall candlesticks stand on a ledge. A book lies closed on the chair. There are other books on the side of the mantlepiece, and above the fireplace the figure of an angel holding a sword, or a lily. Under the table,

a pair of sandals. Death will enter an everyday scene. The house has
not been straightened; things are as they were yesterday, or that
morning. The fire leaps in the fireplace, and the continuous roar can
be heard of the flames being sucked up by the wind. Is the time a late
afternoon in November? Is it dark outside? It is dark. Beneath the
leaping flames, coals; around the coals, the soft ashes, soft as silk; the
whole chamber is the color of ashes, as soft and as sad as ashes. The
paint looks as though it had been mixed with ashes and these ashes
let the light through. When our last hour comes, will we see life shining through the shroud of death? This room in which the Virgin is
preparing to die, this dim, gray room, lit by the candles and the winter fire, is illuminated by a brighter light still.

Mary is lying in bed. A woman arranges her pillow. Before her, at
the foot of the bed, propped on a cushion, the image of her son on
the cross. Her face is lit by a light that comes neither from the fire,
nor from the candle on the round table, nor from the candlesticks.
Around her stand the aged apostles, grieving like any mortals. Peter,
in a chasuble, holds out a taper; and she who bore the Light of the
world takes the luminary as, God willing, we will take it in our own
dying hands. The Heavenly Virgin, the flower of humanity, she who
crushes the Dragon of Darkness and shines like the moon and the
sun, the Virgin Mary, queen of the daughters of Jerusalem, is fashioned from the same clay as we. She does not refuse the anxious
passage, for she is the human race itself. She passes the doors of death
in the footsteps of God made man. The apostles cannot keep from
weeping, even if they tell themselves that their grief might bear witness against their faith.

The figure sleeping, or in rapture, sitting with folded hands near
the fire, and who looks so young, is that John? It is John, to whom
Christ said as he was dying: "Son, this is your Mother," and to
Mary, blinded by tears: "Mother, this is now your son." Why does
he remain apart? Is he exhausted with grief and fatigue? If his eyes
are closed, it is because John the Seer sees Christ and his angels, he
sees their glory showing through the gray ashes where Mary is dying. The light radiating from her and showing in her face, brighter
than the flames leaping on the hearth, is a mere shadow of the sun
in which Christ dwells with his incandescent angels. John contemplates her in a dream as he will see, shining among the rocks of
Patmos, the heavenly Jerusalem, the Eternal City where all tears
will be wiped away, to their very memory. He contemplates the glory
of Christ invisible.

Or: It is John. He is seated on a high-backed chair as though he had just fallen asleep, exhausted from his wake; his hands are folded on the blanket that covers him, and his traveling bag has slipped to the floor. But how is it that he is still so young, while the others are old men? If he is slightly removed, whereas he should be closest to the bed where the Mother of God is receiving the taper and gazing at the crucifix propped before her, it is because he is in another time, another place. He is not really in that room. His mind sees the moment when Mary's soul leaves her body. The picture is his vision. That is why we see, kneeling at the edge of the bed next to the bed curtain and the chest where the oil for the Last Rites stands ready, a monk from the future, a present-day Christian, holding a still-silent bell for the procession and the burial. That is why the women and men huddling beyond the circle of apostles in the shadows of the room are perhaps not inhabitants of Jerusalem, but ourselves, who are soon to die and who believe that Christ is risen.

The date on *The Falling Asleep of the Virgin* is hard to decipher. Bruegel painted it for his friend Abraham Ortelius, the geographer. The few times he painted in this medium, *en grisaille,* using few colors, mixing earth colors with light, give the impression that he was not so much painting as praying. These paintings seem to come from the depths of the heart; he seems to have painted them with his eyes open, like John, somewhere in the dim recesses of his heart lit by the book and the candle flame.

Ortelius may have asked his friend for this Dormition for the fifteenth of August, the Feast of the Assumption, 1565. Perhaps he was thinking of his own death and wanted to have this picture before his eyes each evening, as he murmured: "Now and at the hour of our death," thinking of the instant when these two moments would become one, at the edge of time, and would finally meet like two travelers who have been coming ever closer, and at last embrace; or like our hands when we pray.

Ortelius had a few prints made for his friends. At the bottom, he placed a Latin inscription which he may have composed himself:

Virgin, when you sought the secure realms of your Son, what great joys filled your breast! What had been sweeter to you than to migrate from the prison of the earth to the lofty temples of the longed-for heavens? And when you left the holy band whose support you had been, what sadness sprang up in you; how sad and also how joyful as they watched you going was that pious group of yours. What pleased them more than for you to reign, what was so sad as to do without your face? This picture painted by a master shows the happy bearing of sadness on the faces of the just.

13

THE LAND OF MILK
AND HONEY

Young Peter was never so well behaved as when he was in his father's workshop, perched on his own little stool. Would he remember that grayish afternoon, and the pigeons cooing on the roof? He was three. He bit into a piece of bread and jam. When he finished his afternoon snack, he would return to the sheet on which he was drawing, or painting, like his father and his grandmother; he would return to the print he was coloring. Would he remember this picture taking shape before him, a tale for the eyes? The tree trunk is the foot of a round sloping table, but the jug and the plate never fall. At the base of the tree, sleeping like babes, is a scholar lying on his book and papers, a peasant on his flail, and a soldier on his long jousting pole. The scholar, in white shirt and pink breeches, sprawls on the fur lining of his coat. A simple harvester's garb contents the peasant. The soldier, whose gauntlet is lying in the grass, sports cerise pants with black stripes that match the red pillow cradling his head. The earth turns, carrying them along like figures on a merry-go-round, or a lottery wheel. They have no care for threshing or jousting, no thought for desk or pen. They sleep, slumber, drowse, and dose; they dream and daydream, lost in the clouds. Peacefully they sleep around the foot of the tree with the carefree surrender of sheaves. When they wake to the soft strains of music, they have only to open their mouths, they need only to yawn, and the table is laid. They sleep. Their bodies form a becoming wreath. An afternoon breeze lulls them. The earth provides a soft bed upon which they seem more to float than to weigh. A place is set on the white cloth for a fourth guest. A roast suckling pig with a carving knife close at hand in its belt trots past a cactus made of golden breadrolls. An obliging soft-boiled egg runs by on the lawn, a spoon standing ready in one end. Beneath a lean-to roofed in pies, a knight opens his mouth to a passing roast lark. And so it goes in the Land of Milk and Honey, drifting from repose to repast and from repast to repose.

Peter would spend the rest of his life close to the father he was to know so little. Was it to earn his living that he became his father's copyist, surrounded by a dozen helpers, turning out skating scenes, weddings, and kermises? I personally see an act of piety. He was happy to be instrumental in spreading this work throughout Europe. In his paintings, he sought the father he had hardly known. He saw what his father had seen. His hand followed his father's hand. Sometimes he would sense his father watching as he traced a tree, put in the leaves, poured just the right color into the peasant woman's bowl. His father's painting had become a country whose every blade of grass was familiar to him. His eye and his hand knew exactly how the harvester's hand barely grazed the soldier's red pillow; he had followed the swell of the pillow and savored the curve that was prolonged by the sleeper's leg; he had delighted in the delicious chord struck by the scholar's white shirt and the paper half rolled beneath his lazy head. He knew the fabric of this painting by heart, as an actor knows his role, and the roles of all the others in the play: like no other he appreciates the interplay of rhythms, the interplay of the speeches, the weaving of the episodes, and the allusions echoing from one end to the other of the piece. But his knowledge of his father's invented land was not dulled for all that. He was the indefatigable traveler of this country, its geographer. Were we able to collect and place side by side the images from our sleep, our dreams, our nightmares, and our daydreams, how different from ordinary life would be the one we might come to know. Some painters are visited with an analogous grace. That was the grace Peter Bruegel the Elder had received.

At times Peter would imagine what was happening beyond the frame. The dancers leaping about in the barn, he would set under the trees. He would move the procession climbing Calvary's hill a few steps to the left. He would combine a hill from one picture with a mown field from another and the horizon from yet a third. He would look at the finished painting as a painter looks at the world: choosing the angle and the moment. He knew how far short he fell of his admirable father. Telemachus was no Ulysses; Icarus, no Dædalus. His own grace was to be his father's son, to be intimate with what his father had created and to serve it well. And now that he had reached the age his father was when he died, when he looked at himself in the mirror, or when he looked at his own portrait that van Dyck had recently drawn, he caught his father's features. At times, in a gesture or in the way he had of saying certain words, he would suddenly recognize something of his father.

Evening had come. They were in the workshop even though the hour was late. His father would pick him up and carry him piggyback across the landing, to his room. He would dump him onto the bed like a sack of flour.

"Tell me 'The Land of Milk and Honey.'" His father would sit down by the bed. The lamp lit the ceiling.

"Once upon a time there was a great country called Yesterland, where everyday was Sunday, and the two peoples of the land, the Eetalotts and the Doolittles, lived together in peace. To get there you must go down Storypath and through the Dreamforest. A long time ago, Yesterland reached as far as our house—right to the garden gate. You could open the little green door and see hills made of cakes. You could see the pudding mountains and the waffle castles. You could see the fields of butter and gingerbread houses with nutmeg doors. A wonderland. Fountains of vintage wines and spring of mead flow in peoples' mansions for the asking. Pies grow on oak trees and omelets on birches. You don't have to raise a hand to pick them because they grow right in front of your mouth. Orchards of sugar candy sparkle in the sunlight and gardens of sugarloaves under the moon. Cooked pears pass the time with ripe ones, and in winter it snows powdered sugar. The willow flowers are made of white bread, the hazels bear brioches and the alders *coukestut'*. The rivers flow with milk and the streams with syrup. The stones on the path are made of cheese. When it hails, it hails sugared almonds; when it rains, it rains raisins; and when the wind blows, it smells like fresh-baked bread and the flower of youth. Look! In the meadows they shoot their bows and play at nine-pins all year long! Whoever falls widest of the mark is the winner: that is the law of the Land of Milk and Honey. The last in the race wins the prize. And the Great Snail from the Royal Stables draws his carriage. Everyone takes turn at being king and, during his reign, he dines on desserts and sleeps until noon. Can you see this dreamland? For every tumbler a pilgrim drinks in good company, he receives a denier. If he drinks till the cork soles of his slippers swell, he wins a pistole; if he empties three pots without stopping for breath, and is still on his feet, he gets a carolus and is invited to dinner. In this country all you have to do is say, or even think: Little mouth, what do you fancy? Dear heart, what would you like. And no sooner thought than a laden tray flies in. That was Yesterland, the great land of Your Every Wish, the Empire of Good Humor. All that remains in our countryside are the beribboned poles of plenty, where birds from the Land of Milk and Honey hang wreathes of hams and jugs. Today Yesterland is reduced to an island on the far side of the world. When you get off the boat you must cross a pancake mountain, but you must eat your way through, like a rabbit in its burrow. You have to be a hearty eater."

The boy was falling asleep. Trying to sink into Dreamland. He slipped through the pancake mountain. He saw the Land of Milk and Honey. He barely heard his father's voice saying: "Now we live in the Land of Today. It is a country where you have to work. When children grow up, they leave Yesterland behind."

His father painted this picture as the Bloody Duke tortured villages. Flanders was indeed far from the Land of Milk and Honey! Did he mean that it was time to wake up? But who in Flanders was still asleep? It was a time of vigilance. It was a time of watching and sleepless nights. And yet the interiors were warm, despite the black cloud hanging over the land. Beneath village roofs mothers still rocked their children. Their breasts were the milky streams of the Land of Milk and Honey, their laps the hills. Life went on in those unhappy times like the kernel of wheat beneath the snow and ice. What were the mothers of Bethlehem telling their children when Herod's soldiers kicked in the doors and smashed the windows? Bruegel painted the Land of Milk and Honey the way he told it, on the edge of night, to his son Peter.

14

1567

1

Already a year since the Beggars' Banquet. On the tenth of April, William of Nassau wrote to the king of Spain resigning his post. He was at the town hall. He ran his eyes over the walls of his office and the large world map that hung there. He saw the sun setting over the sea. He saw the ships maneuvering. The next day he received the town dignitaries and a few friends. He was dressed for traveling. It was cold in the big room. Smiles were strained and the guests could not keep back their tears. William hid his at first, and then gave in. He said to those around him: "My friends, the time has come to say: 'From the depths, Lord, I call to thee.'" One by one they came up to him, murmured a few words, took his hand or kissed him. At last he went out. It had started to rain. His horse was led up. No one had anything to add.

What had he done in the last year? After the plundering of the cathedral, he had reestablished order in Antwerp. Of all the rioters arrested, he had punished only three, and these were strangers, to restore calm to the town. He had held negotiations with the Calvinists: he gave them permission to meet, and they vacated the Catholic church. He had protected the monks and priests; he had protected the Catholics. He had put up with quarrelsome letters from the regent: "I told you not to interpret the agreement so broadly!"

He had traveled the length and breadth of his jurisdiction. He had spent the autumn in Holland, Zeeland, and Utrecht, all the while keeping in touch with Antwerp. He had seen that the highways and the seas were made safe. How many times, in Amsterdam, Haarlem, The Hague, Delft, Utrecht, had he met with men on the point of killing each other and persuaded them to live like Christians and to tolerate each other's worship and faith? He became an apologist of the Compromise, and yet he knew that the regent did not consider herself bound, that she claimed to have signed the promises under duress, under threat. She rallied Catholics hostile to any concession, and, on her brother's order, raised troops in Germany. He knew the Spanish army was on its way. Spurred on by Brederode, Louis was preparing an uprising. And he urged William to join them. The latter rejected the proposal as madness. The regent pressed him to keep her informed of the plans of his brother and friends. He would remain loyal as long as he could. It was imperative to hope against hope that the king would reverse his position, and yet they must prepare for war. And therefore they needed the means to rally their troops. In March, after having conferred with his brothers Louis and John, the incumbent count, he had sold his silver plate and precious stones; the money was at Dillenburg.

His face was wet with rain. He could hear the cry of the gulls and the sounds of the waterfront. He mounted his horse and set out. Some sixty burghers escorted him, their capes flattened against their shoulders by the wind and streaming behind them like black banners. They had not reached the city walls when a crowd began to follow, to block their way. William was thinking that he should have left at daybreak. The crowd watched him with worried, reproachful faces. They wanted to know the truth. Was it true that he was abandoning them? Someone laid hold of his horse's bridle. He looked at them with affection. "I'm going to Dillenburg, I'm going hawking."

A woman spoke up. "Sire, a man like you, Prince of Orange, is not about to be satisfied with such paltry game!"

His escort drew around him and opened the way. Their hands released him, their eyes followed him out of sight. Now he was alone on the misty windswept country road.

He rode on. He thought back over the past month, day by day. Brederode had taken Amsterdam and immediately occupied the taverns. John Marnix had led a small band up to Antwerp. The regent's troops had encircled them three miles from the city walls. Instantly the people of Antwerp rose up in arms. John Marnix's wife had run through the streets beseeching men to go to her husband's aid. Two thousand men broke down the gates William had closed and rushed out to battle. They could be of no use to Marnix and would only get themselves killed. William, accompanied by Hoogstraten, spurred his horse to catch them. He intercepted them, shouting:

"You're going to your death. The cavalry will trample you! I'm the one you must help. If you help me, I will stay with you to the death."

He saw the pistols pointed at him and heard shouts of "Traitor!"

"If you believe I'm a traitor, kill me!" He thought that he was about to die. He advanced. They retreated one step at a time. He backed them to the city walls. The crowd then called upon the garrison to open the arsenal.

"You want these arms?" shouted William. "They're yours." And he let the mob in. In the town hall square and at four other locations in Antwerp, he pronounced a declaration which ended with the cry:

"Long live the King!"

The crowds responded: "Long live the Beggars!"

He let it pass. He told himself that he had avoided bloodshed and senseless fighting. But how much longer could he endure the contradiction? He sold what he had left and borrowed large sums from Antwerp financiers who had been offering their help for months. Those who had bought his tapestries and furniture were to take possession as soon as he had gone. He spent the last days like a guest in his own home.

He turned toward Breda. He was pressed for time. At Willebroek, near the canal that links Mechelen and Brussels, Egmont was waiting in the unremitting rain. What remained to be said after their meeting with Louis, Hoorn, and Hoogstraten at Termonde, last October in a hunting lodge? Egmont wanted to convince him that the Spanish king was planning to invade the Low Countries and that the surest way to avoid occupation would be to stop his troops. In short, he wanted to convince him that they should join forces, avoid shows of temper or cruelty, encounter the road-weary troops in time. They needed the Lutheran princes on their side: William's wife was the niece of the Saxony elector, and Egmont's, the sister of the Palatine elector. Would the king of Spain dare flout the rights of the Netherlandish nobility if these German princes put their power and alliance behind them? They looked like two lords with no weightier concerns than some hunting. The autumnal forest rustled and blazed about them. The lodge they had chosen for their secret meeting had only two rooms: a dining room, where the table was laid with crystal and silver that sparkled against the pale tablecloth, amid pyramids of fruits and baskets of grapes; and the kitchen, which was empty because everything had been brought from Brussels. Egmont and William found themselves alone for a moment in the kitchen. Egmont was standing at the window, framed by the fiery leaves. He looked like some gentleman out of a tapestry, a figure from the *Field of the Cloth of Gold*. His humiliation in Madrid had taught him nothing. He wanted to see in Philip II no more than the duke of Burgundy and master of the Golden Fleece: he would remain his vassal. They could only stand there, silent and sad. The glorious autumn which had so recently still enveloped their meeting now took on a funereal aspect, and all seemed stark and bare. They joined the others. "Alas, Egmont," murmured William, "You and all those who think like you are building a bridge for the Spaniards to cross. When they have gained entrance, they will destroy it. Then they will destroy you." What else could he say, there in the irritating April rain. Could they even talk with each other heart to heart? Egmont had been sent by Margaret, and two of the regent's men were watching him. He pleaded with William not to leave the Low Countries. How could William make him understand that the Spanish hawk was hovering and that he wanted to keep his distance in order to return and join battle when the time came, and to liberatè this unhappy land? They searched each other's faces. They would never meet again. Night fell. William longed to be in Breda.

Breda. He bid his vassals and his servants farewell. He exhorted them not to risk their lives foolishly when the Spanish occupier arrived. He told them not to despair, and that he was leaving, but not forsaking them. He gazed at the ramparts and the gray walls of the city outlined against the sky. He rode across wet pastures, along willow-lined streams, through the soft-yellow primroses strewing the path. Covered wagons carried the furnishings from the castle to Dillenburg. William imagined the Spanish soldiers entering the park, occupying every room of the mansion. Then he set out with Anne, his wife, and their three daughters. He wanted to let it be thought that he was returning to Dillenburg only to see his family. He left his son, Philip-William, in Leuwen: his presence was meant to calm suspicions. Philip was named for his godfather, the king of Spain. May that protect him. He was fourteen. William asked about his studies, he encouraged him and reminded him that a gentleman should become educated, not to adorn or amuse himself, but to prepare himself to serve those in his charge. They talked as father and son, seated in the big library of the university or strolling along the paths in the park with bird song soaring on every side. He felt he was leaving his only son as a hostage. Then suddenly before him lay the countryside and the castle of his childhood, the pointed turrets of another age, the vineyards, the woods, the River Dill, with its mill wheels, washhouses, little wooden bridges covered with moss; there lay the plum and cherry orchards with their blackbird population: petty castle, petty estate, petty nobility. Nothing in the background of William of Nassau predestined him to become William of Orange, great lord, great prince, and future liberator of the Netherlands, and to assume a name that Dante had inscribed in his poem. But at the age of eleven, while he was still at the school his parents had opened for the children of the neighboring nobility and their servants, he fell heir to Flanders, Franche-Comté, Dauphiné, Charolais, part of Brabant and Luxembourg, and to rights over the former kingdom of Arles and the duchy of Gravina; he also inherited three Italian principalities, became sixteen times a count, twice a margrave, twice a viscount, some fifty times a baron, and came into some three hundred other estates; finally, he found himself heir to the sovereign principality of Orange. He left Dillenburg and its pie cherries and blackbirds, he left his family and Luther's hymns for the court of Brussels and the emperor's hand on his shoulder as he walked to the throne he was about to abdicate.

2

Was there ever another saint who began, like Paul, by torturing his own people only to take the place of those he had recently been pursuing, enduring insults, prison, and beheading? In his mind Bruegel sees the moment the first martyr dies by stoning, while the future apostle watches over the cloaks of those taking careful aim at that head with its already closed eyes. Come evening, will he be ashamed of having served such brutes? No. He is impatient. Soon he will no longer be content to look after the belongings of those who have rolled up their sleeves to stone a madman, who responds with a blessing. He will no longer be content to watch from a short distance while the stones rain down on the heretic's chest and gash his forehead until at last he falls. He will no longer be content to look at the broken body beneath the bloody cloak, beneath the last rocks and stones. He is growing up. He desires nothing more than to be of service. Despite his youth, he holds an honorable rank. He bears his arms with elegance. He enjoys using them. He is also armed with an incisive tongue. Whether confronting the troops or a single subordinate, his word is already an act. He has the look of a man who is the first to see where to thrust the sword, where to cast the net. He is a Jew, but a Roman Jew. He is a citizen of Rome; his family has paid the price. He often reproaches the Romans for forgetting the glory of their empire and their duty to Cæsar. He looks down on all Jews who have failed to grasp that the grandeur of the children of Abraham proceeds from the universal victory of Rome. He collaborates with all his heart to bring about the new era. The Jews who are still attached to their backwater, he pities. But those who hold one Jesus of Nazareth, crucified according to law and resurrected according to gossip, for the Messiah, those he hates! He hates them with a hatred that surprises even himself. He has enough reason to hate and to kill. They are liars; they raise their eyes to the clouds and bless their killers; they betray the Lord of Israel; they blaspheme; and they bring down on the whole people the impatience of the Romans, who are, after all, concerned only for the welfare of their provinces. The Jews do not see that they have but to be clever and careful, and one day they will rule Rome, which rules the world. They are even less capable than the others of grasping the great plan of the God of Israel and the nearness of his promise. But the hatred he feels in his heart, he is forced to admit, like a fire, like a wound, like some frightful burning sun, like an abscess, a wild animal whose eyes have been put out, this hatred is beyond all reason. It is in his blood, inspired. Had he been at Golgotha at the right moment, he would have snatched the spear from the hands of the soldier who struck a mere routine blow, and he, Saul, would have struck with all his strength and with all his mind and with all his soul!

He wants nothing better than to be useful. He is clever, he is persuasive. He comes from a good family. If only they would give him a squadron, he would show them. Who could refuse this serious young man a command? Who could refuse? The Jews and the Romans are in agreement. Peace throughout the empire! The synagogue and the prefecture understand each other better than people think, on this issue at any rate: the disciples of the so-called Savior of Israel are noxious and a threat. The order is rapidly signed and sealed. The troops are marshalled. And Saul of Tarsus is on his way to root out the malefactors and bring them back, three by three, in chains. Is the road from Jerusalem to Damascus dusty and flat? Bruegel sees Paul crossing the Alps on horseback. In the distance we see the ocean and some tiny ships, the tender green countryside, the villages. The army snakes its way through gorges and among clay-colored rock formations. Some soldiers have a countrified look, helmet in the crook of their arm or pulled down over the eyes, others are regular fashion-plates, dressed in fine fabrics of pale green or gold. All are making good time along the defile. Paul likes the feel of his fighting gear. He likes to rest one hand on his weapon. The smell of the horses and the sweat of men and beasts, the sound of feet and hooves on the rising morning breeze, the noise of an army on the march, its might, the jingling sounds and himself in command with the battle plan in his pocket and in his head, all this gives him a naive pleasure, which he savors. But he is unsmiling. He stops himself from smiling with the pleasure of a man on his mount, surrounded by his men, bound for deeds that will earn him a promotion. He sits like a Roman bust, like an equestrian statue. He shows his troops a model leader. For the time being, everyone is concentrating on the climb, with an occasional glance at the beauty of the world around them, the high outcroppings, the dark-green trees and, in the distance, the silent plain.

The pines are cool. Chains and swords clink. Horses neigh. At that moment, in the rear, the column of men is piling up. Something has happened. The leader has fallen from his horse. A soldier is already speeding to the head of the line to stop them. And yet, someone says, the horse did not make a move. Saul simply fell off. But he is a good horseman. Sunstroke, perhaps? But the air is cool. A dizzy spell; it can happen. And Paul is on the ground ringed in light and darkness. The light is like someone speaking: "Why do you persecute me?" His eyes burn as from the lash of a whip. He answers like a blindfolded man stretching out his hands to feel the door, the passageway. He answers as in a dream: "Who are you?" And the reply is full of sweetness and pain, distant and yet near: "I am Jesus of Nazareth whom you persecute." When they pick him up, when he picks himself up, the light is gone. He is in a dark tunnel. He can feel on his person the blood of the saints he has killed, and now he has been sent to testify that Christ lives. He tries to remount. He knows he must go to Damascus and there someone will have pity on him. A soldier takes him by the hand. He who strutted about working his jaws is now only a blind man whose hands tremble and who must hold them out for others to feed him. And yet the voice of Christ burns softly within him. Higher than the mountains he was crossing are the cliffs of darkness that now surround him. The army mills about, sending rocks tumbling and echoing into the depths, and the trees creak in the wind.

What madness drove him to wish the death of Jesus' disciples, like King Saul the death of David?

Those closest thought they heard a voice speak to Saul. They were astonished not to see anyone. Did they see the light that dazzled Paul? It was almost mid-day. Soon it was only another incident of the trip, which they forgot. Of the light, the sun, the storm that blinded Saul, and more than that and something altogether other than the day star and lightning, the men neither saw nor heard anything out of the way. They noticed nothing of the conflagration that enfolded him like a cloak. Looking at the painting representing the episode, what strikes one first are the mountains, then the army stubbornly wending its way, the standard-bearer's pink banner floating gracefully against the sky, a horseman wearing an odd hat indeed, made of what

looks like leaves and reminiscent of an artichoke. The persecutor's
reversal could well go unseen. A small chip in the paint, and all we
have is an ordinary band crossing the mountains. We would never
know what they were on their way to do; we would never know that
everything hinges on that heart blinded by a light not of this world.
Like Moses, Saul has encountered the Light and the Fire. "I am who
I am," proclaimed the voice from the burning bush. And the Light in
the Damascus mountains: "I am Jesus whom you persecute and
would put in chains." The Light that spoke to Moses took a name, as
we all do. God became one with the flesh tortured by executioners.
The invisible Father of mankind became this man who went among
us, and who is now one with the least among those who suffer.

He who had been breathing threats and death and whose approach filled the messianic community with terror entered Damascus
like a blind beggar whom all were free to smite, as they smote the
blindfolded Christ in the governor's courtyard. He prayed. A man
named Ananias saw him in a dream and came to him. He restored
his sight in the name of God. He said: "Get up. Be baptized and go!
You too must proclaim the good news. Bear witness." And Paul set
out for Antioch. The inner Christ guided him. He no longer lived with
his own life but with the life of Christ who lived in him. What he
knew he had not learned from a human message but from a divine
one. Like Jonah thrown up from the depths, he was on the road
to Nineveh. What he knew he had learned in the darkness and in
its transformation. Without the Spirit, the Books—which he knew
by heart, having memorized them at the feet of the learned Rabbi
Gamaliel—were incomprehensible to him, covered his eyes like a
scale or a film. The Spirit had touched his heart. The Spirit had
changed to faith his capacity for error and crime. The most urgent
task was to sow in the synagogues that he had been ravaging only
the day before. Later he would go up to Jerusalem to pray in the
temple where Jesus had taught. And meet Peter, the head of the apostles. The most urgent was not to seek Peter's authorization: it was
Christ who had appointed him as his messenger and servant.
     Peter Bruegel cherished the liberty which made Paul bow only
before God's own violence. Paul, whose mandate came not from men
but from the Spirit. He looked tenderly at the man, unhorsed on a
mountain trail, minute in the midst of the huge army. When he got
to his feet after his encounter with the lightning, with the fire of love,
his word would go out to the ends of the earth. To Peter, still wrapped
up in rituals, and perhaps more faithful to the old rites than the new,

he said: "You take the Jews. I'll take the rest of mankind, Barbarians, Romans, Greeks." And somewhere out there, Gaul and Flanders! The troops that thought they were marching for Cæsar were the unwitting workers of the borning Church. My God, do you expect me to believe that you always change horror to salvation, and stupidity to intelligence? Alba's army crossing the Alps in the sun and the cold are on their way to persecute the people of Flanders and to erect their pyres at the crossroads where the apostles of the dawning Church once set up the table of Emmaus.

3

Philip II is busy drafting the charter of the Escorial. It is said that his greatest pleasure is to be with the monks, when he lodges in the little house they are using as shelter until the construction is finished. He arrives unannounced, he would like to stay forever. He harries the workmen and the contractors, the *obrero mayor.* Already four years since the groundbreaking! And yet everyone is working *a toda furia.* Philip II wants to be known as the architect of the Eighth Wonder of the World: Juan Bautista de Toledo, disciple of Michelangelo, and Juan de Herrera are mere handymen in comparison. His first plan had been to build a victory temple in honor of Saint Lawrence, who had obtained his victory over the French at Saint Quentin. The death of the emperor gave him the idea of making the temple an imposing tomb for himself and his dynasty. But the white-stone colossus, which the Sierra desert will soon turn gray, is only the base of a vaster, higher spiritual edifice. From this funereal center of the realm will rise a dizzying construction of requiem masses for the repose of royal souls and for those in purgatory. In the rocky, brush-covered wilderness of Guadarrama, a permanent watch will be held for the deceased grandees of Spain, a perpetual vigil until the terrible dawning of Judgment Day. He will come personally each time he has a chance, for the major feasts and despite the atrocious Castilian winters, to pray and watch, like a monk, in his cell which looks onto the never ending mass, onto the host elevated in the priest's hands, onto the Holy Sacrament in its glorious monstrance. He will live as in his tomb. Living, he will attend masses like those that will be celebrated for the repose of his soul when he walks one day in the bitter purgatorial flames, for he knows that his sin is as great as his immense love for God.

Father José de Siguenza—the same who wrote so judiciously on *The Garden of Delights*—once remarked: "It was in the same year, and as good as the same month, that the first stone of the temple was laid and the Council of Trent ended having laid its last stone. In order to confirm and keep the holy dogmas and statutes, the Catholic king laid the first stone of a temple fortress in which they were to be kept and obeyed for all eternity." The king saw himself reflected in this immense work. A new David, fighting for the true Israel, the Church. A new Solomon, builder of this temple and, like Solomon, king of Jerusalem. Another Moses, engraving in stone in the rocky wilderness, before the eyes of an unfaithful rebellious people, God's Law, the Catholic Affirmation. This funereal court, where an emperor would one day lie, became the rival of the Vatican and Rome. While heretics were combatting the monastic life and leveling monasteries, the king of Spain was building his own colossal monastery. While the former were heaping insults on the mass, the latter was planting an infinite forest of masses. While they scorned the splendor of the ceremonies and the holiness of the images, he was canvassing Europe for thousands of painters, weavers, cartoonists, bronzesmiths, ironworkers, bell-casters, goldsmiths, embroiderers of liturgical ornaments, organ-builders; into this crucible he cast the gold of Spain and the New World. While they were throwing relics to the dogs and mocking the worship of saints, he was stocking his Ark of the Covenant with, alongside the arm of Saint Lawrence, the most holy of relics: those of Saint Justus and Saint Pastor, Saint Philip and Saint Bartholomew, Saint James the apostle of Spain, and many more. They arrived by the crateful from all Christendom. Processions traveled the breadth of Spain to lay them in their final reliquary.

A city appeared to be rising in the desert. Twenty cranes and twenty tread wheels lifted stones between the pillars of the church. Trains of wagons drawn by forty oxen slogged through deep mud or raised clouds of white dust, bringing blocks of granite, sculpted capitals, cornices, pilasters. The mountains rang with the ceaseless sound of axes and saws, felling and squaring whole forests of oak and pine. Was it while he was sitting on a rocky perch contemplating the activity that the king considered his plan to crush Flanders like a column of ants beneath his heel? Was it in the fire and the tears of his prayers that he came to the decision? The plundering of the churches gave him the excuse. There is no proof that he provoked it. But nothing we know of his mad criminal soul, of his fine political mind, excludes the idea. The massacre of Flanders is inseparable from the Escorial. He charged the duke of Alba with its execution. The duke set sail on the seventeenth of April, from Cartagena, for Sicily to rally and take command of the *tercios*.

The *tercios* were regiments of three types of fighting men: cavalry mounted on arab horses, armed with swords and lances; foot soldiers armed with pikes and halberds; foot soldiers armed with harquebuses and the latest in weaponry, the musket. They were all simple soldiers, although some were nobles and carried the title *don*, to which not even *hidalgos* are entitled. Each had one or more servants; most were accompanied by their concubine or their wife. Watching them parade by in Lorraine, Brantôme would say: "One would have thought the musketeers were princes, they were so haughty and walked with such arrogance and grace." A later historian would speak of the "horrible Babel of Spanish butchers and Italian sodomites," armies straight from hell. The troops were never garrisoned in Spain; they drilled and bided their time in Sicily and Sardinia, Lombardy, Naples. All the soldiers dressed more or less alike: shirt and doublet, breeches and stockings, shoes, jacket or tunic—the many colors of the costume being a matter of taste or opportunity—and the profusion of plumed hats, ruffs, and collars, purple and green belts, silk and satin sashes over breastplates. They were well fed, and they supplemented their pay by plunder from the towns. If they were unhappy with their officers or their pay was late, they would revolt and immediately choose their own leader. The *tercios* claimed to be descended from the *almugavaros*, those fourteenth-century Catalan soldiers who formed a nomadic military republic and took over a Greek duchy. They were fanatical about their honor. They were reputed to be invincible.

When Europe saw the ten thousand men on the march, she trembled, then bristled. Alba crossed the Alps: Geneva thought Spain had come to destroy the city and prepared to fight. The army gave the town a wide berth. Then Dole and Besançon feared plunder. The army marched away toward Luxembourg. The same terror. Wherever they stopped, the population was forced to provide food and lodging. For countries that had just come through hard times, Alba left famine in his wake. Small villages were submerged by the monstrous flow of armed men. Old terrors revived. The misery was overwhelming. Attics and barns were emptied, the cattle devoured, and sometimes the house burned down, by carelessness or out of spite. The whole country was at the service of these people. Three months before the arrival of the first riders, they collected saltpeter, made powder and fuses and shot, they forged pike irons, built bridges, repaired roads, imported morions and breastplates from Germany. Alba recruited as he went. In the end, perhaps some forty thousand soldiers, together with their wives and valets, were advancing on the Low Countries.

A month yet, a week, before the plague arrived! Brederode had consolidated the ramparts of Vianen and raised an army. The roads teemed with a frightened population fleeing to Germany, England, carrying all they could load onto carts, heavy hearted. Philip Marnix, still in mourning for his brother, stayed to comfort and help the poor people of Emden. Egmont set out to meet Alba. Everyone had seen how he had restored order to Valenciennes, the Spanish way, along with the sinister Noircames. Now he was in Tienen, near Brussels, where the army had stopped. Was it to reciprocate the courtesy the duke had shown him when he was approaching Madrid? Did he feel obliged to greet the king's envoy? Was he hoping to soften the blow? He acted as though he had forgotten what he had suffered on his return from his embassy.

The duke and the count were old acquaintances. Together they had served the emperor. They were with him at the battle of Tunis. Was Egmont aware of Alba's jealousy and hatred? They were now within view of each other.

"Here is my first heretic," said Alba. He took him affectionately by the arm and laid a hand on his shoulder. "At my age, Count, you should have spared me the journey!"

Egmont presented him with several magnificent horses. They crossed the field. Fat drops of rain from a summer storm drummed on the tents, glistened on the metal of arms and canon. The soldiers showed the Flemish lord so little respect that they neither stepped out of his way nor doffed their hats, but stared coldly: some even hissed in a stage whisper "Luther!" or "Traitor!" Beneath the lilac-colored sky, in the pastures and along the woods, herds meandered as they always had.

On the twenty-second of August, in the morning, the duke of Alba entered Brussels.

15

THE PARABLE OF THE
BLIND MEN

1

Sometimes, in fall or winter as the day was ending, Bruegel liked to leave the peaceful house, wander abroad and watch the first fires of evening come alive. Beyond the rooftops, he would let his gaze dwell on the plain, a cart rumbling along the gray road, the smoke rising over villages, the magpies and ravens flying from tree to tree. He could not not think of the hill behind him, that Golgotha with its instruments of torture, like a black sun hanging over the world. He would stand motionless in the silence and the descending shadows. He was dressed warmly, a cap on his head, like a woodsman in the snow. Then he would go back down, taking the friendliest streets, cutting through alleys, small squares. He liked that time of day the French call *entre chien et loup,* the uncertain light, a moment that might be called between ash and ember. He had become a simple passerby, walking in the shadows, and whose breath mingled with the fog of the cold season. He told himself he was traveling his road on earth and that it led, at this precise moment, to this narrow street in Brussels, which passed in front of this particular glowing bakery or that butcher's shop with its great quartered carcasses, in front of this clock shop or that cloth merchant. How many steps were left him here below? He believed he would never again leave Brussels for any length of time. His work and his home had become his life. The only trips he would take now would be his strolls through the streets, his walks in the snow, or in the summertime, never venturing far from the city walls. Even visits from friends had become rare. He wanted to focus more closely on his work, live in the light of Mary and Peter and the other child that was coming. As he delved into the back streets of the city, the thought of his paintings upstairs in the attic and of the house, where Mary was teaching Peter to read, kept him company. Doorways of small pubs opened to the coming evening. He turned into a familiar tavern and was cheered by the babble of voices, this unexpected light in the heart of the falling night. How good it feels to step into the din or the silence, the warmth, the noise of men drinking. You can sit alone and dream. But you can also meet people. People you know, and others. There are travelers. There are local people and neighbors. Conversation flows between the tables. Sometimes there are painters. The names of regular customers are carved on the backrests. Did Bruegel carve his name in one of these taverns? Or did he prefer just to pass through, wherever it was? Did people recognize him when he came down the short flight of steps that led to the long tables in the vaulted room? Did they come up to have a word? Did they know he was a painter? He listened to the sounds, the words. He liked this slower pace, the subterranean lighting, the crowded seating, for lack of space, but no one minded. It was like a shared wake.

The Spanish did not frequent the taverns. Not that they would be in any danger. Here people were not accustomed to slitting throats in cabarets. War is war, and a party is a party. And the tavern was a kind of party, practically a family gathering. People went for the friendly atmosphere, the good cheer, to be together, to rub elbows, and to drink in good company. They went to talk about how things were going and to remember how things used to be, back when they were young. They went to laugh and joke about trivial things. How could the Spanish understand any of that? What business could they have there? It was already enough that their patrols pounded through our streets at all hours of the day and night. No. It was not wariness that kept the Spaniards away. They could have come in well-armed watchful groups. But as soon as they opened the door, they felt like outsiders, and they would promptly leave.

The Chambers of Rhetoric were no longer allowed to meet. Spain found their laughter intolerable, and their secret meetings smacked of revolt. The puppet theaters remained open. But for how long? The Church had never had much patience with these dolls. And it had happened that puppeteers suspected of witchcraft or convicted of sacrilegious remarks were burned at the stake. Bruegel had always enjoyed descending into the tavern cellars with their little square that looked onto the world of dreams, the window onto a world the colors of childhood. Could he formulate what his painting, his vision owed to those representations of universal Death, or the Passion? He would never tire of the *Temptations of Saint Anthony* or *The Time Death nearly Died* or *Duvelor, the Devil Grown Old*. It was time for the show. Everyone was downstairs. They could still hear the muffled noise of the drinkers above, who preferred their game of cards or their melancholy. In the crowded puppet cellar, where people were seated on benches and barrels along the wall green with saltpeter or standing at the back of the room, the lanterns and candles had been doused, except those lighting the little theater. All eyes were on that light and on the painted wooden figures. They called to us, we answered back. And they did not always have the last word. Sometimes they would get mad and run away and hide, refuse to come out. It was all part of the fun. Since the Spanish had come to town, with their frightening stupidity and savagery, new figures had appeared in the magic window, morions on their heads, painted like matamores, or wearing feather-spattered hats. An old man with a long, white beard, Witte de Blanc, but dressed all in black, led the devils with the funny speech. Here everything could be said, among friends, in the secret and the light of these cellars, things that otherwise must not be uttered, must be swallowed down. Such games keep up morale. They would leave. Even the birds of Flanders and Kempen would feel the difference, their songs would be gayer, freer; even the daisies in the pastures would feel easier, and the bushes gladder in the wind. The smoke would rise with a lighter heart from the chimneys to the clouds. There would be no more black smoke from burning pyres, where our loved ones shriek in pain.

Together we would dream. One word leads to another. A joke, a shout from somewhere in the audience, and the story is off to a new start. It is like dreaming with your eyes open. But some things can only be suggested. The pleasure is all the keener. Everyone can swear before the judge that nothing was said, nothing was heard that might possibly give offense. Here is where the stories are invented and passed on that have been the weapon of the oppressed since pharaoh's day.

But they did not arm themselves with dreams and laughter alone. Beneath the puppet cellars no doubt lay other caves, and those long tunnels where they could meet and for once speak their mind. Hardly anyone could descend the short flight to the puppet theater without a glance at the iron door at the far end of the room, at the wooden trap doors that rang hollow under foot and which were used not only as a passage for barrels.

Everyone dreamed about those tunnels, the object of tales and chronicles and which were once only the matter of children's reveries, when they went hunting for skeletons or treasure. Educated people insisted that it was the Gauls who had first dug mile after mile of underground passages between their temples, and that the Romans had enlarged and reinforced the galleries as only they knew how. Now the labyrinth was used as a hiding place and a conspirators' camp. All passages met beneath Brussels, under the very spot where Alba had established his quarters. The entrance was hidden deep in the Forêt de Soignes. A long passage tunneled under roots and rocks and into Germany; another led to the English ships. Through this tunnel passed weapons, books, and money. In these caves were produced pamphlets, Bibles, gunpowder, and harquebuses.

2

The canvas is painted in tempera and bears the Gothic inscription:

> Om dat de Werelt is soe ongetru
> Daer om gha ic in den ru.

The picture is round, like the Proverbs that Bruegel had painted ten years earlier—round like the world. Hood pulled low, hands folded beneath his monkish cloak, an old man utters the bitter words:

> For that the world is so untrue
> Therefore I go about in rue.

His wispy gray beard reaches to his chest. Some four-pointed nails lie in his path: a booby-trap. Behind him, ensconced in the glass globe that represents the world, a thief cuts away at his red, heart-shaped purse. Is it in this purse that he has stashed his heart, and his treasure, this wise man fleeing the world? The countryside is bleak. Near a windmill, a few scattered sheep graze while their shepherd leans stiffly on his staff: the parable, if parable this is, is no longer any more than a far-off voice, lost in time. The hermit resembles the large mourners who bear the death bed of the dukes of Burgundy. What is the meaning of this allegory? And why the reversion to the old manner? Could it be that the power of imagination has failed him for the first time? Cock once published a print by Martin van Heemskerck, inspired perhaps from a page of Erasmus where Folly exclaims: "They endow me with so many shapes and forms, and every day invent so many more that a thousand Democritus would not suffice to mock their foolish ways; and these thousand Democritus, did they exist, might well give a new Democritus something else to mock." On either side of the globe, topped with a cross and draped in a fool's cloak, Democritus was laughing and Heraclitus, crying. The river into which no man steps twice flowed through the land. Perhaps Bruegel has prepared Democritus another canvas. The philosopher's tears and mockery, hung on facing walls, would have held a dialogue. Or does he no longer have the heart to portray the man who laughs at the woes of the world and its folly?

The woes of the world and its folly, here they are, as delicately brushed as a miniature, on a small wood panel. A ballet of five cripples, dragging themselves about on their crutches, stumps, and splints. A courtyard filled with legless beggars, so hideously deformed that we dare not look at their pitiful stumps and imbecile faces, but avert our eyes and toss a coin. These are the Beggars! These are the Cripples! Who could see these toadlike clowns as human beings? Who could look without revulsion on the twisted mouth or the stammering gaze? This is what huddles, growling like dangerous dogs under the stairs of the rich, and holds out remnants of hands at the church door, as we leave with pure hearts, not wanting to know that, if God so wished, we could be in their slimy, stinking place. These are the Poor! The mutilated hand that tugs, pleading, at our dress. Lazarus at the door of the rich man, who never saw him. They hop and stumble on their wooden limbs. They wear foxtails, the leper's mark, and paper mitres, for these wretched creatures have their own— mock—bishop. One of them wears a costume sewn with bells, to give people a chance to make their escape. Bruegel has already painted these figures, when he was composing the *Battle of Carnival and Lent*. He placed them in the procession of the Monday after Epiphany. This time they are the central figures. Where is it set? There are brick walls in the background, church walls perhaps? And there is an archway opening onto a fine-leafed garden. Here unwholesome creatures groveling in the mud; there a garden of delights, springlike peace, which they are forbidden. The back of the panel carries the inscription: *Kruepelen, hooch, dat u nering betern moeg*, which means: "Cripple, may it go better with you!" This is not a piece of derision, but the formula that goes with the giving of alms. It could have read: Look at yourselves, Children of Adam, fallen and woebegone, crippled, forlorn, and fated to die since the day you lost the Garden sublime! Look at yourselves! Those crippled limbs are less unsightly than your hearts. Look at yourselves! You say to yourselves: I am rich, I have everything I desire, I want for nothing; and you do not know that you are unhappy, and wretched, and naked, and blind!" But Bruegel painted the stumps and the grimaces in minute detail, like the bricks and the leaves, thinking of all those other unhappy creatures teeming in the depths of the city and on the outskirts of villages. How dare they take up their Beggar banner while this real band of beggars stares up with wounds for eyes? He thought of the spring at Siloh, of the blind man who had been waiting for years by the miraculous pool, with no hope of being the first to enter, when the waters boiled, and to step out healed. Christ came and raised him to his feet. The Gospels are full of cripples and madmen that God sets free from their ills. But what of the others, all those who were not there at the right time, when Jesus passed, and the multitude of those who would be born later, more numerous than the stars in the sky, who would take their place in the grandstands of the centuries. Even the apostles felt their hearts quail when they leaned over and peered into the black hole of life. "What about him," they asked the Master. "Is he like that because of his sins or because of those of his parents?"

"Neither because of his sins nor those of his parents. But so that the Glory of God might be shown." He, too, was healed. But what about the others, scooting around on their wooden runners and who, like Job, curse the day they were born?

Now where does this figure on the edge of the stream come from? He is pointing to a birdnester in the crotch of a tree, who has just lost his hat. But he does not see that he himself is about to slip and fall into the water. Do not seek the proverb. It is an incident from my childhood. I look back and see the low farm in the distance, and the horse, dreaming, the cart at rest, its arms raised. I can see that pale afternoon sky, the birches, the grass that grows greener beneath the willows; I can hear the rustle of birds chasing through the trees, the whispering of the stream beneath the clumps of grass and the boughs. I can see the pond, the clog-prints in the mud, and the frogs on the stump, a bald, bent willow. I was the boy at play with a treasure of eggs and a terror of birds cupped in his hand. Children cannot imagine pain. Only much later do we measure the friendship of a blackbird perched on our shoulder. And I can see that large, slightly simple boy about to tumble into the stream. Is he still alive? Is he in the barn milking at this very moment? Is he in the woods, with the others, making ready to fight the Spanish? Whenever I think back on my childhood, I see it as an island.

3

The Cripples is a very small painting. Was this because Bruegel had left his workshop? And if he was working on canvas, was it because canvases are easier to carry than wood panels? If Bruegel absented himself from Brussels, in 1568, where did he go? Antwerp, perhaps. He was looking for a ship that would accept him and his family, on the fateful day, and take him to England or Germany. Lucas van

Heere (who used the anagram of his name to make *Schaede leere u,*
"You learn from your sorrows") had taken refuge in London. Other
painters were planning to leave the country—Lucas and Martin
Valckenborgh, Hans Bol, David Vinckeboons, Hoogenbergh, who
published Bruegel's sailing ships and drew maps for Ortelius. A
steady traffic of messages and books flowed between Antwerp and
Amsterdam. Theological pamphlets printed by the Flemish churches
of London were seized aboard English merchantmen or found in
bales of merchandise. Ortelius received many émigrés, who were returning on a mission. I can see Bruegel at the home of his old friend.
The inscription on the back of *The Cripples* is reminiscent of Ortelius.
I can see him surrounded by the maps and books, as of old. One is
making calculations and drawing, the other paints. A word now and
then between the two rooms. The sound of the wind against the
pane. When he leaves, Bruegel presents Ortelius with the painting he
has done. It is an allegory of Charity. The woman carrying a bowl
who passes between the garden and the crippled men and whom we
scarcely notice, is Charity; she is begging in their stead. Charity will
never cease. Bruegel has no doubt left not to prepare his own escape,
but that of those who know, or fear, they are under suspicion. If the
Familia Caritatis still survives under Alba's tyranny, what better task
than to slight the executioner of his victims, to hide the hunted, collect money for those unable to pay their way?

4

He rose without waking Mary. He dressed as though he were going
out. Dawn was breaking. From the window he saw the sky, still almost black. He went into his workshop. Josse was there, waiting for
him. He was not surprised. "Dress warm," Josse told him. "We have
a long road ahead." He took down a traveling cape and a broad-
brimmed hat. It crossed his mind that he was leaving his house forever, and that the time had come to melt away. He looked at the
rough paintings standing in the shadows. There was no time left to
finish them. He thought of waking Mary, of leaving her a note, so
that she would not worry. But Josse was already on his way. He
closed the door softly behind them. Two horses were waiting. They
left by familiar streets. The sentinel on the walls let them by without
asking their names. They passed. They saw the soldiers sleeping or
squatting around a fire, their legs thrown over their weapons, their
elbow resting on their helmet. "It is going to be hard for you, where
we are going," Josse said. Day was breaking cold and gray. The horses

made their way through the brush. The men rode in silence. At times all that could be seen in the distance was a farmer walking in the mist or standing in his doorway holding a pail. The ride was long. Now he recognized the woods near his childhood village. He knew where Josse was taking him and his heart sank. This was the village where his mother lived—he corrected himself: the village where my mother used to live. She had not wanted to leave her home to come to live in Brussels. She had preferred to continue her silent life, her peasant life, her cloistered life in the peace of the trees. He dismounted and looked over the hedge for a glimpse of her blue apron. He caught sight of his mother in a cluster of neighbor women. He had come to the place in the road where the village hove into sight. But what he saw was like a black hole. He saw the charred trees, the burned fields and the skeletons of houses. The church itself had been partly destroyed. He heard Josse telling him what the Spanish had done. They had made the women come out and stand in the square. They had set fire to the houses. They had run the men through with their pikes. They had tied the women to trees, knocked them unconscious and burned them. All of them. And the ashes swirled about the square in the wind, and some scraps of blue cloth. Did he have the strength to pray beneath this wretched, desolate sky. They mounted once more and rode away.

5

They are taking shape on the canvas that is still nearly blank. They are well to the fore. Can they feel us looking at them? They raise their faces to the sky as though they could see. There are five of them. Each with his hand on the shoulder of the next, as in a children's game. The last one looks unconcerned, as though he were walking in his sleep. One hand firmly grasps a staff with which he taps the ground; the other clings to a shorter stick held by the man in front. The latter wears a green hat, and a drinking cup hangs from his belt; a white bead necklace with a crucifix stands out against his dark red shirt. His face is screwed up in a worried look because his hand has slipped from the next man's shoulder. The man in front of him is hanging on, mouth agape, to the shoulder of the third man, in an attempt to retrieve him. His own blank-eyed guide has stumbled and, because he has not let go the stick held by yet another, is about to follow him into the ditch. The one who is falling looks at us with unseeing eyes. In another moment he will have joined his colleague, prostrate in the ditch, his hurdy-gurdy already half submerged in the mud. This miserable procession is painted in delicate tones: the grays, greens, blues, reds of their cloaks and hats; the white of their headgear and stockings; the yellow or purple of a sleeve all harmonize against a background of fine leaves and soft-looking clay. Inside the tranquil houses live those who have never known what it is to go thus in darkness. A church with a green spire and pink-tiled roof stands in the background.

Christ walked on water and cured crowds of their ills. The Pharisees and scribes, who had come from Jerusalem, were scandalized by what they saw and heard. Jesus' disciples did not wash their hands before sitting down to eat, and he himself said things that made no sense at all, like: "What goes into the mouth does not make a man unclean; it is what comes out of the mouth that makes him unclean." When his disciples told him of their indignation, Christ simply said: "Let them be, they are blind men leading blind men; if a blind man leads another blind man, they will both fall into the ditch." And Bruegel heard other things Christ had said: "The eye is the lamp of the body. If your eye is in darkness, your whole body is in darkness." He was thinking of the lamp that must not be hidden under a bushel. He thought of the Wise Virgins, with their lighted lamps, and the Foolish Virgins, whose lamps had gone out and who stayed outside in the dark while the souls of the faithful feasted in the nuptial light, with the Bridegroom, shining like the sun. He thought of Christ transfigured on the mountainside, of his robe whiter than snow, of his face more blinding than the sun. What is the good news but the celebration of the Light and its promise?

The Blind Men, with their gaping faces and bodies of darkness appeared in his life, in his vision. They did not come from the parable. They were not even a recollection of one of Cornelius Massys's prints that he had often seen: four blind men chained together by their hands, one after the other tumbling into a muddy ditch. They did not come from one of the panels of his Flemish *Proverbs*. They did not come from a childhood memory. Or rather, they came from the whole of his memory. But their real source was an anxiety peculiar to man, and to the painter. If he were to lose his sight, what would he be then? Even as he took pleasure in painting the blind men's cloaks and capes, he was hounded by the anxiety of losing his sight. He was gripped by the anxiety of darkness and death. He was not even thinking of those who claimed to come from Christ and who misled the people, when they did not actually torture them. For some time he had known that everyone must listen to his own inner voice; go by his inner light. But sometimes the voice failed, and sometimes one stumbled in the dark. Faith walks with eyes open in the dark, in spite of the dark. Thomas saw, he touched the body of the risen Christ: that is not faith. We walk in the dark night of time, wretched and doubting. We will slip in the mud and fall into the ditch. Can you swear that your eyes will live again at the bottom of the pit, that they will drink in the light?

Bruegel wonders these things, as his second son is being baptized. He watches the child open two blue eyes on the world, bright periwinkles in the dark church. A candle lights the book of questions and answers. His second son's name is John. "There was a man sent by God. His name was John. He came as a witness, to bear witness to the light so that everyone might believe through him. He was not the light, but he came to bear witness to the light. That was the true light, that enlightens all men that come into this world."

16

THE COUNCIL OF BLOOD

Alba quartered the Neapolitan *tercio* at Ghent; the Lombard *tercio* at Liege; the *tercio* from Cerdagne in the province of Hainaut; the Franche-Comté cavalry, near Maestricht. He kept the Sicilian *tercio* with him and occupied the Culemberg mansion, where the Beggars' Banquet had been held. The whole country was in his grip. He showed the regent letters from the king:

The campaign began with the men committing abominable and loathsome deeds, to the constant sound of timbrils; let us therefore make the Duke of Alba our general, representing ourself with all appropriate and customary preeminence, jurisdiction, authority and power, to our captains general. The aforementioned Duke alone will have complete authority to command and to carry out all he deems fit for our service, including punishment, by death, by confiscation of belongings and by all other means, of those whom he finds guilty of the crime of rebellion.

Another letter adds: "Our Sister the Duchess is requested to obey all orders from the Duke of Alba as though it were ourself." That evening Margaret wrote to Philip, presenting her resignation and requesting permission to return to Parma. She would leave Brussels in December.

The Council of Troubles set up by the duke would never be called anything but the Council of Blood by the people. Its members were not jurists because, as the duke said to the king, "Those men of law never hand down a sentence unless they have proof." The council conducted the trials, but the duke alone signed the sentences. If perchance the sentence was less than death, the duke would call a retrial. All the signatories of the Compromise of the Nobility were guilty of lèse-majesté. All were sentenced to death: preachers and members of the consistory, rebels and iconoclasts alike. The only question was how they should die. If he recanted, the condemned man might be spared the rope or the stake. Simply returning to the

Catholic Church saved no one from beheading, which, together with hanging, was the most common form of execution. Anabaptists were burned at the stake. Rarely drawn and quartered. How many victims? Over three thousand in the first months. Fugitives were formally banished.

It was a council of darkness and thuggery. Some enjoyed the cellar tortures and spent the better part of their time feasting their eyes on blood and their ears on victims' screams. Others were no more than obsequious servants, anxious to begin the session on time and to incur no displeasure. Alba's confidential agent was one Vargas, born in Spain, who had left the country after having raped a little girl who was his ward. His devotion had won him clemency. He spoke neither French nor Flemish and had succeeded in having the sentences pronounced in Latin; but he spoke a sort of dog Latin: "Non curamus vestros privilegios" was one of his favorite expressions. His salary was twice that of the rest, sixteen écus a day, paid out of the monies confiscated. But how much did the killers make on the side, from robbery and extortion?

A council that flew in the face of all law, to those who protested against the tyranny and opposed the violation of provincial rights, Alba replied that the crime of lèse-majesté revoked all privileges and customs, and that to dwell on such details would be detrimental to royal sovereignty. The knights of the Golden Fleece were amenable only to the members of the order: but he forbade them to meet, "even to recite the Credo."

The silverware and jewelry, the tapestries and carpets, the paintings, gold and silver of the condemned men and banished victims piled up by the cartload at the Culemberg mansion. The Egmont silver alone filled sixteen chests. The Orange estates were sequestered, and the arsenals and armories of the castles stripped bare, seven barges of pikes and harquebuses, gunpowder, cannonballs, and cannon were stocked in Ghent to be used against the people.

What a marvelous machine! Catholic fanaticism, *raison d'Etat,* and zealous stewardship, together with a taste for personal profit encouraged severity. A death penalty, a banishment meant an inheritance. One suspect burning at the stake meant so much for Alba's coffers and reimbursed the court its costs. A property confiscated paid a regiment, or an officer. What with the plunder, the occupying forces could be financed as long as was needed. What is more, they were fed and housed by the local population.

It was forbidden for burghers, craftsmen and the laboring classes to "take leave and depart alone or with their families, in secret or openly, or to transport by water or by land their furnishings, belongings or merchandise, on pain of being held guilty or suspect of rebellion, and prosecuted, and those belongings being loaded for transport confiscated; boatmen or carters not denouncing emigrants would be considered suspect and as such punished by the confiscation of their boats, carts, and horses." Hardly had the decree been proclaimed than ten burghers from Tournai were arrested on the road, stripped, and returned naked to their homes. Inhabitants of Antwerp were flogged for hiding packages, or merchandise, or clothing bound for England. "Para que cada uno piense que a la noche o a la manana se le puede caer la casa encima," the duke wrote to Madrid: "Day and night every man must live in fear that his roof will fall in on him." A terror that would make the general amnesty all the sweeter, one day, when the whole uprising was over.

The Nassau mansion was searched for weeks. The walls were torn apart, the staircase dismantled in search of caches—secret papers or jewelry. Alba was looking for the pictures he knew William owned, and above all Bosch's *Garden of Delights.* For his master. They tortured Peter Col, the caretaker, to make him betray the prince as well as reveal where the strong-boxes were hidden. He was suspected of having buried the best set of silver in the garden. He refused to talk. In the end, a contingent sounding the walls discovered the triptych. Alba went down, torch in hand, to look at it, as though exhuming a corpse. A few close members of his entourage helped him arrest the work of art, kidnap a wonder from Flanders. Then the painting left for the Escorial.

Egmont had not fled the country. How could he have believed Alba? Hoorn retreated to his castle in Weerdt. He refused to come to Brussels, to participate in this Spanish free-for-all. Alba told his secretary: "I regret that the king did not reward your master fittingly. Great princes are ofttimes slow to recognize a man's worth. If I chance to see the count, I shall prove to him my good will. I am hurt by the nobles' lack of confidence in me. Am I not the friend and servant of all?" Hoorn finally relented. He was hoping for the vice-royalty of Naples. He came to Brussels. Ferdinand of Toledo, Alba's illegitimate son and grand prior of the Order of Saint John, invited him to dinner, with Egmont, their secretaries, Backerzeel and van Laloo, and the burgomaster of Antwerp, van Straelen. At around three o'clock, the duke sent his trumpets to entertain the guests. Sometime later, he asked that the two counts pay him a visit: he wanted their opinion on the plans for the future citadel of Antwerp. Was it then that Alba's son understood the role his father had him play? Was he stricken with shame and remorse? That is something the Spanish sense of honor cannot endure. He wanted to spare his father that disgrace. He saw Egmont, unsuspecting, raise a glass of wine to his lips. He murmured: "Sire Count, saddle the best horse in the stable and flee! I swear that your life is in danger." Egmont rose. He thought back to the moment when Alba had draped his arm around his shoulder as they made their way through the throng of threatening soldiers; once again he felt the same flood of panic. He withdrew into the next room to think and to consult Noircames, his friend. But Noircames had just been named Egmont's judge, when the time came: that was the price for his own life. If the count escaped, what would become of him? He had promised the duke he would condemn him. He laughed, making fun of Egmont's concern. Ferdinand de Toledo's counsel was only a trick to put him to the test: to run away would show his lack of trust and establish him as an enemy. He escorted him back to the banquet table. An hour later, Egmont stepped into the ducal apartments. The engineer unrolled the parchment with the plans of the castle and spread it on the table. Egmont reproached himself for having doubted his host. They examined the drawings. Then Alba withdrew. Egmont prepared to leave the room. At that moment, Sancho de Avila stepped up, placed him under arrest and relieved him of his arms. Hoorn was seized moments later. The secretaries, who would be tortured and made to talk, were arrested at the inn. Van Straelen was incarcerated with Egmont and Hoorn at the citadel in Ghent. Each man was isolated in a blacked-out cell lit by a single candle. They no longer knew how many days they had been held in these conditions. Nothing could be heard through the thick walls that enclosed them. Their sleep was haunted by the fear of death. They woke and saw the walls of their tomb. Twice a night, at the changing of the guard, a captain carrying a torch came to their bedside and peered into their face. Alba's Spain had a genius for policing and drama; a genius for torture and terror.

The trial of Hoorn and Egmont was a lengthy affair. Was Alba hoping that the king would show clemency? They were accused of fomenting rebellion and of treason. Then Louis of Nassau attacked, and his victory over the Spanish at Heiligeslee rang down the sentence. The execution was set for Sunday, the fifth of June, the Feast of Pentecost. The black-draped scaffold was erected in the Grand-Place of Brussels. The square and the adjacent streets were packed with soldiers bristling with their pikes and harquebuses. Egmont and Hoorn were not told until the eve of the day they were to die. There were no farewells. The morning passed, and no one came to their door. Egmont asked that they have done with it. The crowd wept silently as they passed. The facades and roofs reflected the June sky. Egmont advanced, pale but steady; he did not slack his pace. Did he still hope for a royal pardon, or rather for royal justice, and that this whole frightful ceremony was another ruse to put him to the test? Or did he realize what kind of mad cunning animal he had so faithfully tried to serve. He walked with the courage he had always shown in the face of death. He had dressed, as he did for ceremonial occasions, in a crimson damask jacket and black cloak trimmed in gold braid, black taffeta breeches and bronze-colored chamois leggings; his black taffeta hat waved with black and white plumes; the Golden Fleece glittered on his chest. He passed between the ranks assembled as for battle, their banners flying. He saluted and bid farewell to the captains and soldiers, and many wept. At last he saw the scaffold and the chopping block, and the priest holding the cross. He walked to the executioner and knelt. Moments later, Hoorn, who had reached the top of the steps, saw spread on the planks a black velvet cloth spattered with blood. He was heard to murmur: "My friend, is that you, then, lying there?" They had already laid hold of him. For two hours the heads of Egmont and Hoorn lay on view in copper basins. Egmont's body was taken to the convent of Saint Clair. Weeping crowds thronged to kiss the coffin. That night, the duke had the heads placed in ebony boxes, and a heavily guarded carriage set out for Madrid.

The duke watched the execution from the window of one of the houses on the Grand-Place. He stood well back. No one saw him. He was rarely seen. When he went from Brussels to Antwerp, when he traveled from one garrison to another, and even when he crossed Brussels, a curtain of pikes and harquebuses separated him from the others on the road. He was fifty-nine. His body was tall and spare; his face was hard and yellow; his beard thin and gray. He was four when his father had died at the hands of the Moors. From childhood, his grandfather had trained him for war. He was clever at masking with polite words and manners the fits of rage that would come over him. Close-mouthed, inflexible, proud. His loyalty to the king outweighed his submission to the pope, whom he fought upon occasion. He burned with hatred for the Flemish people, and their country. Was he a cruel man? He was a loyal soldier: ordered to crucify, crucify he would. Personally he might have preferred moderation.

"The people are so good natured," he wrote to the king, "that Your Majesty's clemency will make them as willing in the future to accept obedience as today they are loath. The executions have left their minds so terrified that they think this bloody rule will last forever. As long as your subjects live with this idea, they will never love the King." When the countess of Egmont was flinging herself upon altars and doors, dishevelled and barefoot, pleading for her husband's life, the duke did not turn a hair. Duty forbade it. But he sent a letter to the king with the post that carried the ebony boxes: "I have the greatest compassion for the countess of Egmont and her children. I beseech Your Majesty to grant them a stipend that will enable them to eat. I do not know how she will dine this evening, such is her isolation and poverty. I believe there is nothing sadder on the face of the earth." And as the king had responded that he had recommended the family to God and ordered prayers to be said throughout Spain, the duke continued: "The Countess would starve to death together with her children were I not to give her a small sum of money." Pity, perhaps. But once he received his orders, he carried them out. And the orders were to stamp out rebellion, even if it meant crushing every sign of life in the Low Countries; if it meant destroying every last village. One of the decrees concerning suspects (but who was not suspect in the eyes of the maddened Spaniard) read: "It must be ascertained with all possible dispatch who and where they are; and the first to be found, be they man or woman, hanged and choked to death forthwith, and their houses destroyed and pulled down, in order by this fervid demonstration to strike terror into their hearts and make them docile, and to keep them from carrying on their evil business."

He made no pretense of punishing heresy, only disorder and insurrection. But there are those who think that it is better to destroy a kingdom by preserving it for God and the king, through war, than to keep it intact, through peace, for the devil and his heretic disciples. Who did he see when he looked in the mirror that morning, as he prepared to preside over the council? Did he see an aging man, detained far from his country, far from Toledo, far from his orange trees and the mansions along the Tage, by his duty to Spain and to God? Did he see himself as an angel of death, the exterminating angel? The incarnation of terror? Or did he even recognize his own face?

Alba forced the people of Brussels to quarter as many as six Spaniards in a single house. These soldiers and officers, billeted out to families and behaving as though they were the masters, were so many ears and eyes in the service of the king. It was unwise to speak openly, and often, even when they were alone in the room, no one spoke at all: next door the Spaniard was listening. There was no more visiting back and forth between friends. The Spanish night penetrated the very heart of people's homes. The only speech was an occasional glance. The archives have preserved a document dispensing "maestereen van Pieter Bruegel" from quartering soldiers. Did this refer to the painter or to a doctor of the same name? If he was excused from lodging soldiers, was it because the city wanted to spare his work and his talent? Bruegel's health had suddenly begun to fail. He was subject to spells of fatigue and fainting. One day, as he was working, he had vomited blood. Was this why the Brussels aldermen had placed Bruegel's household under their protection?

That autumn, William of Orange, having at last put together an army, crossed into the Low Countries. Three of the divisions, the northern, central, and southern armies, were defeated in rapid succession. When he encountered the duke of Alba, who had fresh troops, he was no longer capable of winning. His army numbered no fewer than the adversary, but it was a ragtag company of mercenaries who were only as loyal as their last pay and who helped themselves from farms, castles, and churches. Alba confronted this band with his self-assured, faultlessly disciplined troops. Finally, in the face of an enemy that harassed him but refused to fight, William was forced to retreat. He was bankrupt. Winter had set in. William's famished army withdrew to the French border, pillaging as they went. The peasants refused all aid and set upon stragglers with pitchforks and sticks. Alba's cavalry, fresh and well fed, harried William's stumbling, starving men. When William reached Strasbourg, on the first of January 1569, he had not eaten for several days. Feverish and ill, he could no longer stay on his horse. His mercenary commanders forced his door and threatened to kill him if they were not paid. He sold his last cannons to the aldermen, left his baggage, and crossed the Rhine that night on a darkened barge.

Alba wrote to the king that the prince of Orange was now a dead man. Henceforth the Low Countries could be governed by even a sheriff. The duke's entourage saw him as "the true instrument chosen by God to chastise those devils." Earlier the pope had urged moderation on the king, but the executions of June delighted him. In Rome he celebrated the victory over Louis of Nassau at Jemmingen with processions and receptions. He had offered to make a financial contribution to the upkeep of the soldiers and the keeping of the faith. The nuncio declared the duke of Alba the Sword of God. Spain's final victory filled Pius V with joy. It was the custom of the sovereign pontiff at Christmas to bless a hat and a sword and to send them to one of the illustrious princes of Christendom: the sword as a sign of temporal power in the service of Christ; the hat as a sign of the protection Christ granted those who fought for him. Paul III had granted Philip II these honors in 1549, when he came to Brussels, carrying a brief exhorting him to destroy heresy. Pius V bestowed the same honors on the duke. Piously, Alba strapped on the tuck by its diamond-studded belt; he donned the gray velvet hat trimmed in ermine and set with pearls. Later, in the citadel in Antwerp, on an impressive pedestal he erected a statue cast from the Silent's canons representing himself quelling Rebellion and Heresy. One side of the monument bore a pompous Latin inscription. The other showed Dawn—*alba* in Spanish—hunting nocturnal beasts and thieves. The insult, the vanity, the lie had to be endured. Every day the lesson had to be learned, in one's flesh: one does not have to succeed in order to persevere, nor hope to undertake. One had to learn to hope against all hope.

17

JONAH

Now when he takes the Book in his hands, they sometimes tremble. "I'm getting old," he thinks. But he does not believe it. He is not yet fifty. How old was Pieter van Aalst when he died? Not fifty either. When he looks in the mirror, he is surprised to see his face suddenly hollow cheeked and pale, the streaks of white in his gray hair, his beard gone nearly white. The Mechelen fishermen's guild has commissioned a Jonah. How old was Jonah when God sent him to Nineveh? (Nineveh—you might as well say Babylon and Babel, since Nimrod ruled them, too.) He was probably no longer young. On his straw-bottomed chair, drawn up to the fire as soon as fall set in, listening for the wind along the roof and glad not to have to be outdoors, he was starting to show his age. He was beginning to feel the rain and the winter in his shoulder. The last years of life can be sweet. And now God wants him to go to Nineveh.

Bruegel sketches Jonah thrown up on the wet sand, catching his breath and enjoying the cool breeze on his back before setting out. He is nearly naked and he has a head as bald as a newborn baby's; if his hands are joined, is it to thank God for saving him from the sea and the monster or to ask for the courage not to turn away a second time? The monster is still visible with its tiny eyes and huge gullet. The time is one gray morning. Nineveh is at the other end of the world. The cries of seagulls speed through the air beneath the clouds. It would be nice to stay here, to build a hut in the dunes, live on crabs and mussels and fish. He would hang a lantern on the door, like a ferryman. He would pray, fast, and become a holy man in his sandy hermitage, edifying sailors and voyagers. He would be the providence of castaways on stormy nights. Is that not sacrifice enough when you think of the home he has lost? One day rain-laden winds would sweep his grave as today they sweep the sea and the deserted sands. But Jonah gets to his feet. The whale has sounded. All he can see now is a dot on the horizon. The big fish is returning to its seaweed

pastures. And Jonah advances toward the people of Cham. They have
learned nothing from the flood. One small lonely man against the
violent city? The north wind whips his tattered clothes.

The Bible speaks only of the ship from which Jonah is to be
thrown into the sea. But Bruegel sees a hundred ships with black or
white sails, depending on how the light strikes them, all caught in
the storm. He sees the sky black with rain. He sees the swollen waves,
crashing together, knotting up, striking out with fin and tail. The big
fish that can be seen in the foam look like mere waves endowed with
life. Some black-and-white birds, blown off course, flee the winds. In
the distance, landfall; and in an archway of calm, even a harbor and
a church. But so distant. A patch of green water cuts a triangle in the
midst of the convulsed waves. Is this oil spread by some boat to calm
the waters? Is it a supernatural light from the heights of the sky or
the depths of the sea? A whale follows a ship, playing with a barrel.
No doubt the sailors have thrown over the crates they had carefully
stowed in the hold, their tuns, the merchandise, and everything not
tied down, to better their chances of riding out the storm. That is the
way it is: when death comes, the detachment is sudden, absolute. But
the whale is not to be put off by a barrel. It waits for Jonah with a
gaping red maw.

But is this about Jonah? The boat is only one of many, all caught
in the storm. In such weather and from such a distance, no one is
visible in the rigging or on deck. It is a sorely tried fleet that hangs on
as best it can, buffeted by the winds and tossed by the waves. But
Jonah has drawn Bruegel into himself. Had he ever before painted
ships in such weather? He used to paint them sailing beneath azure
skies. He used to paint them bathed in light. He was unaware that he
had been painting his own youth, then, and his strength. Today he
faces the gray hours, the dangerous hours of the sea. He sees his life
as a crossing that ends in lowering gales.

Was it fatigue that stayed his hand? The painting has an unfinished
look. The primer shows through the last layer of sky. One cannot tell
whether the brushstrokes were meant to disappear or whether they
indicate the downpour.

18

THE SPIRIT IS NO LONGER
OF THIS BODY

Ortelius came to see Bruegel. He was pained to see him so pale, so thin and weak. Bruegel rarely left his armchair. Nevertheless, they went upstairs to the workshop, but Bruegel found it hard to stand in front of his paintings for any length of time. Within a few months he had become an old man. Sometimes he spoke so softly that one needed to listen hard. His beard was more white than gray, like his hair. But his smile retained its inner force.

Ortelius talked about his work. Next year the *Theatrum orbis ter-rum,* his opus, would come out. Bruegel told Ortelius how impatient he was. How happy he would be to hold the book in his hands. Next year . . . But both of them knew he would never see it.

They talked about the ills that plagued the country, about their friends, and about those who had left for other lands and those who had been arrested. "The Catholic evil, the Beggars' fever, and the Huguenot dysentery," as Ortelius used to say. What would he say today?

They were in the workshop. Ortelius took his time looking at the Peasant paintings: the Dance, the Wedding Feast in the barn. Had Bruegel ever painted the world so near? He had placed himself just a few steps from the figures, and in their midst. Never had his colors been stronger. But was this joy? Ortelius looked at the face of one of the dancers: prematurely old and devoid of tenderness, he brings down a heavy dancing foot onto two pieces of straw, that form a cross. Had Bruegel, unthinkingly, unwittingly, placed this tiny straw cross—Nativity and Calvary—under the foot of the dancing man?

A large, nearly square painting stood on the easel. In the center, on a clay mound, a gallows, empty. The hump of land on which the gallows stands resembles a skull. In one of the eye sockets, the skull of a horse, like the one we see in *The Bearing of the Cross,* and some

bones. By rights, this should be a place to avoid, but a group of dancing peasants is coming up on the left—men and women holding
hands in groups of two or three, stepping in circles or lines: they are
shown from above, more figurines than figures. Do they not see the
gallows? Or have they forgotten it? Are the bad times over? Has this
evil place at last been returned to nature? The peasants come from a
peaceful village that can be glimpsed through the trees. A castle melts
into the blue haze. A few birds soar in the sky.

On top of the gallows is a magpie, near the center of the picture.
This is not a symbol for gossips or thieves, but simply a black-and-
white bird, the colors of day and night, the image of time. Neither
raven nor dove: a magpie, the median bird. It sits in the middle of the
picture like the hub of the wheel of days. Below, at the foot of the
gallows stands its mate. A magpie couple, a peasant couple.

All this takes place amid vegetation, trees, woods. At the foot of
the hill, a stream flows, turning a mill wheel, another sign of passing
time. But the mill says that the grain of the seasons will be made into
life: the dancing peasants, the mill and its stream, and the land that
surrounds and feeds them.

"My testament," says Bruegel.

Between the gallows and the mill stands a cross, like the roadside
calvaries. The countryside is infinitely mild. In the middle distance,
the stream flows into the immense gentle river. The blue-green land
is still the Garden of Eden.

"I painted this picture for Mary."

The doctor came today. He comes nearly every day. Bruegel knows
he is dying. But when? A few weeks, a few months, maybe a year?

Has he told Mary? Not yet. But he will live like a man departing.

He is conscious of his dying.

Sometimes feeble, sometimes less.

Sometimes he can paint, sometimes not.

He works against time. And yet he is preparing to step out of time.
He is astonished to have come to the days preceding his death, and
he sets about dying as a job to be done, not to cry out as though
it were some extraordinary misfortune, some incomprehensible,
unique piece of injustice. Know that this is the true road. And take
it. Endure the company of that deteriorating body now constantly
racked with pain.

Bruegel senses he is about to die. It has begun to snow. Little by
little he grows unconscious of his surroundings. Once again he sees

his Triumph of Death. But this time it is not simply a picture. And then the scene is traversed by a procession which he fails to recognize at first: it is Christ on his way to Golgotha. For an instant, Christ looks up, through the sweat and the blood, and their eyes meet.

Someone—Mary—enters the room, arranges his pillow, cools his brow. She gives him a sip of herbal tea. He tries to say something. He is unable to speak.

A detailed vision of the Tower of Babel. He sees the thousands of jobs he has done, his work, his travels, his childhood. The Tower of Babel and the world he has known are one. The movement and the details of his life pass before his eyes. Once more he meets those he has known—and some have already died.

He has left Babel. He passes through villages and fields. Babel is barely visible on the horizon. He crosses a desert. In the distance a caravan appears. Camels and elephants, the wisemen's train. Night has fallen. A strange star is shining overhead. Someone helps him to his feet. He was lying in a ditch. The stones were digging into his spine. He falls into step with the others. The procession has come from a far country, from the far reaches of time; you can tell by their curious caps. The procession makes its way down the mountain toward a tiny village, the clustered roofs of a hamlet.

Still in the world of the living. Bells. Noises. Bells—or the sound of an anvil in his childhood village—today blackened ashes. Sounds from today's day. Someone is talking. Someone is reciting a prayer in Latin. Someone is speaking to him. He replies. He does not know if they hear him. His children are standing at the foot of the bed, awed and silent. Can they see that he is smiling at them. He is unable to bring himself back closer to them.

They have come to the run-down stable. Who is it? A shepherd—or perhaps a child. He sees the Nativity, just as he had always imagined it, as he painted it. But this one is *real*. He tells himself that he has seen this place, this scene, like a garden through a frosted window. Now the window is opening; he sees in truth what he has seen in his dreams. A crowd presses around the figures of Christmas and Epiphany, the paupers and beggars of Flanders, a tattered throng, and the poor wretches with their crutches or lying on a board, and the peoples of America, just as wretched. And surrounding the crowd, soldiers and police—helmets, lances, knives—a monstrous encircling army. The crowd knows that if this child dies, the gates of heaven will close.

The snow falls in gasps. A man, a woman on a donkey holding a child wrapped up in her cloak. Flight in the darkness and the snow. The passage.

Now the workshop stands empty. He will never again rise at dawn to paint, to stand there dreaming the truth. A young woman with her two children will have to accustom themselves to the silence overhead, to the absence. He could have lived nearly twice as long as he did. Many painters continue until the last snows of old age, and their last work sings as never before. They are like navigators who, on their last voyage, discover the true island paradise. Their body is in pain, feeble, their hands gnarled; they paint, they have traveled the world, and they are not yet done; there is a greater freedom still to come. But Bruegel did not reach fifty. He died on the fifth of September 1569. The bells of Notre-Dame de la Chapelle rang for him that day. The mirrors were veiled. Were the paintings also veiled, as was the custom, in the house of the deceased? The workshop would be set to rights tomorrow, or later. As long as the easels and palettes and tables and brushes and chalks are left *as before,* it is as though some warmth were left in the body that has just breathed its last. The birds light on the windowsill as though Bruegel were alive. The garden is filled with the same light, which astonishes our grief. Somewhere within, Bruegel must have known how little time he had to live: whence the energy with which he painted for those few years. Who came during those days to view his closed face? Who came to pray by the bed? The bell of Notre-Dame de la Chapelle tolled one last time. The spirit, no longer of this body, set out on a new journey.

REFERENCES

Author's sources

The Guicciardini quotations are adapted from *Description de tous les Pays Bas*, French translation of *Description of All the Lowlands*, edited by Paule Ciselet and Marie Delcourt (Brussels, 1943); the Van Mander quotations are adapted from Robert Genaille's edition of *Le Livre de peinture* (Paris: Hermann, 1965).

D'Aubarède, Gabriel. *La Révolution des Saints, 1520–1536*. Paris: Gallimard, 1946.

Baie, Eugène. *Le Siècle des Gugex—Histoire de la sensibilité flamande sous la Renaissance*. Brussels: Librairie Van der Linden, 1928; Brussels: Anc. Etablis. d'Imprimerie, Th. De Warichet; Paris: Librairie Fischbacher, 1932–58 (8 vols. published by various publishers).

Bertrand, Louis. *Philippe II. Une ténébreuse affaire*. Paris: Grasset, 1929.

———. *Philippe II à l'Escorial*. Paris: L'Artisan du Livre, 1929.

Braudel, Fernand. *Civilization matérielle, économie et capitalisme, xvie–xviiie siècle*. Paris: Armand Colin, 1979.

Chastel, André. *Le Sac de Rome, 1527*. Paris: Gallimard, 1984.

Cohn, Norman. *Les Fanatiques de l'Apocalypse*. Paris: Payot, 1983.

Eekhoud, Georges. *Les Libertins d'Anvers*. Paris: Mercure de France, 1912.

Febvre, Lucien. *Philippe II et la Franche-Comté*. Paris: Flammarion, 1970.

Forneron, H. *Histoire de Philippe II*. Paris: Plon, 1881–82.

Gossart, Ernest. *L'Etablissement du régime espagnol dans les Pays-Bas et l'Insurrection*. Brussels, 1905.

Jacquot, Jean, and Elie Koningson. *Les Fêtes de la Renaissance*, vols. 1–3. Paris: Centre national de la recherche scientifique, 1973–75.

Lesure François. *La Renaissance dans les Provinces du Nord*. Paris: Centre national de la recherche scientifique, 1956.

Madariaga, Salvador de. *Charles Quint*. Paris: Albin Michel, 1969.

Saunders, J. B. de C. M., and Charles D. O'Malley, *The Illustrations from the Works of Andreas Vesalius of Brussels*. New York: Dover Publications, 1973.

Verheyden, Alphonse L. E. *Le Conseil des Troubles*. Flavion-Florennes, Belgium: Editions le Phare, 1981.

Wedgwood, Cicely Veronica. *Guillaume le Taciturne*. Paris: Librairie Jules Tal-
landier, 1978. (Translation of *William the Silent* [Atlantic Highlands, N.J.:
Humanities Press, 1960.])

Works in English on Peter Bruegel the Elder

Gibson, Michael. *Bruegel*. Secausus, N.J.: Wellfleet Press, 1989.
Klein, H. Arthur. *Graphic Worlds of Peter Bruegel the Elder*. New York: Dover
Publications, 1963.
Stechow, Wolfgang. *Pieter Bruegel the Elder*. New York: Harry N. Abrams,
1970.